Adam's Contract with God

A Story of One Man's Struggle of Living with Schizophrenia

by Heidi Custin
Cover Illustration by Michael Brown

Cover Design by: Michael Brown

Printed in the United States of America

ISBN – 978-0-578-62835-6

Acknowledgments

There are so many people in my life I wish to thank for making this book possible. To my friend, Tomas Hernandez, who encouraged me to write this story, sent me daily messages of empowerment and introduced me to my editor, Leanna Brunner. To Leanna, who sat down with me for coffee and on the day we first met, told me I had a story to tell, which needed to be told.

To my longtime friend, Lorna Hesskamp, who spent hours by my side or on the phone, calming me down and from a great distance guiding me through crisis after crisis.

To my friend, Michael Brown, who wrote me daily to make sure I was functioning okay. He was never one to tell me to "suck it up!" or "get over it already!" or "move on!" He was gentle and encouraging and also encouraged me to write this story. He, along with Tomas Hernandez, had such an impact on Adam's life.

To my teacher, mentor and friend, Bob Marolf, whose knowledge in the mental health field far surpasses anything I could have understood on my own, who keeps me on my toes with encouraging support.

To my family, to whom I owe so much! So many people in our shoes have told me that the family support or support of the spouse is not there. I am so blessed to have Joe for my husband. His endless love and support for me and what I needed to do is remarkable, as is his faith that I can do anything I put my mind to! My brother, Martin, and sisters, Ann and Kristina, who listen to me whenever I need to let it out, who hold me when I fall. My daughter, Stephanie, who listened without judgment and gave me positive vibes and feedback; she gets me!

To my brother-in-law, Steve, his wife, Connie, and Joe's sister, Debbie, who travel from miles away in an instant to help us hold it together and make decisions we cannot emotionally handle alone. Debbie, who often sends me messages of love and hope, understanding that the loss of a child does not go away in a few months, a year or more, and who also travels from miles away without question. To my sister-in-law, Suzanne, who took precious time away from her family to be by our side during a very difficult time when her husband—my brother Jimmy—could not.

To my niece, Jessica, who understands the loss of suicide from losing so many close to her, who allows me to say whatever I need to without judgment and offers words of peace.

To my friend, Mac McDonald, who has given me spiritual peace and helped me along my path to spirituality.

To my cousin, prayer warrior Pastor Gary Powell, who stood by Adam and our family through the years, offering comfort and understanding. To my cousin, Bev, the card warrior, who sends continuous messages of love and support and lifts up our souls through her wonderful cards.

To the many counselors, social workers, doctors, and nurses, who worked so hard to help Adam through his pain and suffering, including Nick Pinnell, Tyler Sharpe, Aimee Johnson, Tess Fekas, Dr. David Galbreath, Dr. James Southwell, Jennifer Brown, AJ and Jillian Ledford, and our friend, the dentist, Dr. Jennifer McArroy, and her wonderful staff. Monica Roe with Job One who gave Adam confidence and worked with him to get him employed and mentored him along the way. Richard, his boss, who passed away from kidney failure. We never got to meet him but are forever thankful to him for being a friend and mentor.

To the friends who stood by Adam and picked up the phone to listen when he felt defeated and down, and during the times he had senseless rantings through the night, including Elise (Megan) Rainey, Kara Rainey, April Stafford, Cary Williams, Sam Vining, Nikki Riley, Ben Ledford, Betsy Adams, Nathan Michaud, and some I didn't know about. Thank you for loving Adam for who he is and for not turning away during the difficult times. To other Tulsa friends of Adam, Harley Harrington, Sabi Rhi, Michelle Banks, Tim and Lauren Harmon, who loved Adam without judgment.

To Brad and Tracy Young, who for more than thirty years have supported us in prayer, comfort, and presence and lived near us everywhere we go, who offer friendship, fellowship, spiritual guidance, love and support in so many ways I could never adequately thank you for! To the friends who loved him his whole life: The Fairfax gang, Alex Foster, Bryce and John Green, Nathan Michaud, Carson Pevey, and Nick Ogden. To the parents of those children and other adult friends of Tulsa, who held us up during the hard times in Oklahoma: Joe and Tracy Foster, Glen and Susie Green, Mike and Kathleen Michaud, Carol Ogden and Danny, Rene (Tess Ogden), Keli O'Neal, Ben Tedder, Craig and Leslie Jones (now in Texas), Deb Carroll, and her lovely girls, Kaitlyn, Jordan, and Taylor, Jacy Hesskamp, Julie Easley.

To my NAMI friends, who guided us through the mess we were in and helped us sort it out: Jennifer Boyden, Laura Denkler, Becky Beers, Holly Behrens, Liz and Greg Muleski, Clay and Annette Hugill, Janet Moyer, Don and Deb Davis, Cynthia Keele Johnson, Todd and Alice Wilhelmus, Elizabeth Wilson, Tomas Hernandez, Francie Hughes, Kristen Springer, Cathy Simonds, Felice McDaniels, the late Nikk Thompson, Guyla Stidmon, Isabelle Abarr, Jonathon Light, Nina Kaminski, Lisa Ann Bailey, Saundra Morman, Vanessa Welchen, Cynthia Keele Johnson, and so many more!

To all the families who have lived through tragedy, child loss or suicide, yet gave us comfort when we needed it: Dawn Gominsky, Guy Hulen, Lisa Cable, the late Jerry Ausburn, JoAnn Ausburn, Monica Wilkens, Camille McClain, Jim and Sharon Parcel, Jennifer Burnett, Lynn Wright, Jim and Jeanne Finnegan, Kris Remus, Fred and Shelly Brandenburg, Sherry Elbs, Tim Brown, cousins Doug and Valerie Powell, and Kathy and Sam Vining.

To the people we met after our move to Kansas City who stood by us through so much: Kristen Springer, Sarah Boyce, Monica Wilkens, Craig and Lisa Peterson, Ted Wilkens, Tyler Wilkens, Josie Wilkens, Nick and Sadie Peterson, Tim and Lorrie Gordon, John Ambrose, Tony and Karen Kehrees, Mary DeVore, and too many others to name!

To all the first responders we have had the privilege of meeting through Crisis Intervention Trainings, including police officers, fire fighters, social workers, and dispatchers. We also thank the chaplains and pastors who are making an effort to implement mental health programs in their churches to better serve their congregations. To name a few: Kevin Hardy, Sgt. Greg Smith and Officer Jon Benet, Dawn Morris, Officer Mark Cherry, Captain Chris Looney, Sally Boone, Officer J.D. Pettey, Officer Sean Hess, and the late Nikk Thompson.

To the people we didn't know yet, who picked up the pieces of our lives and helped us put them back together, including Krissy and Mike Revert, Terry and Becky Luna, Mac McDonald, Jerry and Robbin Loftin, Pastor Chris Pinion, Mike and Mindy Horton, Jim and Sharon Parcel, Marty Sexton, Tricia Wear, Leon and Linda Schoor, Tim and Amy Goulet, Dan and Debbie Braun, Don and Dana Bass, Jeff Kroenlein, Mylissa Russell, Avis and Lloyd Curphey, Angela Bolinger, Laney

Allison, Ryan and Olivia Luna, Matt and Penny Mills, Bill and Mary Fort, Bill and Cindy Wilmurth, George and Dawn Farrill, Zach Gardoski , Shawn and Sue Teagarden. Basically, most LifeQuest people and the folks from the VFW in Lee's Summit, Missouri. People who did not even know our son, who came into our lives during the aftermath and loved and continue to love us fiercely. Love is the key, and it keeps us all alive. Remember this when someone you love is suffering. Love conquers all!

Most of all, I thank Adam for coming into my life, for blessing me as a mother and teaching me so much more than any school could. I loved you from the day I first felt you in my womb. I love you still and will love you forever!

Prologue

I journaled for over four years before I finally began to write this story: the story of me, my husband, my daughter, my family, and friends who have taken this journey with us: Adam's story. In the beginning, I could not define a starting point. What is the purpose of recording our story, other than for the selfish reason of wanting the world to meet and know our son, Adam, and his complicated, yet brilliant life? Is it for the purpose of renewing faith among people in our shattered world through relating miracles our family has experienced time and time again? Is it to help people recognize mental illness as a physical malady, which needs to be treated with the same respect, care, and compassion as diabetes, hypertension, or cancer? Of helping to eliminate the stigma surrounding mental illness so that others might not be afraid to seek help? Or to help promote the organization we are so proudly a part of, the National Alliance on Mental Illness?

It is really for all of these reasons. Yes, we want to give meaning to Adam's life; to shout to the world about all of the gifts he has given us. Through his life, we have learned so much. The greatest lessons we have been given have been an acceptance of others, embracing our differences, and discarding the word "normal", because none of us are! He taught us to be thankful for the little things in life, and for those who have walked with us. He taught us love. Love is where it begins and where it ends.

My daughter Stephanie recently said to me, "Mom, I figured it out, why we are all here. It is to love. It is that simple. Without love, we have nothing." Adam taught us that. Every path we have walked upon, whether we chose it or it fell upon us, whether it was good or bad, has shaped us into who we were meant to become. I can search my soul for all the reasons we were chosen for this journey, and although it seems like it was thrust upon us suddenly at some point, we have all been on the path together from day one.

I read a book by Mary C.Neal M.D. about a woman who drowned in a kayaking accident, went to heaven to experience God's love and peace, then returned to this world to tell her story. Neal challenged her readers to keep a journal of the consequences they met with in their own lives, dividing them into two columns. In the first column, they were to list the detail of each major event in their lives (such as marriage, attending college, choosing where to live, etc.) and take note of every time they fell into place easily. In the second column, they were to record every time they experienced a struggle and the outcome of that struggle. Then they were to write what happened as an indirect result of these challenges and the lessons that were learned. Neal's thesis was that all the events in our lives are interconnected and are indicative of a plan God has set before us. We are to see that there really are no negative consequences, but rather miracles to show us that God is with us in times of sorrow and struggle.

After reading her book, I began to make a list of the major events in my life, and I saw patterns emerging that I had never paid attention to before. It really began with the day I was born, or maybe even before that, on the day of my husband's birth. I have concluded that Dr. Neal is correct in her assessment. There are no consequences, good or bad. Like it or not, everything that happens to us is meant to happen, and we are all connected in this life. As I look back at my own life, from childhood through adulthood, before Adam, during his struggles and afterwards, I see these connections and understand why people were brought into my life at the time they appeared. I see and feel it

9

all over again as I write these pages of the story about my son, Adam. I also now understand that it isn't what happens to you, good or bad. It is what you do with it. How you live your life and connect with others makes all the difference.

Chapter 1
First Miracles

"Mom!" I was awakened by a very angry fifteen-year-old. My daughter Stephanie was standing over me with an insulin bottle in one hand and a syringe in the other.

"What was Adam doing with this?"

Years prior, in August of 2000, Stephanie was just shy of her eleventh birthday in September. We were traveling in a caravan with my sister Ann, her sons, Christopher, Tad, and William, her cousins Brittney and Jessica, my husband Joe, and our two children, Stephanie and Adam. Our goal was to travel in two vans from Tulsa, Oklahoma (where we then resided), to Missouri, where we would meet up with Ann and the gang, and drive through Illinois, Michigan, and finally into Canada.

We stopped every half hour or so because Stephanie had to pee. We were all frustrated as the drive to our destination was taking so long. We suggested she not drink so much in the van. We were blind to what was happening before us, as most of us are when faced with an illness we have never been exposed to and know nothing about. That wasn't the first time we would be ignorant to an illness taking over one of our children, and it certainly would not be the last!

It didn't take Ann long to figure out the problem. Growing up as a group of five children, we used to joke that Ann should have been in the medical field. She read every medical journal she could get her hands on, and having a seemingly photographic memory, she had a great retention of anything she read or saw. "She has Type One Diabetes," Ann announced as if she was stating a fact.

My first instinct was to kid around. "Okay, Dr. Shultz," I replied, yet the seriousness in her tone stopped me short. Suddenly, what was an annoying stop-and-go adventure with Stephanie became frightening.

Ann began to tell us about her friend from Kansas City, whose child—who was about the same age as Steph—had gone into a coma and was found to be a Type One Diabetic, just the week prior to our trip. She explained the symptoms of excessive thirst, frequent urination, unexplained weight loss, and fatigue. She went on and on. Every symptom she mentioned we could identify with Stephanie.

At that time, we were spending the night in a campground far from any city or town, and I vowed to get her to the nearest hospital in the morning.

We reviewed the summer up to that point. I had a home daycare for infants through the age of five at that time. My children were nine and ten years old that year and certainly didn't want to spend their summer with a bunch of little kids! Our neighborhood was rich with friends who had children of the same age as ours. The children would spend much of their time outdoors, going from house to house. It was the greatest neighborhood watch around. They were safe and parented by all of us. I recalled Adam coming home for lunch several times that summer, without being accompanied by Stephanie. She had been a healthy, stocky young child, who wasn't picky about food. I would ask him if she was hungry, and his response was, "She is taking a nap in the tree house."

Noticing throughout the summer how thin Stephanie was getting, I broached the subject of anorexia with her. She flat out laughed at me. "Mom! Seriously?" she replied. "I love to eat. I would never starve myself!" Yet, I was concerned that this was what was going on. Like I said, I am often ignorant of an illness until someone I love has it, and as a teen, I did have a friend who suffered from anorexia. I just decided to keep an eye on Stephanie.

But at that campsite, listening to Ann, it all began to make sense. I recalled the events of the prior day. We had all climbed sand dunes in the heat. Stephanie had struggled up those hills, downing water like there was no tomorrow! Why hadn't I seen it?

The next day, we came upon Traverse City, Michigan, a gorgeous place that Joe, Stephanie, and I did not have the pleasure of exploring. It is located on the shores of East Grand Traverse Bay and West Grand Traverse Bay, which both flow into lake Michigan.

We drove straight to Munson Medical Center and very quickly discovered that Ann had been correct in her diagnosis. We also learned that we had just had our first recognizable miracle (in reviewing our lives, this was one of many): Stephanie walked into that hospital. Her blood sugar was over 1,000 mg/dL! It was off the charts. The medical staff told us that the normal level was between 70 and 120. It wasn't long before we realized that this was very serious, and that we could actually lose our child!

Joe and I spent a week at Munson with Stephanie while Ann continued the vacation with six children! She took Adam, too.

We were thrust into classes about Type 1 Juvenile Diabetes and had an overwhelming amount of information shoved down our throats. Learning about what our daughter had to do for the rest of her life to stay alive was overwhelming and devastating: taking blood sugar measurements, figuring out meal plans, and deciding how many units of insulin to give her—and that was just the beginning! What if her blood sugar was low? High? What about school? Sleepovers? Life in general? We did learn that Type 1 was different from Type 2 in the respect that she (or we) didn't do this to Stephanie. It wasn't caused by a poor diet or lifestyle choices.

One doctor told us that some children are just born with it. Other doctors believed that a previous illness with raging fevers may have destroyed her pancreas and caused this. Stephanie had suffered from a rare tick-borne illness at the age of six, which had caused her to have 106-degree temperatures over the course of a month, before it was discovered that she had Tularemia, a disease that can be fatal if not treated. Given that she had suffered with that for a month and survived, I guess you could say that it had been the first miracle!

Joe and I had to administer a shot of saline solution into our own bellies in front of Stephanie to show her that we were not scared of the injection process. Really? I fainted at the sight of blood or having blood drawn. Joe quietly said, "You can, and will, do this." Of course I did, because this was our child. I would step in front of a train for my child, no questions asked.

We made it through that week and began our long journey home. Stephanie seemed more on top of things than we were. This child was insistent that she would draw her own blood, test it, and administer her own injections. We were in such awe of her!

We were traveling back to Tulsa through Chicago during rush hour, when from the back of the van, Steph calmly proclaimed, "I have a low blood sugar."

I began to panic. Where's the food? I thought. Oh my God, what if she passes out?

Joe grabbed my leg. "Calm down," he said. "You can't help her if you are freaking out. Remain calm." Years later, he would use the phrase, "You must put the oxygen mask on yourself first, and then on your child." He loved airplanes and had a pilot's license when we met, so he was all about phrases and analogies that had to do with flying.

By the time I had leaped into the back seat, Stephanie already had things under control. She just looked at me like I was crazy. "Everything is fine, Mom," she said. "I've got this."

We finally made our way home to a bedroom stuffed with balloons and giggling girls. A huge sign read, "Welcome Home, Stephanie!". My good friend, Lorna Hesskamp, who also had a home daycare and was my Girl Scout co-leader at the time, arranged the welcome home party.

We all felt very loved and supported as people in our community came together to help us and learn about Stephanie's new life so they could help her continue to do the things other children did. Parents came to our home to be educated so that she could have sleepovers at their homes. Teachers were compassionate, and counselors rushed to our aid. We were touched by the support a community gives when your child is ill...as long as the illness resides in the body, not the brain, which we would learn a few years down the road.

Chapter 2
The Wakeup Call

So, there we were five years later, and Steph was standing over me, angrily waving the syringe and insulin above my head as I lay in bed. Still groggy, I asked her what she was talking about.

Apparently, Stephanie had awoken in the middle of the night with a feeling that something was not quite right. She said that Adam was in the shower. "Something" had told her to go into his room and go to his desk. It was one of those old roll top desks we had received from Joe's mom and had once belonged to her mother. It had at least a dozen small drawers. That "something" drew Steph to open one particular drawer to discover it contained her insulin and one syringe.

I was confused, and both of us wondered why he would have taken that. (During the years that followed, Stephanie and I both had a special connection and knew things we couldn't explain where Adam was concerned.)

Adam was not in his room. He was taking a shower in the middle of the night. I waited, listening from my room across the hall until he went to bed. I could hear him rustling around in the desk drawers. Then there was only quiet. I went to sleep.

I got up the next morning and looked in on my still sleeping son. He was breathing and appeared to be okay. It was a summer day, so the kids were not in school, but it was a work day for me, so I had to get breakfast going for the children who were soon to wake up.

In 1989, I earned a BS in education from the University of Missouri in Columbia, Missouri, and received my teaching certificate for K-8 that same year. Joe was transferred to Tulsa, Oklahoma, that same summer. I stayed through early October as I gave birth to Stephanie in September. Not knowing anyone I could trust in a new city and state, I opted to stay home with her, and eight months later, I started my day-care business.

I began teaching the little ones once they reached preschool age, and later earned my Child Development degree. Later, when our kids were in school, Joe renovated the garage into a classroom, and I changed my focus to teaching from our home.

Along the edges of my classroom, the exterior of the garage had a door leading into it that served as an alternate exit. I kept a freezer and extra refrigerator out there to store food for the preschool.

That morning, I walked out there to retrieve something from the fridge, and on the floor beside it I found a pair of Adam's black jeans with a huge hole in one leg. I smelled bleach on them. Baffled, I picked them up. Underneath the pants I discovered vomit. In a panic, I rushed back into the house and woke up Joe. I canceled preschool for the day, and we discussed what we should do. That early summer morning was our first wakeup call that something was wrong with our son.

At that time we knew nothing about mental illness. That subject was the furthest thought from our minds, especially in relation to Adam. We wondered: at that time he had a girlfriend named Shelby. Had they broken up or had an argument? Why would he do this? He seemed happy enough to us. His girlfriend was beautiful and sweet. He was good looking and had tons of friends. Why was this happening?

We soon learned that Adam had intended to kill himself that night and had thought it would be easy to do if he took a heavy dose of insulin. What we couldn't understand was, why? Why did this beautiful, popular kid want to die?

Chapter 3
Babies and Toddlers

Stephanie and Adam had been born seventeen months apart. They were inseparable from each other from the day we brought Adam home. Both births were traumatic for me. Stephanie had her umbilical cord wrapped around her neck, and Adam had a bowel movement while in the birth canal and breathed in toxic fumes. Both were taken for observation immediately following birth. It took longer to get Adam back than it had with Stephanie. It was a very stressful time. I had already lost one baby in the womb at four-and-a-half months. Her brain had stopped developing, so the doctor had to put me under and surgically remove the baby. I never knew for sure if that baby had been a girl or a boy, but I felt in my heart that she was a girl.

Now, panic was rearing its ugly head, as I had not yet seen my baby boy. Joe assured me he was in good hands and that everything would be okay.

My mom spent two weeks with us when Adam was born: the week prior to and the week following. With the exception of one other time when she had visited with my father and we hung out with our close friends, the Michauds, that was her only visit during the twenty years we lived there.

Still, I was grateful, and she was a huge help. Stephanie had a blast with her and was always close to her in her heart. My mom had trouble showing affection but did so well those two weeks. I think that was ingrained in Steph's brain forever after that. Mom got to be there and witness the birth of our son, too.

Finally, I was holding my nine-pound, four-ounce baby boy in my arms! Student nurses asked to come see the woman who had given birth to this big baby and were surprised to see a little woman who had only gained seventeen pounds during her entire pregnancy lying there. My pregnancy with Adam had been difficult. I'd had extreme morning sickness the entire first trimester and a viral infection during the second trimester. Putting on weight had been difficult.

Adam was a large baby, but his growth leveled off at about six months. From that point on, he was a small boy. At his adult height, he was five foot six inches tall and weighed from 135 to 145 pounds. Adam was one of those angelic looking babies, and later on, he was an angelic looking child. He had huge, bright blue eyes and white-blond hair.

When Adam was a baby, Joe told me that he was going to be an extraordinary person. I remember asking him why he had said that. He said that looking into Adam's eyes, he saw a spark of something special; an intelligence he could not define. He said Adam had a good soul, and he could feel it.

Adam was a sweet baby. He had a rough first two months. He cried a lot. Daddy took him for nightly walks on his shoulder to calm him down. I rocked him in the night and sang him a John Denver song, "For Baby (For Bobbie)". That was my song; Adam's baby song, our song. Years later, this song would have an even greater impact on me than I could ever have imagined.

I foolishly returned to work two weeks after Adam's birth. I was breastfeeding, and we didn't have the wonderful pumps they have today, so it was up to me to get up in the night to care for him. By around the sixth week, I was so exhausted I cried out to Joe. "I can't do this anymore. I cannot get out of the bed." For the remaining days, Joe dutifully got out of bed and brought our son to me so I wouldn't have to get up. Two weeks later, Adam slept peacefully through the night.

From that point on, he was a delightful baby. He had this infectious laugh. He loved his sister, Steph, who was still a baby herself. Two babies together; a girl and a boy. It was the greatest time in our lives. They were seriously picture-perfect babies. We would joke about it as people constantly stopped us in public to tell us how beautiful they were. We wondered aloud how we had such beautiful children. I would say, looking at Joe, "They got their looks from you." He would say the same thing to me. When people would comment, we wanted to say, "We know," then laughed, saying how arrogant that sounded. Yet, they were gorgeous!

We had so much joy with those two. I saw in Joe such pride and love. Joe had been adopted at nine months of age. He talked about how strange it was to never see yourself in another person. Bearing no resemblance to anyone. He talked about how he would look at total strangers as a child and wonder if they were his mother, sister, brother, dad. But he saw his reflection in both of our children. One day, his close friend Jim Finnegan was playing with baby Stephanie on our living room floor when he suddenly, dramatically cried out, "Ahh! I was just kissing Joe!" We laughed, but she did look just like him! Jim and Joe had been roommates in Columbia when we met. We transferred to Tulsa the next year. He later married Jeanne and had two children, Kaitlyn and Kevin, both of whom I took care of during my first few years in day care.

Joe was awesome with our two. We had decided early on that we would have a big family. I was born into a big family, and Joe longed to see himself in others. Sadly, I had two more losses like before, one with the same situation in which the baby's brain stopped developing halfway through the pregnancy. I miscarried the last one into the toilet.

We decided to stop trying, as the pregnancies were taking a toll on my body and my mental health. I had bladder surgery in my early thirties due to the stress from the pregnancies. And though I tended not to gain much weight while pregnant, my babies were both born larger than average. Joe and I joked (though it was not funny in reality) that during every year of our marriage, someone was hospitalized. Twenty-eight years in a row! Year twenty-nine we finally broke the trend.

On weekends, I would grocery shop for home and day care. It was my break away from the children and Joe and the kids' bonding time. Often I would come home to see them all frozen in various modes in the living room, hair disheveled. I knew they were up to no good but definitely having fun. I was the worrier, the cautious parent, always putting safety first. Joe was the fun guy, throwing caution to the wind. We were a good team, and we had a great balance, both as parents and in our marriage. We were and continue to be blessed that way.

I later learned of a game they would play when I left, called 'Purdy Milk'. Back when we were kids, milk was delivered to your door in glass bottles. When you emptied out the bottles, you rinsed them out, placed them outside your door, and received newly filled bottles. In Tennessee where Joe had lived, the brand of milk was Purdy. So the game, as they explained it, was Dad laying on his back on the floor, feet up in the air, knees bent. He would place one of the kids on his feet, yell out "Purdy Milk!" and basically catapult them through the air onto the couch, like milk spewing forth from the bottle. One of these times I walked in and they all looked scared. I guess Adam had flown a bit too hard and hit the wall and then the floor. They all agreed, "Don't tell Mom." Oh, those crazy kids, all three of them.

Chapter 4
Denial

After the discovery of the insulin, the syringe, the pants, and the vomit, Joe called Laureate Psychiatric in Tulsa to inquire what we should do. We suspected that Stephanie's discovery the night before had interfered with a possible suicide attempt, although we had no idea why. They suggested we bring him in for an evaluation.

We calmly woke Adam up. I told him what I had found outside my classroom in the garage. He actually admitted to us that he was going to take the insulin to end his life but couldn't find where he had hidden it. He had taken the shower to prepare himself for death! When he could not locate the insulin, he had decided to swallow bleach! I still shudder today at that thought. He accidentally spilled it on his jeans and when the hole formed, it scared him to think of how painful that would be to ingest. So he swallowed an entire bottle of hydrogen peroxide instead. It obviously didn't kill him, but it made him vomit throughout the night.

We took Adam to Laureate for an evaluation. We let him know how much we loved him and just wanted to help him get through what-ever it was that was bothering him enough to make him want to die at fourteen!

Adam was evaluated and determined to be a danger to himself. He was admitted to Laureate. If memory serves me correctly, I believe he stayed there a week. Forgive me for that lapse in memory, but he would subsequently have so many psychiatric hospital stays, and at that time, I guess I figured it would be the first and the last. Surely, I thought, this was just a bump in the road—a phase, and we would fix it as we did everything else because that is what parents do, right? What I do remember about that first hospital stay is that no one brought it up. There were no welcome home signs. No balloons. No casseroles. Adam's illness was treated so much differently than Stephanie's.

I thought back to three people I'd known in my past. Steve Gibbs, a high school friend, had taken his life. The day before he did it, he had been giving things away and telling us, "Good luck" on this and that. No one had thought anything of it. These had been signs that we didn't see. When it happened, it seemed surreal. A group of us had been out a few nights before. I'd had my bare feet on the back of the front seats and he'd played "This Little Piggy" on my toes. How do you act normal like that and then take your life? What signs had Adam given? I have no idea!

A high school friend of mine named Mel found her mother in the garage. She had taken her life in the family car by inhaling carbon monoxide fumes. Another friend in college came from a large Catholic family. Her brother had taken his life, and the church had refused to hold a Mass for him. I couldn't comprehend these events then, nor could I now.

We were Catholic. When we went to church, our priest told Adam point blank, "You do realize that if you had completed suicide, you would be in Hell right now?" I stood by and said nothing. I was scared. I wanted support as a mother and wanted it for my son, and that is what I received.

Adam was diagnosed with depression, prescribed medications, and put on suicide watch. He went through intensive individual and group therapies. We were allowed to visit him during the evenings. He hated it there and just wanted to come home. We wanted him home yet were terrified to be placed back in charge of our own child! We had not signed up for this. What had happened to our beautiful, carefree, full-of-life, son? Was it something we had said or something we had done? Had we been too easy on him? Too hard? Where did this sadness come from? Suddenly, everything we had ever done as parents, as a family, every decision we had ever made, was questioned. And not just by ourselves, but by our family, some of our friends, and people in our church. Where had we taken a wrong turn?

Reflecting back on visiting Adam in Laureate, I feel a bit foolish. We were a happy, well-rounded family, who lived in a great neighborhood. Something like this did not happen to people like us. I am ashamed to admit today that at that moment in time, I really did feel like "this too shall pass". I felt like I wasn't one of those people. I didn't belong with that group of parents. Adam didn't belong with that group of kids. We were nothing like them because we were good people who were involved with our children, who belonged to a church family, who prayed, who helped others, and who volunteered countless hours of our time for others. We loved our children.

Why did I feel as if the others did not do or feel any of those things? Did I seriously believe that mental illness strikes only a select group of people? Who then? The poor? The homeless? The uneducated? The ungodly? Looking back, I was the picture-perfect example of someone stigmatizing those who suffered from mental illness. In my ignorance, I guess I thought that somehow, someone else caused a person to become mentally ill, and I couldn't see that in our own family. So, I chose to think that whatever Adam's problem was, it would be over soon, and we would be able to move on with our lives.

Chapter 5
B.A. Bonds

We raised our children in Broken Arrow, Oklahoma (B.A. as the residents call it), which is the largest suburb of Tulsa. We built our first house, a three-bedroom, ranch style, in 1990 and moved in with our baby girl in January. Adam joined our family in March of 1991. Our home was in a new neighborhood. The backyard butted up against a field with a pond and some woods in the background. It was a peaceful place during the early years. We had a huge backyard full of play equipment for the day care and our children. We considered the fields and woods a playground as well, and the kids often explored back there with their dad. We had two Blue Russian cats, Smokey and Sugar Bear.

Smokey was five years older than Bear (as we ended up calling him) and ruled the roost. His name was shortened to Key, The Key… more like the King. He liked to hide in dark places, leap, and attack ankles without warning. Bear was, as you might have guessed, sweet as sugar. They roamed the property and beyond as well. Sadly, The Key was hit by a car and killed our fifth year in B.A. He had been ten years old.

About four years later, Bear went out one night and didn't return until ten days later. When he did, he was a shadow of his former self, with the contents of his belly hanging out. Miraculously, he was healed and went on to live to the age of nineteen. Ten more years! We did keep our cats inside from that day on.

We added Fred, a gray tabby, when Bear was ten. Stephanie claimed him as her husband, and she and all my Girl Scouts argued over whom he loved the most. He gave her so much joy and helped her through her adjustment with juvenile diabetes, as animals have a way of doing.

I have the fondest memories of Broken Arrow in the nineties. I believe that during that decade, we were all truly happy. We quickly established bonds with the neighbors. Many had children around the age of ours. Mostly boys lived the closest and almost all of them were in Adam's grade. Stephanie was a bit of a tomboy, so it didn't bother her to hang out with them, too. On our street alone lived the McCurdys, who had a son named Charlie, the Ogdens, with their son Nick, and the Peveys with their son Carson. Carson was a bit younger than the other boys but hung out with them. Later, the Michauds would move into our street, bringing their son Nathan, who was a year younger than Adam. On the street that teed into ours lived Adam's best friend, Alex Foster, and around the bend a block or so down, Bryce Green. Through the years, a few others joined the pack. Bryce later moved to the Kansas City area, but most of the boys grew up together.

It was the ideal place with the ideal people. Joe and Traci Foster, Mike and Kathleen Michaud, Carol Ogden, Glen and Susie Green, Craig and Leslie Jones (who later moved, but remain close friends to this day) all became the best of friends, and it was our children who brought us all together!

I remember the day I met Tracy Foster and her son, Alex. It was the summer of Adam's third year. I had enrolled him and Stephanie in a mother's day out program at our church, St. Benedict's in Broken Arrow, the previous school year. I had been teaching them, along with the other preschool children, but had had some conflicts. Stephanie, my smarty pants, wanted to run the show. Looking back, I am sure she did not want to share her Mama with other children! And Adam was painfully shy. I was concerned that Steph needed to have another authority figure in her life so she would be better prepared for kindergarten, and Adam needed socialization away from my leg, which he was so fond of clinging to.

Adam and I were taking a walk that summer, when in the distance, I saw another little boy running in our direction. I remember this moment in slow motion, like in the movies. The boy was calling, "Adam! Adam!" And my boy was calling, "Alex! Alex!" They finally met, embracing one another like two long-lost friends. I looked at his mother. She said, "Is that the Adam?"

I asked, "Is that the Alex?" Both boys had talked on and on about their best friend all school year. I said, "You live in this neighborhood?"

Nodding, she pointed down the T in our street, which ran into our house. She only lived four doors down! These boys were inseparable from that day on. Joe and Traci hit it off with my Joe and me. We spent many weekends together, both home and away. The Joes, along with our friend, Craig Jones, played golf together. We met Craig and Leslie through Shirley Billingsley, who worked for the builder who had constructed our home. She became a great friend, too. Craig and Leslie needed child care, so I took care of Spencer (and later, Schyler) until they moved away when Spencer was four. The women played Bunco. There was so much joy and laughter in those days.

The first time we invited Joe and Traci over to play dominoes, my Joe and I were beating them. Traci joked that we were the "Cheatin' Custins" and that we had invited them over to make ourselves look good. We laughed and laughed. The next day, Traci called to apologize. Her Joe thought she had offended us. I asked her why, and she said it was because she had called us the Cheatin' Custins. I told her we'd loved it. It actually broke the ice to a new and lifelong friendship.

We also met Nick Ogden and Charlie McCurdy that year. They car-pooled with Ronnie McCurdy, Charlie's mom, to St. Benedict's for pre-school. Soon we were all getting together for evenings of fun while the gang of kids played. Life was perfect!

The year the Jones moved away, the Greens moved into the neighborhood. They were looking for childcare and got a referral for me. Their boys were in kindergarten. Bryce, who was Adam's age, and his younger brother John joined the pack.

When Adam was in first grade, he joined the Cub Scouts. All the boys his age did. The same year, the Michauds moved in a few doors down, and like the other parents before them, they were looking for childcare for their baby girl, and for Nathan, who was in kinder-garten. They also had another baby on the way. The Michauds became an important family in our lives and a great support system for us for many years to come. When the boys joined the scouts, Joe, Mike Mi-chaud, Carol Ogden, and Susie Green became den leaders.

The gang bonded. The bond between the boys, the families, and Joe and Adam grew even stronger. Eventually, Adam got into sports. He tried baseball, football, basketball, and so on. He was always the smallest boy, so often these sports were tough to compete in.

I remember Adam trying out t-ball at a young age. He was so tiny. He made it to first base. The umpire called "safe". On the way to first base, Adam had lost a shoe. After being called safe, he ran back to get it and got tagged out. The coach yelled and screamed at him over this. He put his head down, looking so forlorn. I wanted to run out and hold him but didn't want to cause further embarrassment.

From that point on, Joe always participated as co-coach for both kids' sports teams, and Adam and Joe continued with scouts. Finally, Adam found a sport he could compete in on equal grounds. He became a wrestler in the lighter weight division and did quite well with it. Coaches joked that he would always begin a round by smiling really big and friendly at his opponent. They would tell him not to do that, as it made him appear weak. He was simply an all-around nice kid, and his genuine smile reflected that. Funny thing: most of the time he ended up taking that opponent down and winning! Maybe that smile made them let their guard down and they thought they had him! All I know is it worked for him!

Chapter 6
Family and Independence

Since we made the choice to move to Oklahoma, it put some distance (in miles) between us and our families. It some ways this was a good thing. We were able to live our lives independently and make our own decisions without anyone telling us what we should or should not do. We had to make our own way and our own set of friends apart from those we had known back in Missouri. It took us out of our comfort zone. It was a huge step for me, as I had lived my entire life in Missouri and had never considered living anywhere else. I was shy and relied on my family or Joe, my close-knit circle, to lead me. I never considered that I could be a leader myself. Moving away pushed me in ways I never thought were possible. I had my own business. I had to talk to people to sell myself on my own. And I had a successful business for twenty years, up until Joe got a promotion, which caused us to move back to Missouri.

Joe worked for State Farm in Personal Lines Underwriting when we'd made the move to Broken Arrow in 1989. His father Cliff was previously a Regional Deputy Vice President of the company. The move had given Joe his own identity within the company, separate from his father. Luckily for him, just about everyone he had worked with in Columbia moved with him. That worked for me too, because I began my day care business with State Farm families, who in turn became friends of mine, as well. Our work-related folk and neighbors became our family away from home.

Meanwhile, we made every possible effort to connect with both our Custin family and our Shultz family, as we both felt that the bond of family was important. One downside of living so far away was that we missed things due to distances to drive for a day event or such. So, most vacation time was spent with our immediate family. Another was that people would make assumptions about our parenting—which they did not witness—and much blame was placed on us later on for our children's health issues.

We eventually owned two vans: one for scouting events and one for transporting children and travel. Christmases were spent either driving to Atlanta, Georgia, to be with Joe's brother's family, or to Florida during the years Joe's folks, Mimi and Popi, wintered there, or later on to Harlingen, Texas, or back to Columbia, Missouri, where my side of the family, the Shultzes resided. For a time we also went to Lake of the Ozarks, where Mimi and Popi had a house. It was a long haul no matter where we went, but it kept us close. Visiting and maintaining these bonds with our family would later bring about even more miracles than we could ever have imagined.

Thanksgiving was always in Columbia at Mom and Papa's house. It was a big to-do, with all five of us siblings and our children. We often had a visit from Papa's sister, beloved Aunt Jane, who was more like a mom to us, and her kids if they were in town. As children, we celebrated holidays with them, so our family later carried on the same tradition.

Fourth of July was often at the Lake of the Ozarks when Mimi and Popi lived there. We took the boat out on the lake with seemingly millions of other boats to watch the fireworks. The kids would swim in the lake like fish with their Custin cousins.

Our children had many cousins from both sides of the family, several of them close to their ages. The times we gathered together were memorable ones, full of joy and lots of love and giggles. It reminded me of my own youth and time spent with my own cousins.

When I was younger, we spent a lot of time outdoors, and one of our favorite activities was camping and canoing. Papa organized these events. I passed this on to Joe, who years later became more of a canoeist than I had ever been.

We took our children on their first canoe trip, out on the Buffalo River in Arkansas, when they were three and four years old. Papa and I had Adam in our canoe, and Joe partnered with nephew Chris, ten at the time, with Stephanie sitting in the middle. It was a big family affair, and we questioned whether we should be taking the children yet. My mom was supposed to watch them at the cabin she was staying in, but she decided not to at the last minute. So, we took them.

Papa was an expert canoeist, and I felt we were safe in his canoe. Joe was just as good, so I felt confident that Stephanie would be safe with him.

The group left the put-in point one at a time, and Papa waited to take the back. We entered into the river and immediately ran right smack into some rapids. We watched as the other canoes had a bit of difficulty making it through, but they did. Then we took off. Our canoe landed on top of a large boulder almost right away and began spinning around. Then, Papa dropped his paddle into the water, and it floated downstream. I quickly gave him mine, as the person in the back of the canoe controls the direction of the canoe. As I handed him the paddle, I saw Adam's huge, trusting, blue eyes staring at me. When I looked forward, I saw and heard Stephanie from the canoe in front of us as she screamed in terror that her brother—her "Adam Boy", as she called him—would surely perish in the waters of the Buffalo River! Joe retrieved the paddle, and by some miracle, we made it through, and the rest of the day was a blast.

Our kids loved the water and went on many float trips in the years to come. So, our time visiting and spending time with family was fun and carefree and created great memories.

Aside from the Michigan trip, the kids always traveled with Aunt Ann and Papa, as it was difficult for me to take time away from my business in addition to the vacations I spent with family.

We believed these life experiences would shape our children into well-rounded individuals, who would soar to great heights. They had advantages and life experiences that many other children did not. So, no, I didn't think anything bad was ever going to happen to our family.

Chapter 7
The Four of Us

Aside from sports, church, friends and family life, our own family of four had our special times together, as well. When the children were little, we walked a lot. We would frequently walk in the parks, one in a stroller, one in a backpack carrier. We camped a lot, too. We often went to airshows or simply sat outside the Tulsa Airport and watched the planes come and go.

On September 11, 2001, we—along with the rest of the world—watched in horror as the Twin Towers were struck by terrorists. In October, as Halloween approached, many concerned parents wondered if our children were safe to trick-or-treat. A group of parents in our circle decided to do something different that year. Several of us chose an activity in our homes for the kids to do. They would also be allowed to collect goodies from each house. We loaded both of our vans with children and started the night at our house. We bobbed for apples there, handed out treats, and headed to the next place. Our friends, the Burgesses, had created a haunted house. It was fantastic. Their daughter Elizabeth was one of my Girl Scouts and one of Stephanie's best friends. Our final destination was at Susie and Glenn Green's house.

The next morning, Joe told me we needed to go to Susie's house because there was something there he needed to show me. I had been so wrapped up in corralling the children the night before that I hadn't noticed the new addition to their household: a sweet, terrified puppy lying in a corner, shaking. Glen and Susie had two dogs already and needed to find a home for this one. Susie had found her in the streets of downtown Tulsa during morning rush hour. Someone had filled her belly with stew and dropped her there. Susie had taken her into her office, where she had thrown up the stew and laid under her desk all day.

Joe and I had both been raised with dogs, and I think the question passed through both of our minds why we never had a dog before in our marriage. This girl was white in the legs and face with a black back and belly and a black stripe down her face and along her top. She reminded me of an Alaskan husky with brown eyes. I quickly said, "She looks like Alaska."

Joe said, "You think she is from Alaska?"

I knew when I saw her, he had wanted her from the moment he had laid eyes on her. I instantly felt the same. We never discussed it. We just knew she belonged with us.

"No," I replied, "her name should be Alaska."

Funny thing: a few months after we took her home, she began to look more like a mix of lab or shepherd. She lost the black fur on her face and belly. People always asked why we named her that.

We took her home. She threw up again on the way across the neighborhood. She had been through something awful; we never would know exactly what. She feared men in ball caps. She shook when she encountered anyone new, even the cats. She sniffed Bear, and he hissed and slapped her with his paws on both sides of her face. She cried. Years later, we would joke about how it didn't take her long to get over that and become a sassy, bossy girl. She retained her sweetness, however. She was very protective over the children in my care, the scouts, and our own two.

Stephanie had become so attached to cats, she adamantly told us she was not happy we were bringing home a dog. She said she didn't like dogs. She changed the thought dramatically after Alaska arrived and immediately told us she loved her. She has been a dog lover ever since and is never without one in her life.

The following spring, I was sitting outside with Stephanie and the end-of-the-day pickups from day care, when a man jogged by, followed by two dogs. The one in the rear, a black puppy with a small patch of white on her neck, around four months old, retreated from the jogging team, ran up to us, and began kissing Stephanie and me. I called out to the man that he had left his dog behind.

He replied, "Oh, that one is not mine. She has been following us for a few miles."

This was back before you could make news go viral and advertise missing animals and such online. So, we posted in nearby neighborhoods about the lost dog. No one answered, so Nellie became our second dog and Alaska's sister. She appeared to be a lab/chow mix. Now our family was complete with two parents, two kids, two cats, and two dogs. Oh, yeah and a tank full of fish! Who could ask for more?

When I turned forty in 2002, we traveled to Cozumel, a Mexican island in the Caribbean Sea. Adam was eleven and Stephanie was twelve at the time. We stayed at a resort near the ocean with a pool and cabana. You could see both from our hotel room window, which was up high.

Stephanie was sick most of the trip and stayed in the room. She had been living with type 1 Diabetes for a year and a half, and traveling somehow got her blood sugars all out of whack. She would get really nauseated. She would occasionally watch us from the window, and we checked on her often.

Adam swam with the sea life, literally. We felt safe and secure in that place. Joe and I would hang out at the cabana, and Adam would head down to the ocean to swim. He made many adult friends on that trip while swimming. One evening at dinner in the town, he ran into a couple and introduced them to us. We all had a great time, thanks to Adam. He was like that everywhere he went: he smiled that smile, batted those baby blues, and reeled them in. He knew all the wait staff, the bartenders, and cooks. He would come up from the ocean to get a drink. "I would like a Coke, please," he'd say.

"One rum and Coke for the boy," the bartender would say, rolling his r's. We would laugh, as we knew he was only getting a Coke, and that was a treat, as we didn't let the kids have pop very often. Then, off to the ocean he would return.

One day he was followed by a school of baby jellyfish and got stung multiple times. He came running back to the cabana with the news. The bartender sent him to the cook, who treated the stings with meat tenderizer. (Who knew that worked?) He had already arrived in Cozumel with a family of seed ticks covering his private parts from a scouting trip a few days earlier. We joked that he had smuggled them in and probably contributed to a future tick infestation in Cozumel. I recall that I had been the chosen one to pick off the ticks. Not so much fun. We later joked that Adam was a tick magnet.

This was our happy life. We had fun. We loved one another. We worked hard and played hard. It was our normal. When Adam became sick at fourteen, our world changed forever. All we had left of our previous life were these precious memories. Some days we wonder if they ever happened at all, yet like everyone else, we have pictures to prove these life events took place.

Chapter 8
School Years

The kids attended Anderson Elementary School in Broken Arrow. Our area had a small-town feel. They walked about three blocks to and from school. All along the way, there were homes with children who attended with them, and they would join the group as they walked towards their location. Some of us had a sticker on our front windows indicating we were a pre-approved safe house. If any child felt unsafe or threatened in any way, they knew they could go to one of these locations. It was one of those neighborhoods where everyone knew everyone else. I only remember one time when someone came to us. It was an adult on his way to work on a cold, snowy day who did not know us personally, but through reputation. He found a small boy of around two-and-a-half who spoke no English, walking barefoot in the snow. He said he knew the boy would be safe with us, and we would somehow figure it out. Apparently, the mother felt it was okay to sneak out early in the morning, run a short errand, and find her way back before the child awoke. He had awoken looking for his mother and wandered into the snow. They were shortly reunited, and the lesson was learned.

Anderson had a great group of teachers, many of whom I had the pleasure of knowing personally. One was a co-leader when I first began teaching Girl Scouts. Some were parents of the children to whom I taught preschool. As time went on, I became familiar through referrals to my preschool with four of the Union public elementary schools in the district to which Anderson belonged. Union encompassed part of Broken Arrow and part of Tulsa. There was another district in our city, Broken Arrow Public Schools, but we were near the cutoff, so our kids attended Union.

When Adam entered first grade, Joe followed suit as a scout leader with the boys. They enjoyed that time together. Looking back, I would say those were the best years the two of them had. Girl Scout rules were a lot stricter than those of the Boy Scouts. The boys had a lot more freedom to get out and do things. Adventures included day camps during the early years, where they fished, shot guns, practiced archery, did woodworking, and learned basic skills of rope tying and campfire building, among many other things.

Adam looked forward to these days, and so did Joe. He would take off work for all the camps, whether they were long or short. Every year we had the pinewood derby contest and many celebrations as boys advanced higher in scouts. Joe was an excellent leader, along with Susie Green, Mike Michaud, and Carol Ogden, as they guided the boys to advancement. As Adam became older, there were longer trips, such as one to Sea Base. We once took a ski trip in North Kansas City area with the Boy Scouts and went on many, many camp outs. I got to go on a few hikes with them, one on the Katy Trail near Rocheport, Missouri, and once in the mountains of Arkansas. That one was cold, wet, and treacherous, but we made it safely to the top, camped overnight, and returned down the mountain the next day.

Our kids were outgoing and made friends with everyone. I felt they took after their dad, who had been popular throughout his school years. I, on the other hand, had been shy and reclusive.

Adam ended up with all of his closest friends in the same kindergarten class. After that year, I am certain they were very careful to separate the boys as much as possible, as they were having too much fun. Adam was a bit of a class clown, but the teachers loved him. He was so cute and little, it was difficult to become angry with him or stay that way for too long.

In second or third grade, we had a parent/teacher conference. The teacher was concerned that Adam might have Attention Deficit/ Hyperactivity Disorder, as he was continually disorganized and distracted. We didn't see it the way she did. We figured he was all boy and enjoyed playing too hard and clowning around. His room at home was disorganized too, but I felt maybe I did too much for him, and perhaps I was part of the problem. I vowed to give him more responsibility for cleaning up after himself. We said we would talk with Adam and work on these skills at home. The teacher jokingly told us not to worry too much, as he was very bright, especially with his math skills. She said he would be a very rich man one day because he would make a lot of money with the knowledge he had. That made us feel very proud.

Years later, I would learn from many other families who had a child with mental illness, that the first diagnosis at an early age was that they had ADHD or Attention Deficit Disorder. This certainly does not mean that if your child has this diagnosis, he or she will develop bipolarity, schizophrenia, or another more serious mental illness later on. I just wish I had been aware early on of the potential signs. Maybe Adam didn't have ADHD. Maybe he was showing the early signs of what was yet to come.

In the Union School District, the elementary schools merged into the 6th and 7th grade center following the primary years. Here the students transitioned from about 100 students from the elementary school to a class of around 1,000. The chances of finding someone you knew in one of those classes was slim. Still, both Stephanie and Adam made it through these grades seemingly unscathed.

Eighth grade center followed. I always thought it odd that that one particular grade got its own building. It wasn't until years later after some reflection, that I realized how difficult that year could be for children. It seemed to be the year of big changes. That was the year children turned thirteen. Puberty hit big time. The children were caught somewhere between childhood and young adulthood. The girls began to have periods. Some kids got acne. Adam suffered terribly from it. He was also the second smallest boy in the class. His friends thought it was cute to carry him around. He later said he felt embarrassed to be so small and didn't want attention drawn to him. Still, he was a bit of a class clown and didn't let that show to his buddies.

Adam was still going strong in wrestling and Boy Scouts. He still hung around the guys in the neighborhood, even though they didn't see each other too much in school. At school, he also made new friends like everyone else. Now kids were choosing groups based on similar interests, be it sports, academics, or whatever else they had a proclivity for.

Stephanie was in ninth grade at Union Intermediate High School. Both she and Adam seemed to be changing and struggling a bit and losing interest in school. Stephanie had gotten an insulin pump, which was attached by a small needle to her hip. The high school had three thousand kids milling about. Often she would get knocked accidentally and the pump would come out. Very frustrated, she began to isolate herself from the kids she had known for many years. We became pretty focused on her and her needs, thinking Adam was doing fine. The same year she was taken advantage of by her first boyfriend and began cutting herself.

Joe walked into her room and caught her doing it. She jumped out the window and ran away. We took her to Laureate Psychiatric Hospital, where they evaluated her. They determined she was not trying to kill herself as we had initially thought. They released her. She never was admitted after that. We figured it was a phase that maybe kids those days went through. We got an education on cutting that year.

Apparently, when a person feels strong emotional pain, the cutting actually makes them feel better. Most people who inflict self-harm do it to relieve themselves of all the pent-up emotions they are feeling and to feel in control of something. It may distract them from difficult life events, relieve guilt, or be used as self-punishment. It helps them deal with negative emotions like depression, rage, guilt, emptiness, and self-hatred. Often it becomes addicting.

The prognosis made sense to us, considering her feelings about having diabetes at such a young age and the assault from the boyfriend. Naturally, we were concerned and focused a lot on her. This was our first taste of understanding that we had symptoms of mental illness in our family. Still, we had hope that she would be okay. She suffered greatly from anxiety at her school and eventually attended Union's Alternative School, where there were fewer students, so she could complete her studies in a less stressful environment. She passed high school with good grades and graduated a semester ahead of her class. She began working at sixteen years old and was responsible for a good period of time. It was when we were beginning to worry less about Stephanie that the insulin event with Adam took place.

Chapter 9
The Fight Begins

Following Adam's stay at Laureate in 2005 at the age of fourteen, our lives changed drastically. As a mother, I no longer slept through the night. It was as if the children were infants all over again. Adam changed dramatically. He no longer associated with his childhood friends. He dressed in black. He hung around kids that dressed just like him. We didn't like it. We tried to stop it. He would simply tell us, "Everybody does this." Joe made the comment at an open house at Union when Adam was in the ninth grade that out of 1,000 kids, he saw maybe twelve who looked like Adam.

Adam became withdrawn. He no longer showed interest in sports or scouting. One of the last events I recall him participating in was a ski trip to a resort north of Kansas City in Weston, Missouri. We stayed in some houses owned by Heartland Presbyterian Church. While the boys were skiing, I was organizing our family's things and found cigars in Adam's luggage. Apparently, he had stolen them from a gas station on the way there. I remember Joe and I ranting on and on about how scouts don't steal or smoke. We were angry and disappointed. Little did we know, he had already been smoking cigarettes and had soon after found a reliable pot dealer in the halls of Union High School to help alleviate the symptoms of his depression.

We couldn't understand why we could steer Stephanie somewhat back on track, but not Adam. It seemed that no matter how we tried, he just pushed back and got worse.

That same summer, Joe took Adam to Sea Base with the Boy Scouts. The boys had to pass rigorous tests in order to participate. Adam passed them all. Joe explained to me later that the boys had canoed out to an island off the coast of Florida. They then parked the canoes at a certain point and waded through sargassum and sea creatures.

One of the guides had pulled a barracuda from the water, punched it in the face, torn out its eyes, and dared someone to eat one of them. You guessed it: Adam did it on a dare and money bet. He didn't follow the safety rules, including the wearing of sunscreen, and he got a very intense sunburn, almost earning him a trip back home. Who knows why he was allowed to stay? It could be because Joe had accompanied him on the trip. He was becoming more and more careless and reckless with his own safety. He was not the Boy Scout we knew from earlier years who had been elected by Order of The Arrow, along with Joe. (Only a very select few are voted to do this.)

We got Adam to a wonderful doctor in Tulsa who specialized in child and adolescent psychiatry. Since he was still a minor, we had access to all of his records, although Dr. Puls did keep much of what was said between himself and Adam private.

I loved how he would work a session. Adam would go in and see him first, alone. Then I would. Then both of us. At that time, Dr. Puls agreed that Adam had depression—clinical depression, which is characterized as a constant sense of hopelessness and despair. It can make it difficult for those who suffer from it to sleep, work, study, and enjoy friends and activities. Symptoms include fatigue, feelings of worthlessness or guilt, impaired concentration, indecisiveness, insomnia, restlessness or feeling slowed down, markedly diminished interest or pleasure in almost all activities, recurring thoughts of death or suicide, and significant weight loss or gain. Adam exhibited all of these symptoms, including the weight loss. He was painfully thin.

Adam also became increasingly agitated when asked about how

he was feeling. He was quickly building a wall between our family and himself.

We were very developing a thick file on Adam filled with his suicide attempts, mental illness symptoms, drug use, and so on. We started this in 2005 with the insulin incident and hospitalizations due to psychotic episodes and overdoses or threats of suicide. We quickly learned the importance of documentation to have credibility if you want to have someone hospitalized in a mental health facility. If there is no proof of a threat to their own person or others, they are sent home.

Our son's life was important to us, so even if it meant he would be angry or withdrawn from us because we "put him away", we did what we had to do for his safety. Looking through his files and at his behavior, I began to doubt that depression was the sole thing we were dealing with. Unfortunately, during the teenage years, young men's brains are still developing, so it is difficult to determine what the true diagnosis is. Not wanting to label a child with schizophrenia or bipolar disorder, for example, many doctors are hesitant. So, you wonder if they just have poor behavior or if the poor behavior is a symptom of illness. It is very frustrating for doctors and parents alike.

Chapter 10
The Stress Affects Everyone Involved

In 2006, Adam was fifteen years old. He was still struggling, in spite of psychiatric treatments and our support, love, and understanding. All the while, we were attempting to hold it together and keep up a positive front to our friends and family and for the sake of our jobs. We were both feeling the stress. Joe felt he wasn't doing enough as a dad to discipline his kids. He didn't want anyone at his job to know what was going on. Neither did I, but I was open about it because my business was all about children. If anyone judged me or Joe for what Adam was going through or felt we were somehow at fault for it, the natural reaction would be to remove their child from my care.

At the same time, I constantly felt the pressure of my reputation being on the line. Inside, I constantly worried that Adam would be accused of something involving the children who had been entrusted to me because in our society, many people believe that all those with mental illness are going to kill or harm us. This is not true; they are more likely to become the victims of a crime than to commit one. I worried that many years of hard work building trust with families and having an excellent track record and reputation would be wasted because everyone knows the parents are ultimately to blame for their children's problems, right? Of course this isn't true, but it is what we are told.

My mother-in-law actually said, "Send him to Aunt Alicia's (sorry, Alicia) for a week, and she will straighten him out," insinuating that we couldn't raise our kids right. Someone on my side suggested that we send him to my brother Jimmy and his wife Suzanne, for the same reason. Sorry, guys. No offense, it's just what we were told. Don't think for one moment we didn't consider it so that others would actually see where we were coming from. A week? Good luck with that!

In everyone's eyes, we were to blame. It's easy to blame someone when you are on the outside looking in, living hours away, not witnessing for yourself that they are doing everything in their power to change the outcome of self-destruction. Did we beat our kids, as someone suggested we did? No. We did not believe in that. Did we discipline them? Of course! We took away privileges and grounded them. Did that work? Of course not! What works within a normal (typical) situation does not work for a child with mental illness! The rules of the game change. They escape. They run away. They do not concern themselves with consequences. Did we "let" that happen? No, we stayed awake at night to ensure Adam stayed put for as long as we possibly could. Eventually, we'd crash because our bodies needed sleep to survive. Sleep deprivation takes a toll on a person, and it affects the decision-making faculty, as well. Suddenly, you wonder if it really is YOU who is to blame.

I was actually very lucky, as far as the parents of the children under my care were concerned. I had built so much trust through our family lines over the years that they knew me well. Only one parent removed their children from my care (a social worker, of all professions) out of concern for them. I loved those children and felt very protective over them, but I couldn't argue with her. I had many social workers and teachers throughout the previous years and years to come who more than made up for the hurt and pain of that loss. They backed me up and stood by me through so many trials. I thank them all! When that family left, they offered a nanny job to my kindergarten transporter, so she quit working for me, and neither told me the truth. I found out through others. Both of them were women I loved and respected (and still do), but it hurt. This is life for families like us. Just one small example. It was sad and scary at the same time.

I told each and every prospective family after that my story, and you know what? I enrolled each and every one of them! They knew me through someone else or were related to a previous family. My job still stood solid. I was blessed.

At the same time, I couldn't help as a parent to blame myself. And I couldn't blame my transporter for leaving, either. What would I have done in her place? She was there taking over the supervision of the kids any time I had an Adam emergency or had to take him to the psychiatrist. I know this was traumatic for my assistant. After how many such instances did I expect her to stay and helplessly look on?

She was one of the kindest people I have ever known and very gentle with the children. I missed her terribly but had to understand how helpless she must have felt because she was powerless to help solve the problem.

Chapter 11
The Second Year

By 2006 we hadn't "fixed" the problem, but we'd somehow deluded ourselves into thinking that if we did everything right, it would all work out. We belonged to the same congregation, St. Benedict's Catholic Church, for many years in Broken Arrow. We had developed many friendships through our church community and were very involved in activities there. The children went from Mother's Day Out in the early years to Religious Education (R.E.) on Wednesdays and Sundays through the later years. Joe and I volunteered for Adoration on Thursday nights. Joe and I joined a prayer group of three other couples to whom we soon became close. Joe had been Adam's Boy Scout leader since first grade, and I had been Stephanie's Girl Scout leader since she was in kindergarten. I was the Girl Scout Cookie Coordinator for our service unit in the Tulsa metro area. We felt that if we led by example, our kids would be fine.

One area I know I failed at was in giving them enough responsibility for tasks such as keeping their rooms clean and helping in the kitchen, the yard, or whatever. I felt like I had worked so hard as a child that I missed out on being a kid and didn't want my kids to feel that way. I wanted them to be kids since that phase of life passes so quickly. I think you can go too far on either end of the spectrum. At one point, I felt sure I was responsible for the mental illness because they didn't know how to take care of themselves. When your child is sick with a mental illness, you can come up with many ways to self-blame. But of course, what a parent does or doesn't do does not cause mental illness. In our journey over the next several years, we met so many people from different walks of life: some were rich, some were poor; some were understanding, kind, and loving; and some were not. It made no difference to the ultimate outcome.

So, there we were every Thursday night at church, lighting candles, praying, praying, praying. We were filled with hope, knowing that we were doing it right! And, we continued to send the kids to R.E. Little did we know that when we dropped them off at the front of the building, they exited through the back. Occasionally, we'd receive a call from the church staff saying they missed our kids, and then we'd make an extra effort to make sure they stayed put. We'd wait and watch at the entrance to the church until we knew they were there. But then we'd stop, and then the cycle would begin again.

With Adam, the same thing was happening at school. He skipped often, sometimes hiding in some wooded area around the school until it was let out, and then he would catch the bus home. Rarely were we contacted by the school. We first learned of this behavior when the grade reports came out. We called for conferences with all of his teachers. I can remember showing up to one such meeting where only one teacher showed up. They did not seem to care at all! He wasn't important enough for them to show up for, yet they expected him to show up in class. During the meetings when some of them showed up, they were rude and disrespectful to us as parents, as if we were condoning his behavior. We did everything we could possibly do. We just didn't understand (and neither did they) that he wasn't just some bad kid with behavior issues. He was sick inside his mind. The behavior was a result of the chaos in his brain, yet it took us so many years to figure it out.

During 2006, Adam made his second suicide attempt, a drug overdose. Kids would go to a pharmacy and steal over-the-counter medications such as Robitussin and Delsym cough suppressants to get high. Adam used these, along with other drugs. During that year, he overdosed several times on them and landed in St. Francis Hospital. Blood tests revealed other street drugs in his system, as well. We were overwhelmed with this information. Where in the world could a fifteen-year-old get a hold of that? Oh, we were so naive. Apparently, kids sold them in school. According to the kids, you could access them at any corner of the hallways at school. Union public high schools had police on campus patrolling the halls. I couldn't for the life of me figure out why the kids knew where to get it, but the police apparently didn't.

Following these hospitalizations, we did not receive a welcome-home party or balloons. No food was delivered; there were no phone calls. Joe and I felt alone and ashamed. I can only imagine how Adam felt. He had wanted to die, and it seemed like most people didn't care. (An example of stigma!) We know that no one meant any harm; no one knew what to say or do. Neither did we! Everyone had their idea of what this was, even if they were aware it was mental illness. Our belief system is so screwed up in regard to what we think is happening and what is causing it. We are way off. It took many years of learning and living the life to take away the stigma in our own hearts and minds.

We had one visitor at the hospital from a lady in our prayer group, whom I will call Diane to protect her identity. She was my rock and comfort, assuring me that we were doing everything right. I also have another wonderful friend, Deb Carroll, who had small children at home she had to care for at the time. She did make sure I took time for myself, and once a month, she and I would go to dinner, a movie, or both. I don't know if she knew what she was doing, but she got me through some really tough times. I had cared for all of her girls over the years, and somehow, despite my obvious lousy parenting skills, she still trusted me! Her girls even insisted on spending summers with me beyond early childhood. They were all a Godsend. I also have a long-time friend, Lorna Hesskamp, who lives in Louisiana and was always a phone call away. She talked me through many a crisis and continues to do so today!

Following his second attempt, Adam was sent to a place called Shadow Mountain Behavioral Health Facility in Tulsa. Its purpose is to treat various mental health disorders and behavioral issues. (It is funny to me now that it is named "behavioral health" rather than "mental health". It led us to believe it was all due to bad behavior and that we had somehow caused it. We were the parents!) In reality, it is the mental health issue that causes the acting out. There was a dormitory for boys Adam's age, as well as ones for girls and kids of various ages. I was shocked to see kids as young as four moving around in groups. It was heartbreaking.

Adam was placed in their residential treatment program. He was supervised by some pretty tough-looking, bulked-up guys who looked like they would beat the crap out of you if you stepped out of line. Adam went through counseling and drug rehabilitation there, while he continued his schooling. He pretty much did what he was told. We know he hated it there and wanted to come home, but we hoped this place would "nip the problem in the bud". After all, we were following through as parents with the discipline that Adam needed, just like everyone kept shoving down our throats.

When visiting our son, we had to come at a specific time and go directly to the dormitory. One of the tough guys would retrieve Adam from his room and usher him into a meeting room, where we could talk. Adam was still small for his age and was apparently being pushed and shoved around by some of the other boys who were bigger than he was.

He told us a story about this on one of our visitations. I asked him about the supervisors. He said they were pretty cool, actually. He said that one day that week, they had been moved from the dorm to an activity in formation. As they had gone up an outside stairway, one particular kid who had been bullying him kept pushing and hitting him when no one was watching. Adam had let this fester for days, until finally he'd had enough. He hit the guy back, and he took a fall down the stairs. The supervisor witnessed this and said nothing. He later told Adam that that was one of the things he needed to work on: standing up for himself. He felt that the other kid had deserved it, so he had looked the other way. Adam got along fine with the boys after that. I don't know that the other boy deserved it. In my heart, I had to wonder what he had been through to behave like that.

Adam came home and seemed to level out for a while. We came to learn he would do better for a short time because he feared being placed somewhere again. We didn't ever want to have to use that option, but we feared for his safety and felt it was the only way sometimes to keep him safe from himself. Every time we left a place like Laureate or Shadow Mountain, we felt a renewed hope that this time Adam would be on the right path and that everything would be okay. This was just a phase, we thought, and it too would pass.

Boy, were we wrong. The phase that passed was just the honeymoon we had when Adam came home. We came to understand that he was self-medicating at this point, with some hard core drugs, cocaine being one of them. Once again, he was placed in Laureate following an overdose. He really did not want to live! How could our sweet little Adam, once so full of life, want to die? Where had we gone wrong? Were we going to keep on placing him in hospitals for years to come? Was this his/our life? Could we change the outcome?

There were many nights we all went to bed, and once everyone was asleep, Adam would open his window and climb out, disappearing into the night, doing God knows what. I would wake up and check on him to find him missing. It was frightening. Sometimes a police officer would bring him home as he broke curfew, a rule established in Broken Arrow for those under eighteen years of age. Other times, we would get a call to retrieve him from a friend's residence, where the police had arrested anyone over seventeen and called the parents to pick up the younger ones. At least we had that going for us: no jail time.

One late morning after a cold winter night, Adam wandered through the front door.

"Where have you been?" I demanded. "I was worried sick."

"I fell asleep," he responded.

"Where?" I asked.

"In a big field," he told me. "It was beautiful and peaceful." How he kept from freezing to death is beyond me!

We began to feel desperate about what to do next. We were still trying to protect our reputation, and it was getting more and more difficult. At some point, Joe bought a 1991 Harley Sportster from a friend. Whenever we could, we would escape on that bike and ride it all over the Tulsa area and beyond. If only for a brief time, it gave us relief from the pain. I don't know how it started, but in our own way, we began to self-medicate, too. We ate all the comfort foods we could stuff into our bodies (fried foods, bar foods, the bad fats, sugars, beer, etc.).

Chapter 12
A Home and a Preschool—
the Next "Solution"

Joe and I were desperate to save our son. It seemed like nothing we tried was working. No amount of love was sinking in. What was causing this? What was happening to our precious son and our lives as we knew them? What had gone wrong? What was it that set Adam apart from his friends? We lived in a one-story house. Most of his friends lived in bigger homes. Could that have been it? Did he feel like he was less than they were? (I know we were grasping at straws, but we were looking for an "out" somewhere.) Or could it have been having to share myself and my work with our family?

Joe and I decided we needed to split the preschool business from our home life. We built a beautiful two-story home in the Broken Arrow School District and completely turned the one-story into a preschool, utilizing all the rooms for various activities. We thought that letting the children have their own space away from Mom's work would be ideal. Stephanie and Adam had bedrooms upstairs with their own living room, and Joe had a music room up there to accommodate his drum set, keyboard, and guitar. We had an air hockey table and a pinball machine. It was ideal! Or so we thought.

Downstairs we had two guest rooms, our bedroom, a wonderfully large kitchen that opened up to a great living area, a formal dining room, and a nook, plus extras. Yes, this new home had to make them happy! They could still attend Union, since we owned houses in both districts, but they had the option of attending Broken Arrow High if they chose.

Everyone seemed excited about the change. I took the kids to work with me. They caught the bus from there and returned to me after school, and we rode home together. At the preschool, I used what had once been the master bedroom to lay mats down for naps and music activities, since it was usually bare. I kept my desk in the back of the room by the windows.

One afternoon, Adam came home from school and went in there to use my computer. When I went in to check on him, I found him seated in my chair doing a complete back bend over one of its arms. In a panic, I rushed to him. He was about 120 pounds. So was I. I lifted that boy with superhuman strength and half carried/half dragged him out the door. At the time, a friend named Trina was helping me with the kids. She called Joe, who rushed over to meet me. I was dragging Adam through the neighborhood when he drove up to me. Luckily, he didn't work too far away. The hospital was close by, too. Adam had inhaled air-duster and had become unconscious.

Prior to this incident, I knew nothing about inhaling chemical products. Air duster products, used to clean computer keyboards, were popular among kids to get high with during my children's teenage years. The act is called "huffing". The purpose is to attain a feeling of euphoria or mental high by inhaling the chemical vapors. The user may feel intoxicated, as if they are drinking alcohol. Initial symptoms include drowsiness, lightheadedness, and inhibition. Continued use can lead to dizziness, hallucinations or delusions, belligerence, apathy, and impaired judgment.

Long-term users can suffer damaging health consequences, including depression and mood changes, weight loss, inattentiveness, lack of coordination, irritability, and physical weakness. More serious consequences may result in permanent damage to the brain or even death, as well as irreversible damage to the heart, liver, kidney, lungs, and brain. We did learn later on that a lady I knew in Broken Arrow who also ran a day care had had a son who tried air duster just one time his first year of college ... just for fun. He died.

We took Adam to the hospital and he came around. Was this another suicide attempt, or simply a way to avoid the pain of depression—a possible escape from his reality? Once again Adam was evaluated, and we continued to seek professional help. He was now entering the phase of self-medicating. When someone with a mental illness self-medicates, they are attempting to alleviate the pain or feel this is a way to make it all go away. They try to escape from their reality. Often, they choose the self-medication over the prescribed route, which in turn can make the symptoms of the illness magnify.

Taking both prescriptions and illegal substances doesn't help either, as self-medication often cancels out the treatment the person is receiving. It can be very frustrating for the families who try to help their loved ones, which is why so many of our homeless or our prison population suffer from mental illness. It seems to create a domino effect, from self-medication or not taking prescribed medications, to their families giving up on them, to them living in the streets, and/or resorting to crime to survive.

As parents, Joe and I were terrified. We feared that the ultimate outcome of all of this was surely death, either from suicide or from accidental overdose of an illegal drug.

Because of the move and owning two houses, we ended up in two school districts. The old house, although in Broken Arrow, crossed over a division that was in the Union Public School District. The new house, although only a few miles away, landed in the Broken Arrow Public School District. Our children could attend either since both houses were considered residences. Stephanie continued to attend Union until she graduated. We sent Adam to Broken Arrow, thinking a change of scenery (and friends?) would be just the thing he needed. The parent of one of my preschool children taught at Union, but her husband was a principal at Broken Arrow. His oldest son was in Joe's scout troop. Surely, Adam would do so much better there.

Here's the thing about mental illness and troubled youth that we didn't understand: they will find like-minded people, no matter where they go! If they are self-medicating, they will find drugs wherever they go! Adam was still sneaking out of school, but instead of retreating to a wooded area, he simply came home while we worked. It was close enough to walk to, and the house was big enough to hide in if one of us showed up in the middle of the day. Stephanie's closet had a secret hideaway behind it. Adam had a leveled roof jutting out from under his room, and he climbed out his window to sit and smoke on it. There were small attic access points. Besides, if we came home, we were not likely to go around searching the house for anything suspicious.

Chapter 13
Adam is Sixteen, Year Three

For many years, I worked long hours at the preschool, beginning at 5:30 a.m. for set up and certain early arranged arrivals. The regular hours were 7:00 a.m. to 5:30 p.m., Monday through Friday. For eighteen years, I worked over sixty hours per week, cleaning and shopping on weekends. When I opened up the school and took on more students, I hired others to help me. This made my days more manageable.

I worked Monday through Thursday from 5:30 a.m. to 3:30 p.m., and on Fridays, I left at 1 p.m. Saturdays were spent cleaning the preschool and shopping, planning, etc., so I still got in about 45-50 hours, which was more bearable than 70-plus! It upset some parents, who complained because I wasn't there at pickup time. Usually, parents who dropped their children off at the beginning of the day, then got off work and went shopping or whatever until the last minute, couldn't understand why twelve-hour days and dealing with sick children was taxing on my health.

So, one Friday I left for home around one. Usually, I would clean my own house on Fridays, but that day I was going to meet Joe for lunch and have an early start to our weekend. We met at home. Shortly after our arrival we heard a loud thud coming from upstairs … Adam's room!

We both bolted up the stairs. We found him lying on the floor, his skin as red as a lobster. He had fallen out of his bed, obviously having taken something very toxic into his system. He looked up at us, dazed and confused, and asked, "Who are you?"

We went into panic mode. Oh, dear God! I thought. Is he seriously brain damaged at this point? Joe literally carried Adam down the stairs and into our truck, and once again, we drove him to the emergency room. He had overdosed on Delsym cough syrup of all things! Would this be what takes out our boy? Cough syrup? Once the drug had passed through his system and ample fluids had been given intravenously, Adam recognized us. We felt we had dodged a big bullet this time.

Of course, after such an attempt, Adam was once again placed in a mental health facility to "level him out", put him on some new medication, and send him home after a week. I am not sure if this ever did Adam any good. What it did for us was give us a break, let us sleep through the night for a few nights, and recharge, without worry over where he was or what he was doing.

We visited Adam every evening when he was in one of these places. He was always happy to see us and enjoyed us bringing in his favorite foods or candy. At the same time, he would beg us to get him out of there, promising to change. When he came home, it seemed things were good for a little while. We would get false hope, and bang! The cycle would start all over again.

Chapter 14
Adolescent Outpatient Drug Rehab Fallout

Following the cough syrup overdose began yet another inpatient stay at Laureate. Now we were looking at possible drug addiction, and we were referred to Associate Centers for Therapy in Tulsa. Yes, I say we, because as his parents, we had to participate in the program, an outpatient group therapy for drug abuse, which lasted for five weeks. I was fortunate to have notes and documentation during this time.

The suffering child self-medicates to feel "normal" or to dull the pain and distract their senses from what is happening in their minds. If you are one of those parents, I hope you will understand through this that it is not your fault!

Adam was actually working the program pretty well at first. He was given incentives and coins that were earned for progress through the program. Smoking was not allowed on the premises, so on break, the kids would walk to a spot on the perimeter of the grounds and smoke so they wouldn't get into trouble with their superiors. Adam was close to the end of the process—just days away—when he was caught smoking on that perimeter and was thrown out of the program. We pleaded and begged on his behalf. He felt so proud of himself for not using drugs for weeks on end, and he really wanted that coin for validation. Even we as parents did not understand the No Smoking period. We understood it to be on the grounds only. Now, you are probably thinking why in the world would we want our sixteen-year-old smoking cigarettes, anyway? What fools were we to condone it?

Years later we would be facilitating a support group for families of the mentally ill. A good friend, Becky Beers, said it best of all. As

61

she talked about her life versus the life of her son, she said, "When I was growing up, I followed every rule. I was a 'good girl'. I went to school, studied, did what made my parents happy and proud. I did that because I could. I didn't smoke or drink. Never crossed my mind to do that. I was not of age. The bar was set at a certain level we understood. You will go to school. You will make good grades, and you will attend college. No one questioned that. I never even tried an alcoholic drink until I was twenty-one and still really don't drink. We set those same rules for our boys as responsible parents do.

"When our son became ill with Bipolar Disorder, we had to 'lower the bar' to adjust to his behaviors caused by the illness, even though it was not at our comfort level."

Lowering the bar! I love that term, and when I think of our family and others like ours, we all do it. We walk on eggshells, afraid to set our loved one off into psychosis or depression, never wanting to be the cause of something going horribly wrong, like in our case, what if Adam was successful at one of his suicide attempts? Was taking a cigarette away from him worth it? So, here is how our "bar" went from the highest level to basically laying on the floor to step over:

Rules

• You will go to school, do your homework, turn it in, and make good grades.
• You will wear respectable clothes.
• You will keep your hair cut at a decent length.
• You will shower every day.
• You will hang around parent-approved friends.
• You will attend church on Sundays and receive religious education.
• You will not smoke, drink, do drugs, or engage in inappropriate sexual behavior.

• You will not cuss.

• You will use a respectable tone when speaking to parents, teachers, and other adults.

• You will keep your room clean.

This is how the bar gradually lowered until it was on the floor: something you simply stepped or tripped over, until it disappeared altogether.

• From: You will go to school most of the time, try to do your homework, and make passing grades. To: Hopefully get a GED.

• From: You will wear clothes that cover your bottom; no, not all black clothes. To: At least you have clothes on.

• From: You will cut your hair. You may not color it black! To: It will grow out eventually, and he will outgrow this phase. It is only hair, after all.

• From: You will shower and wear clean clothes three days a week. To: At least once a week.

• From: You will not hang out with those people. To: Ultimately not liking the situation, but having no control over it at all.

• From: Trying to no avail to keep the kids in class at church. To: Finally giving up and going to church alone.

• From: You may not smoke cigarettes in the house or on our property. To: You may smoke on the back patio (hidden from others).

• From: Pushing against drinking and the use of drugs. To: Finally letting it become the same thing as cigarettes. Only with pot, and not in the house. (This was actually when he was of age; we forbade it when he was underage).

• From: Do not cuss. To: Do not cuss around the children.

• From: Please be respectful to your elders. To: Please be respectful to your elders other than us. We just endured it at home in the hope that he would get it out of his system.

• From: You will clean your room. To: I will clean your room if it gets to a really bad place and I can't stand it anymore. Or just close the door.

Anyway, taking the possibility of the coin away, along with never being allowed in the program again—not even to start over—was devastating to Adam and to us, as well. We had a great almost five weeks at home because of this program, and we all felt hopeless. We were hurt and angry. It set Adam way back on a new course of self-destruction.

Traveling to the group daily for five weeks had taken a toll on our family, as it was. Joe and I have always been close and never try to hurt the other's feelings. During that time in our lives, we kept what we were feeling to ourselves. You would probably guess we were each blaming the other spouse, but to the contrary, internally we were blaming ourselves almost to the point of our own self destruction!

We had a daily plan: I would leave work, have someone cover for me, and drop Adam off at the location, and Joe would pick him up on his return home, as I closed the preschool at 5:30 and didn't have time to make it back by six, the rehab closing time. One evening when I got home, Joe was there. I went in and asked how Adam had done that day.

"Adam?" he snarled. He had forgotten to get him. I went into a panic because they had said they would contact the Department of Human Services if anyone was late picking up their child. Joe told me to pick up my own "f%#&ing child" and left, peeling out of the driveway. At the time I was so angry, wondering, "What in the hell just happened?" Stephanie was mad, too.

Looking back, I can see what a toll everything took on Joe. It is heartbreaking to see your loved one try and try until they go into an ultimate breakdown like that. I loaded clothes, pillows, blankets, Stephanie, and the dogs into the car to get Adam. (Fred, our remaining cat, lived at the preschool.) We picked up Adam and went to the little house to spend the night. Oh, yes! I was going to make a statement. I was going to let Joe worry about all of us!

We spent the night restless on uncomfortable surfaces. Early the next morning, I drove over to the house to pick up the newspaper, and Joe was not home! He had never returned. I guess we both had the same idea in mind, but neither of us knew that the other had left. It was almost laughable!

I called our friend, Ben Tedder, who was had been Joe's drum instructor before turning into a great friend to all of us. He was our most trusted person when Joe and I had to travel. He stayed with our kids and had a great relationship with them. He said he would try to get in touch with Joe, make sure he was okay, and calm him down.

On my lunch break, I drove past the house again. Joe's pickup truck was in the driveway, and the windshield was smashed. Had he been in an accident? Was he hurt? Still angry, I did not enter the house. I figured if the car was there, he was okay.

Ben got in touch with him, and before I left work, Joe called me to say he was sorry. He was so overwhelmed with grief over who our son was, and he felt powerless. He had driven somewhere with some beer and woke up not knowing where he was. Evidence on his knuckles proved he had punched the window. I went home and we just held each other sobbing. We vowed nothing like that would ever happen again, and it never did.

2007 was one of the most difficult years for us. We had a few suicide attempts that year. People were beginning to think Adam was only looking for attention, but the things he consumed and the methods he tried … it was a miracle he lived through any of them.

During April of 2007, we received a call from our cousin, Pastor Gary, that two of his brother Doug's children had been in a horrible car accident in Bowling Green, Missouri. One had survived but was badly injured and hospitalized in a nearby town. Lacey, who was nineteen at the time, had died on impact. It really scared me. My heart was breaking for Doug. We had grown up with these cousins like siblings. I couldn't imagine anything like this happening to any of us. I recall at her funeral turning to Adam in tears and begging him, "Please don't ever do this to me! I couldn't bear losing you!"

He looked at me and told me to stop worrying. "That will never happen," he said.

Adam turned sixteen that year and got his driver's license, which added another element of fear to our lives. We let him pick up his sister at work to give him some responsibility, and it helped us out. Adam also got a job, over and over. He would start one, work a couple of weeks, quit, and after a while, he would get another one and repeat the pattern.

Visiting with other families years later, we learned that this is common with people living with mental illness. It is not laziness or an unwillingness to work. Mental illness is so overwhelming that it not only drains their mental energy, but their physical, as well. That is the reason behind the lack of interest in school, occupations, or other activities, as well as the neglecting of self-care.

I would get reports around the neighborhood we first lived in about Adam and Stephanie sightings in my van. It would be speeding through the neighborhood with Adam on its roof holding onto the luggage rack!

Another time he left with his friend, Cary. I came upon a grizzly accident at an intersection near our home, with a car that looked like Cary's. A boy with dyed black hair was dangling from the passenger side, blood running from his body. Police were at the scene. I called Adam's number. It was not them! Thank God!

For a while, Joe took on a paper route so he and Adam could do that together. One night, after curfew (the exceptions of which were if you were working at a job or were with a parent), Joe and Adam were in a QuikTrip getting a drink. A familiar Broken Arrow police officer came in. Yes, sad but true, we were beginning to know who all the officers were. He saw Adam, and Adam quickly said, "I got a job!" The officer saw Joe and everyone had to laugh.

That same year we received a call to pick up Adam from JCPenney. He had stolen merchandise (to support his cigarette, drug, and alcohol addictions). He would steal and then sell to a local consignment shop with the tags still on the merchandise! You would think they would recognize it was a racket and report it, but hey, they were making money! The same thing happened with Stephanie. We were so upset over this. "We" don't steal!

One day, I was at work on my break, doing payroll on my computer. When we changed the location, I was able to increase the number of children we served and hire helpers. Rene Ogden, Jessica Cook, Kelli King, and Keli O'Neal rotated shifts. My friend from my church group, Diane, wanted some work, too. She was a certified teacher, but due to horrible migraines and depression, she couldn't work a full-time job. So she helped transport the kids who went to afternoon programs. Jessica was Steph's age, so she was still in high school, as was Kelli, who had younger siblings in my care. They worked afternoons, and Rene and Keli helped during the day.

Adam had a MySpace account at the time. One of the younger girls was on hers and was friends with Adam. She immediately pulled me aside to see what he had written: "I have a gun. At a friend's house. I am done. Good-bye, everyone!"

Of course, I went into sheer panic. The ladies working told me to leave and go find him, and not to worry about the kids. They had it under control. I left, not knowing where he was or if I could possibly find him in time. Was it too late? If I found him, what would I see? Would I recognize my boy?

Joe had told me earlier in the week that Adam had been spending time at a house in the older neighborhood that was attached to our newer one. Apparently, the mom of that home let teenage boys come in and party there. She partied right along with them. I entered the older neighborhood through the street that connected ours to it. Suddenly, it was as if someone else had taken over the wheel—and my mind. Something or someone led me to a street I had never driven on and took me to a particular house. Was it an angel? Was it God Himself? I looked at the house and was certain that Adam was in this random house! Then I heard very loud screamo type music coming from that very house. It had to be it. Oh, God! He must have turned up the music to cover up the sound of the gunshot! I called the police and Joe and said I was going into the house. I rang the bell and banged on the door and no one answered. Please don't let me be too late! I prayed. I was crying and screaming, and suddenly there were arms around me, gently moving me away.

"Ma'am, please go back to your van," a man's voice said. "We will take care of this."

I complied. Then Joe appeared and confirmed that this was the house Adam was in. I had to pee so bad. He said to go back to the house and then come back. Reluctantly, I left.

When I returned, it looked like the entire police department was there. This was the day Adam had dyed his hair from blond to black. Standing in the middle of a group of officers was a young man I didn't recognize from behind. His hands were cuffed behind his back. His blond curls were straight and black, along with his clothes. As if it were a slow motion scene, as I rounded the corner, he turned to face me, and it was Adam's face! He had attempted suicide by police officer. How they had gotten him out of there alive is beyond me, but oh, I was so very grateful! So was Joe. Naturally, they took him to the mental health hospital for another week-long stay. How many times are we going to come out of this alive, we thought? We have to do something!

As if that wasn't enough, my dear friend Diane's husband called me before the school year was out to let me know that she was in the hospital due to an overdose. He believed it was an attempt on her life, but she said it was an accident. Another friend took over as driver for the rest of the school year.

By the end of the school year, Rene quit, which saddened me, too. Luckily, Jessica was out of school and able to take her place.

Naturally, more judgment kept coming from some family members. How does he get out? Don't we pay attention? Well, we did have him on the second floor this time, and we kept our bedroom door open in case he came by or exited out the front door, but he didn't leave that way. He climbed out his window and jumped from the roof. He told us once he thought of diving off the roof as a suicide but figured he would be badly injured or confined to a wheelchair, and that would be even worse. I wondered how many ways he thought of. All I knew was, my boy did not want to be here, and I didn't really understand why.

He also told me at some point that he didn't like living in the "big" house. "I loved our childhood home," he said. "It was perfect." I did agree that he could lose himself in this house, but I learned that he was just fine with not competing with the Joneses. I was beginning to understand that this was a bigger issue than we had thought.

Joe wasn't quite on board yet. He was the dad, the one who was supposed to make us feel safe. He felt it was probably a discipline issue, yet ordinary discipline did not work. Adam did not fear consequences in the least. Heck, if you want to die, why would you care if you got grounded or had a privilege taken away?

Joe continued with scouting and helped lead many boys to Eagle Scouts. Adam had been well on his way but had given that up, too. Absolutely nothing made him happy. None of us was happy, but we put on a facade to function in our daily lives. It was almost a relief to be at work, a break from reality, yet we worried the entire time we were there.

I was so blessed with families those last years in Broken Arrow during Adam's teen years. Everyone knew what was going on and helped in any way they could to offer support, love, and prayer.

Also during that year, Adam spent a lot of time online. One day I had several charges on my debit card that had to do with gaming of some sort. Another addictive behavior. My bank removed the charges on that account, but later I found charges on my credit card for the same thing that amounted to a few thousand dollars! The same bank did not remove those charges. It was so frustrating! For both Joe and me. We were paying mortgages on two houses and had astronomical medical bills (even with great insurance). In those days, mental health was only covered for so many days per year for inpatient services, and we far exceeded it every year.

In addition to that, I had to pay others to do my job during times of doctor visits, hospital stays, etc. So, adding this to my credit card really set me back. Yet, Adam never had any idea how harmful any of this was to Joe or me. We hid our struggles from him as best we could. The last thing we wanted was to give Adam an excuse to kill himself. He had enough reasons already.

Another dramatic attempt occurred that year. Adam stole my van. I used the van for transportation and he took it. And he didn't return. We filed a police report. Joe reported the van stolen, but we also filed a missing person's report. I went to area drug stores with copies of Adam's picture, asking them to look out for this guy. "He will steal drugs and wants to kill himself," I told them. "He is missing. Call 911 if you see him. He's been missing for a couple of days."

One of my preschool moms, April Price, let me use her jeep to transport. "What if I have an accident?" I asked.

"That's what we have insurance for!" she said. Her oldest son was a friend of Adam's, and they had been dealing with some stuff with him, too. It seems as he got older he outgrew it, thank God! I cared for his little brother, Jack.

I was transporting Jack and another boy, Michael, home from kindergarten on day three when I was approaching Union High School, which both kids previously attended. A voice in my head suddenly told me to pull into the parking lot. "You will find your son," it said.

My logical mind said, "This is crazy. He is long gone. A friend told us he was headed to California to kill himself on a beach."

I pulled in anyway and drove all the way around the building. No van. No Adam. Stupid me, I was thinking. As I headed toward the exit, there came Adam, driving my van into the parking lot!

What? I thought. Have I been spirit-led? Twice? Or is this some strange mother's intuition? How is this possible?

I turned the jeep to follow him. He sped through the lot. He had seen my face. A high-speed chase ensued. He turned into a circular drive blocked by school buses. I blocked him in on the other side. I ran out. "Get out of the van!" I screamed at him.

He stumbled out, obviously high on something. I hauled him into the school, where there were police on site with two little boys in tow. I asked for help. They told me to move the vehicles. Those buses needed to get to a football game. No one wanted to help. He no longer attended this school, after all. (Not like anyone helped him when he did!) Just ignore the boy with mental illness. Not our problem! I told them, "Help me or I don't move any vehicles!" The principal asked the officer for help. Adam was taken to the police station and later released to a mental health hospital once again.

Adam had been listed as a missing person with the police department. He told us the following story: During the time he was gone with the van, he had pulled up in front of a local grocery store. (We thought at the time he was long gone from Tulsa.) I am not sure why he parked in front of the building, but a police officer came to the window and asked for his driver's license, then asked him why he was parked there.

He replied, "My mom just went into the store and I am waiting to pick her up."

The officer told Adam that he was listed as a missing person.

Adam told him it had all been a misunderstanding. "My mom is in the store," he repeated.

The officer did not check it out and let him go! That could have resulted in a serious outcome if he had indeed made it out of the city before I had cornered him at Union High School!

Chapter 15
Diane

At the beginning of 2007, Diane decided she wanted to come back to work. Rene had recently returned also. I explained to Diane that I only had a budget for ten hours and could really use her during the middle of the day following lunch, for story time and the beginning of naptime. She was very creative and artistic and a great story teller. I figured while I transported children, she would be good at settling little ones down for a nap. We had just begun taking infants again the previous August, so the extra hand during that time was great.

I had taken on a three-year-old child in 2006. I will call him "Z". His mother was a friend of a friend. Z had been dismissed from a few daycare centers due to behavior. I felt with the help I had, I could help her and hopefully her son as well. I had no idea that taking him on during a very stressful time in my family life would cause such a domino effect in my business and personal life.

Z was the most difficult child I had ever cared for. His parents were divorced and both so appreciative of me taking him on. They were very supportive and good to me, and I felt I couldn't let them down, so I persevered. While Z wasn't unkind to the other children, he was very disrespectful of adults, women in particular. He didn't really interact with the other children. He preferred to play alone and would become agitated if one showed up in an area of play he had chosen. When an adult intervened and let him know that, for example, four children could play in the block area at the same time, he became belligerent—and even violent—towards the adult. The language that little boy could spew would make a sailor blush.

73

"Misses Heidi, I am going to take this f-ing chair and throw it through the f-ing window and take a piece of glass and slit your f-ing throat and watch you bleed to death," was typical of the kinds of things he would say to me. He would punch me, hit me, you name it. Thank goodness, he didn't do this to the other children, but we did have to remove him from the room due to the language alone. Any time it escalated, I would call his parents, and they would come right away.

One particular time, it got really ugly. I was at my wits' end trying to prevent outbursts and separate him from others while still following the rules of DHS. He refused to go into the other room. That day I called his parents. I was on the phone with one of them and they said, "Just put him outside. I am on the way."

It was a pleasant day outside. He was standing on one side of the glass door, and I was on the other. I was literally inches away from his face. I couldn't leave the other person in the house with eleven kids alone (DHS rules). Nor could I leave him alone. So, I decided this was the best solution for what we were dealing with. He is screaming like crazy. Within moments, the parent arrived. No harm was done.

Well, around the same time, my sister Kristina was organizing a group cruise, something we did every couple of years or so. "Family and Friends," she called it. We all invited others and it grew every year. I invited all my helpers, including Diane. She thought about it and decided she couldn't go. Rene and Keli were on board to go, however. During the same time, Diane was asking to work different shifts. I put her at the end of the day. While she was great with the children, she sometimes set the parents off. She liked to tell them what they should and should not do with their children, a big no-no in early childhood services.

We had a new boy, a cousin of a longtime family, there. His first day was rough. At pick-up time, according to his parents, Diane roughly handed him over and complained about how horrible he had been. He was a great kid, by the way—just scared on his first day.

This wasn't the only complaint I heard. I talked with her about it, and she said she would work on it. I ended up putting her back to the middle of the day, when she didn't have to interact with parents and could do what she did best. I had her back and let the parents know I wasn't letting her go. The children loved her, and she was good with them, especially Z. The parents trusted me and didn't question it.

Around the time Kristina was putting the cruise together (for August 2008), Diane asked me for more hours. As a matter of fact, she wanted to partner with me on the business. I told her I couldn't afford to do that, but it wasn't enough explanation for her. How could I tell her that due to new tax laws, the debt we were incurring medically and paying help, I was making less than I did with a home daycare and fewer children. I was barely breaking even. I was ashamed. We were still trying to act like everything else at home was okay, when our entire world was being ripped apart.

Towards the middle of May 2007, all hell broke loose. Diane wrote me an email saying it wasn't fair that Rene got more hours than her. After all, she had quit and come back. I replied that she had come back before Diane did. I was so worried that I would push her into another overdose because I was dealing with so much of that with Adam, that I didn't tell her that parents were still complaining. I thought I was protecting her. Then she sent an email that just set me off: "You just like Rene and Keli more than me and want them to afford to spend money on the cruise." I thought it was absurd, and that is exactly what I told her. She ended our friendship and quit. She said I was dishonest with her. I guess I was. I wanted her to feel good about herself and have some time with the kids, and I didn't tell her everything. But it wasn't what she thought. I just loved her and thought if I didn't say anything, she wouldn't be hurt or try to hurt herself. I already felt so responsible for our son's life. I didn't want to feel responsible for someone else's. How could I possibly tell her that?

Some parents came to me shortly after that showing me a questionnaire she had mailed out, a survey about her. None of them would respond. I pleaded with them to do it because she had told me she thought I had asked them not to reply. She thought I lied about that, too. The parents were mostly angry because she had looked through my files for their addresses without my permission. I never had the opportunity to tell her that. I wanted to make it right and restore our friendship. I truly loved her and just wanted to help her.

That same week, Joe and I were on a motorcycle ride, and I burned my right calf badly on the bike. We are talking a third-degree burn, which took a year to heal. We traveled to southern Missouri that weekend to visit my brother Jimmy and other family members for Memorial Day. When we returned that Monday, I opened my email to find an accusation that I had thrown a boulder-sized rock through Diane's front window, narrowly missing her child and friends during a sleepover. My first thought was, Oh my God! How horrible! I hope the girls are okay. Then, realization crept in that I was the one being accused. She said, "I don't know what kind of evil got into you this weekend that caused you to throw the rock through our window! I was going to apologize and try to mend our friendship, but after this, no!" I was in shock. I was hurt. First of all, anyone who knows me knows I am a rule follower and that I fear the law.

Second of all, I would never do anything like that! I wasn't even angry enough to come close to an act like that. I can't imagine what would push me to that point. It hurt because I realized then that she didn't really know me at all. She also had to tell me that I didn't handle the Z situation very well. Maybe not, but I had no idea what to do about that and relied on a parent's decision. I explained to her that our family had been traveling when the incident with the rock had happened. I hadn't even been in town. I had joint issues in my hands and could barely walk with my injured leg. She went on to tell me that Adam's friends must have been involved. Adam could not have cared less what went on in my personal life at that point in time; he was so consumed with his mental illness. He only cared about one thing, ending his life.

I didn't tell her that either because I didn't want to trigger her. She had no idea that I had been told that she had tried to end her life with pills, so I could never bring it up. So, that ended our friendship. I have long since forgiven her. She was hurting inside, and hurt people hurt people. I am not sure she has forgiven me, but I can live with that. I know inside that I was only trying to protect multiple people, and it backfired on me.

Soon after our falling out, I received a visit from DHS. I had been reported for putting Z outside the door for ten minutes and not being out there with him. There were only two possibilities as to who had reported that. My neighbor, who could have heard him screaming (but couldn't have known the details about what had happened inside), or Diane, who had been there. She denied it, of course. She claimed a parent had done it, yet every single parent wrote DHS to defend me, including Z's parents.

Nevertheless, I was written up. It went into my file, along with the parents' letters. I asked my caseworker what the main thing I had done wrong was. It was putting him outside alone. I asked, what if I had gone outside and left the other caregiver alone with eleven children?

Either way, I would have been written up. It was a no-win situation. I asked her what she would have done, and she said "Probably the same thing you did."

She made me give notice to Z's parents. They were totally understanding. I remain friends with his mom to this day. I later received an update on Z. He was tested for allergies and was allergic to many foods and things in his environment. When that was remedied, he became a new kid. I rejoiced with her! If only it would have been that simple with Adam. It has made me question the impact food and the environment have on the brain.

Diane has had some successes with employment since and then some health issues. I continue to pray for her healing daily and am very sorry for the ending of our friendship all based on a misunderstanding.

Chapter 16
Questions about Origins

Joe and I were doing a lot of soul searching during this time. We were plagued with guilt, the possibility that we did or did not do something, which must have caused this to happen to our child. Both children, really? Why did our children have to be born into suffering? Why did we? Why? Why? Why? Hadn't we done everything we were supposed to do to prevent this sort of thing from happening? We discussed the things we had accomplished thus far as parents; all the things we felt were the positives:

1. We built our home in a great, safe, neighborhood, with a low crime rate.
2. Our children went to good schools.
3. We took our children to church and enrolled them in religious education.
4. We set examples of serving God by volunteering at church through Adoration and prayer group.
5. We made sure the children were rich in experiences. They tried basketball, football, baseball, dance (Steph), wrestling (Adam), and scouting.
6. We didn't just enroll them in these; we became coaches and leaders so we could spend more time with them.
7. I made my business from home so I could have them there with me.
8. We gave them the gift of travel so they could see the world and experience various cultures.
9. We taught them love and acceptance of all people.

10. We made sure they were clothed and had proper nutrition and exercise, and we led by example.

11. Most of all, we LOVED them with all our hearts and never gave up on them, through good times and bad.

So, if we had done everything right, what had gone wrong? Did we carry a gene for mental illness? Did we pass it on to our children? We talked some more about our own pasts, our own skeletons, in an attempt for answers. Some theorize that mental illness is hereditary, so perhaps we had just passed this on.

Examining one's own life can be very painful emotionally. The guilt that follows the acknowledgment that perhaps you did all the right things, but were at fault just by bringing a child into the world is overwhelming. Writing my own story of my life, I see clearly the emergence of mental illness. Through this experience, I was finally able to gain some closure over the loss of three babies. Two of them had issues with their brains. Did God already know that these two would be mentally ill, as well? Did he take them back because he only gives us what we can handle? Was it because he knew the road would be long and difficult with Adam, and we would need every bit of physical and emotional strength to make it through our journey?

Chapter 17
My Beginnings

My husband said to me one day, "I don't feel normal." Really? I thought. What is normal? None of us are normal. We just believe that we are and judge the rest of the world and others by what our individual standard of "normal" is.

It's laughable, really, to think I have believed I'm normal my entire life with abnormal people or unusual events happening to me directly or in my environment. Is normal how I react? How I behave? How I look? My size? The truth is, I have tried my entire life to prove I am "normal" despite my circumstances.

I was born in Kansas City, Missouri, in 1962 to educated, but sometimes misguided parents, who met in the travel industry. Mom worked for United Airlines. Papa worked for Pan American Airlines. They both lived in Washington D.C. They met over the phone and eventually became friends, although they never saw one another's faces. Papa was still married to his first wife and going through a nasty divorce. Mom told me she wanted to learn German, and Papa was fluent and had a book he wanted to give her to help her learn. They were married shortly after the day he brought her the book, as soon as his divorce was final. After that, she never studied German!

I lived in K.C. the first seven years of my life. By then, my older sister Ann, was eight, and the baby sister, Kristina, was four. Those were probably the most carefree years of my life. Though some of my memories have been tucked away somewhere in my brain due to a later childhood trauma, I rely on Ann to fill in the gaps sometimes. I do, however, remember good vibes during this phase of my life.

When I was born, we lived in a small house, just Ann, Mama, Papa and I. Then we moved into a spacious two-story house with a basement and a fenced-in backyard. In my memory, I shared a long, narrow bedroom upstairs with Ann and Kristina. It looked like the lane of a bowling alley, and Mama and Papa's room was across the hall. It seemed like our folks were doing well financially at the time. Papa went into business with a woman who owned a travel agency in the Plaza area in Kansas City. It was one of those clay, shingled buildings.

I remember during those happy years Papa used to pull us girls on a long, wooden sled through Swope Park during the snowy winters. I remember playing soccer in our backyard and digging foxholes in a designated area set aside for such destruction. I didn't really know what a foxhole was until many years later when Papa explained how they would dig them to hide in during the Korean War. I literally thought it was for a fox! I remember tornado storms and being afraid to walk down the wooden basement stairs for fear I would fall through the spaces. I remember when the power would go out and the house was pitch black. Papa would hide in a closet with glow-in-the-dark Halloween teeth and jump out and scare us. We would scream with glee, like little girls do. Then he would scoop us up onto his shoulders and dance around.

I remember my first friend, Stephanie Carr. She lived across the street and down a few houses and had a cat and a bird. The bird hung from the rafters in the basement in a cage and the cat would search for routes to get to it. I recall that cat scratching up Ann's legs really badly and Mom putting Mecuricome, a dark red topical antiseptic containing mercury, all over her legs. It was a medicine commonly used during those times. It stung like razors cutting into you and Ann screamed and screamed. She didn't care for cats after that.

I was pretty accident prone (I still am), and I recall two accidents in K.C. One of them was when I fell on a wooden rocking horse and tore my Maxillary Frenum, the little piece of tissue that connects the upper lip to the gum between the two front teeth. That took care of that. I no longer have that. I drank milkshakes for days afterwards! The second was when I fell from the top of the stairs (ironically, not the wooden basement ones I feared I would fall through). I was carrying a load of stuffed animals with a slinky on top. The slinky fell and did its thing one step at a time. I leaned over to grab it.

The next thing I knew, I was waking up in the front of the car with my head in Papa's lap. He had one hand on the steering wheel, the other on the cloth on my forehead to stop the bleeding. "You are going to be okay," I heard him say, but he sounded scared. I passed out again, and the second time I woke up, I was lying on a table getting ready for stitches. "No, no!" Papa said. "No anesthesia! What if she has an allergic reaction?"

I was lying down, very still, terrified to move, not understanding why I had to suffer the pain. What was he thinking? Only after being a parent myself, could I fully understand his decision that day, how he truly feared for the life of his little girl. When we returned home, my mom asked how I did. Papa said I was very brave. Still somewhat in shock, I said in a monotone voice, "I was scared."

Looking back through my childhood, I thought these were the most traumatic events of my life. I had to hold on to my seat, as the ride was about to become more challenging and traumatic than I ever thought possible. These, like I said, were the good years. Those were the times I felt safe from harm as all children should. I felt Papa would protect me from all evil.

During those years, my mother was a stay-at-home mom. She

loved to dance and sing. She tried to pass along these gifts to her three girls, but I for one had two left feet, like my father! Still, we had fun with it. That was her good, happy side. In her early years, she dreamed of becoming a performer on stage and participated in theatre during her high school years. A swimming accident had changed all of that with a broken neck. She spent her college years in traction. She earned her degree in journalism and Spanish instead and never missed a chance to let us all know how her life was over with the change in plans. She spent the rest of her life lamenting over the past and drowning it in bottles of booze.

We did enjoy productions at the Starlight Theatre in Kansas City, our enthusiasm inspired by Mom. We also spent many an evening watching Papa play first chair violin in the Kansas City Philharmonic Orchestra.

Birthdays were special events. We chose our own dinner cooked by our father, who could challenge any chef in the world. As a world traveler, he experimented with the various cuisines he had experienced from other worlds. On my third birthday, I chose lobster tails in butter sauce! And that is what I got!

Papa spoke a lot of German in the home and it was expected that we did, too. As time went on, he developed a talent for learning many other languages, as well.

I don't remember much about school in K.C., just vague memories of my kindergarten classroom. I picture this huge wooden structure that resembled a wide canoe with a rounded bend in the middle. A bench sat on either side, and two children could rock back and forth. I remember having a nap mat. I also remember making an ashtray for my mother out of clay, baking it, and painting it. Both parents smoked during that era, drank a lot, and hosted and attended many social parties. All of this was normal for us. No one today would make an ashtray for their mother. It simply would not be approved of or appropriate!

In relating these events, I can already see patterns emerge in Dr. Neal's chart of life events. I can also see the beginnings of mental illness. It did not begin with my own son, Adam. It began in my own world the day I was born.

Chapter 18
My First Move to a New Town:
First New "Normal"

Ann was eight, I was seven, and Kristina was four when our parents said we had to move out of Kansas City. The story that was told to us children was that crime was getting out of control in the big city, so a move to the country would be better. We moved to a tiny farmhouse in the country in Warrensburg, Missouri. It was a two-bedroom house, with one for the parents, one for the kids, and one bathroom in between.

We had a large garden where we learned to grow, can, and freeze our own vegetables. For a short time, we raised chickens for eggs. Unfortunately, foxes and snakes eventually killed off the chickens. We had a pond to ice skate on and fish in. Mom, having grown up on Lake Erie in Toledo, Ohio, was an expert figure skater. She taught us how to skate. There was land with fields and woods to roam in. The landlord/neighbor had a pasture with cows and horses.

The positives would be having less crime and living close to our Grandpa and Grandma Shultz. Grandma was an elementary school music teacher and taught at Whiteman Air Force Base. Grandpa worked for Central Missouri State University as an academic advisor. They were both active in the Methodist Church, and soon we were too.

Being so young, we didn't question why our family was growing (our brother, Jimmy was born shortly after the move), yet our house was getting smaller and life was getting harder. We didn't question why our parents had once been homeowners in K.C. but now had a landlord. We didn't question why our pet dogs, Ludwig (Luddie) and Inga (Papa named the animals German names), were now breeders of puppies to make extra money to survive. We now owned guns and had to learn how to shoot.

Our "normal" was evolving into something else. Ample free playtime turned into work—lots of work! The children worked the garden, collected eggs, cleaned up after the animals, mowed the property, and learned to cook and clean. Suddenly, we were the mother to our little brother, and we were still in elementary school!

Many years later, it is my understanding that the woman my father was in business with at that time had cheated him somehow. He left the business, and she sued him for breach of contract. Part of the agreement was that he could not live in Kansas City and steal her potential clients.

While we had lived in K.C., he worked two jobs. The second job was as a bartender at the Buttonwood Tree. He continued to work there when we moved to the farm in Warrensburg. Following the move, he was offered a job at Atlantic Travel School. While teaching there, he flunked a student whose father was a leader of the NAACP and possibly the Black Panther Movement. One night while working at the bar, they busted up his car and threatened him and our family. I wonder if that was the turning point after which he began to make racist comments. I never understood why he spoke so fondly of his black nanny and her family and his love for her, only to later change his feelings toward black people.

Atlantic School made him a sales rep for potential students. His area was in the Northern United States, but he lived in Canada until it was deemed safe for him to return home. After his return, he continued working for Atlantic School as a sales rep and drove all over Missouri and the Midwest searching for potential students. Papa began to work with other travel agencies again in Kansas City, taking groups all over the world, and he eventually quit working for Atlantic School. He continued to commute. At one point, Papa was ranked number ten among the best tour conductors in the world.

But despite Papa's hard work, life seemed to be a struggle at home. There never seemed to be enough money. Our parents drank more and more. Mom slept a lot during the day. Our happy family was changing. Papa suddenly had a temper. All the stress of Kansas City seemed to take its toll on him.

Being so young, I didn't realize Papa had also fought in a war, the Korean War. It wasn't until later years that he opened up about his experiences. One, he was in a terrible accident in which the jeep he was riding was blown up. He was the sole survivor and was badly injured in the face, having to have his jaw reconstructed. The comical side to that story is that his group had actually been going on a beer run!

Another story he told was about being awakened in his tent one night by the enemy. A man came into the tent and tried to kill him, and my father shot him, killing him instead. He spoke of how that haunted him because this was a man with a family, too—a human being.

Knowing what I know now as an adult about mental illness, I can clearly see he suffered from Post-Traumatic Stress Disorder from his war battles, and it was later triggered by the daily stresses of work and life.

Apparently, he had a problem with faithfulness in marriage. His travels introduced him to many women from all over the world. He was knowledgeable on many subjects, including world history, geography, religions of the world. He also spoke many languages. Women were drawn to him. Our own mother was an attractive lady and well spoken, yet she drank too much. For reasons I cannot comprehend, my parents stayed together until my father's death in 2014. My mother grew to hate him. They both became argumentative, angry, bitter people.

Life in Warrensburg was a turning point in our young development. We were witnessing our first view of mental illness in our young lives, but wouldn't fully grasp it until many years into adulthood.

Taking from Dr. Neal's book on charting one's life, these were lessons learned on the farm: you work for everything you get. You raise your food, cook it, freeze and can it, and grownups get the credit. Mom has babies and that is your responsibility, as well. Parents drink a lot of alcohol, but that is "normal" until Grandpa and Grandma visit, and it is also the kids' responsibility to hide it somewhere. Papa gets angry easily and becomes physical. You become a people pleaser or a rebel. Ann and I learned to please as a means of survival. Kristina and Jimmy were still young but later became rebels, yet another mechanism for survival. At this point, all of us girls were doing well in school. It was mandatory!

From Warrensburg I have a memory of one friend, Janet Bodenhammer, who was my age. I remember my fifth-grade teacher of the same name because she was her aunt; no other reason. I remember no one else from school. No teachers, no students. All those memories are tucked neatly away somewhere in the recesses of my brain. I once spent the night at Janet's house. She had tons of Barbie dolls and accessories: the houses and cars. I was in awe of her many toys, as we had a doll or two, school books from Grandma Shultz, and blocks. She never came to my house. We never had friends over, not once.

Cousins came during the summer—the Powell boys, sons of Papa's only sibling, Aunt Jane. Doug, Jeff and Gary and another cousin, Mike Smith. All played significant roles throughout my life and the lives of my future children. Aunt Jane and her husband, Uncle Don,

Mike's mom, cousin Bev, and my Shultz grandparents were the positive role models in our lives. In later years, as I studied brain development in early childhood and the negative impact abuse can have on the developing brain of the child, it became clear to me that the sole reason our brains developed into caring, functional, human beings later in life was due to these nurturing adults in our world.

Although I don't remember many people, I remember earning the Presidential Physical Fitness award and being the top girl among about one hundred students in my fifth-grade class in Warrensburg. I still had a shred of self-esteem at this point in my life.

Chapter 19
A New Form of Trauma Becomes the Norm

During the middle of my fifth-grade year, my father was offered a job at Columbia College in Columbia, Missouri, to start a travel program. He agreed as long as he could still take his tour groups and travel the globe. Mom was hired on as well. They co-taught the travel program at Columbia College.

We lived at the KOA campground near Rocheport, Missouri, for a while as my parents searched for a rental house. The luxury of a swimming pool was really all we cared about at that time.

We moved into another farmhouse outside of Rocheport, a small historic town near Columbia, established in 1825. During our residence there, not much was happening in that old town. There was an old post office and a tiny general store. We would ride our bikes along old 40 Highway leading into the town, buy a glass bottle of Coke, and share it. We walked along the railroad tracks and looked at the bluffs above. It was quiet and peaceful. An elderly couple lived at the top of a hill in a shack. They would sit on rocking chairs, rock and wave to those who passed by, smiling as if they hadn't a care in the world. Years later, the shack burned down, they perished and thousands of dollars were discovered buried in tin cans in the mud floor of the shack.

Today, Rocheport is a happening place as part of the Katy Trail, featuring bed and breakfasts, winery, shops, restaurants, and antique shops. By coincidence, we know one of the owners, Diane Dunn. Recently retired, she worked with my husband for many years for State Farm Insurance. Today we are all friends. Occasionally, we visit the Old General Store, gather with friends, and listen to bands.

The "new" farm we moved into was an old three-bedroom house (upgrade!) with one bathroom. Our family grew to seven as our youngest brother, Martin, was born that year. He was born with his feet twisted abnormally. The doctors said he was club-footed, yet his feet did not take on the shape of club feet. As I married a man with two of them, I know what they look like! Martin was put in leg casts as a baby, gradually moving his feet into the correct position. The boy could later run like the wind, so seemingly no harm had been done.

All five of us seemed "normal", or at least we thought we were, which was an amazing miracle, as our mother smoked and drank throughout each of her pregnancies. She began to sleep more during the day. I became the assigned mother to baby Martin. I was ten and a half when he was born.

Along with the same responsibilities we'd had in Warrensburg, we now had added ones and stresses no child should have to endure. We now had a Dachshund puppy-making business to run, as well. We walked them all daily. In addition to that, we had two bigger mutts dumped on the road in Warrensburg, who came with us. Brownie and Blackie protected us everywhere we went. We also chopped wood during the winter for the fireplace to keep us warm. We had no running hot water, so we boiled water in large metal buckets on the stove for dishes and baths—one bath a week with shared bath water. We rose before the dawn to care for the garden and do outdoor chores.

We burned our paper trash and toted the rest up a long trail to a dump. It didn't seem to matter to our parents that Kristina had one of the buckets fall on her and burned her stomach badly with boiling water, or that the fire she was attending for trash one day took off and nearly burned down the entire farmland. The adults still didn't question whether or not children should be responsible for this kind of work! In addition to all this, we were expected to earn high marks in school.

Ah, school! A small, country school. There were maybe 22 kids in my entire class. Back in Warrensburg, we were shipped to town, so this was a new experience. We were considered city folk, which seemed laughable to us as many of these kids lived in a neighborhood, not a farm, near the school. They had no idea how truly country we had become.

My first day, the principal walked me into the classroom and introduced me, "Heidi Ho-ho". He made fun of my name in front of my future classmates, which set the tone for many years to come. They all laughed and snickered. I was humiliated. The teacher put me in the last desk at the end of the middle row. As I made the walk of shame through the center of the room, my cheeks burned and tears filled my eyes. I almost made it to my desk, when a boy named Ricky stuck out his cowboy boot and tripped me. I fell flat on my face. The class roared. No one said or did a thing about it.

On the playground, I was taunted and teased. One day, two boys, Chris and Jimmy, shoved my face into a pole and broke my nose, causing blood to pour from my face. The teacher looked the other way, basically telling me to suck it up. In gym class, no one picked me for their teams. At first I wanted to scream, "I won the Presidential Fitness Award! I can do this!" As time went on, I lost all self-confidence, hated gym, and hated school. It was a prison to me. In my ten-year-old mind, I was no longer self-confident or capable of success. I began to cower and fear everything around me.

The only really kind person in the whole classroom was a girl named Sherri Wise. She was well liked by the entire group and went out of her way to be nice to me. I have always wanted to tell her that her kindness was what got me through those years; just knowing that one person cared. The framework for my own mental instability, the shaping of my own brain for who I was to become, was evolving. Mental illness was already showing a trend in our family from PTSD (Papa), alcoholism and possible undiagnosed depression (Mom), to now the beginnings of childhood PTSD (post-traumatic stress disorder).

Chapter 20
Life Keeps Changing in Rocheport

The travel department at Columbia College was becoming a success. As kids living in the seventies, we witnessed the drinking and drug use of the era through our parents' students. Our folks were the "cool" teachers, who hosted parties on the farm. Back in the deep woods ran a creek with many rock banks. Kegs were set up, there were bottles of booze, and of course some of the students brought along marijuana and who knows what else. We were still young and a bit oblivious to every detail and we were good, well-behaved children. The students were friendly and kind to us, many acting like older siblings. Some became babysitters while our parents traveled; strangely enough, always male students. They were great.

One would go on adventures with us all over the land, in and out of abandoned barns and sheds, through the woods, and along the creek. He had special names for us. I was Eliza Jane. I wish I could remember his name. I probably changed it so many times during our imaginary play that I forgot what it really was!

Two others, Vince and Brent, stayed with us one winter. Vince was big and burly with a full, black beard, who should have frightened us. But he was kind; a gentle bear of a man. Brent liked to smoke a lot of pot, had messy, curly wild hair, and was legally blind. I remember they made us snow ice cream. They were wonderful. Another one, Dave Bleu, became so close to us that after he graduated, he would return once a year throughout my college years to squeeze us all into his Volkswagen Bug and take us to McDonald's for lunch. And Ron Schweer, an older student, was our parents' age. He had Schizophrenia, something I didn't know or understand at the time, although sadly, I would become more familiar with that illness later in life. Later, during the adolescent and teen years of us girls, we became close to Rick Skrivan, Jeff Berbrick, and Mark Tatelman, who still continue to be close during these later years of our lives. These are the adults outside of my family who I credit for giving us security, fun, and love without a price.

During the school year, our parents would teach at the college. They held onto the travel department from the time I was ten in 1972 through 1982, my second year of college. During summer breaks, Christmas breaks, and spring breaks, Papa would take tour groups around the world. During this time period, it was mainly travel students.

He took turns taking one of us with him. Oh, the irony. Poor kids, wearing tattered clothing, traveling the world with this man, our Papa, in his tailor-made suits made of the finest silk in China. Still, we didn't see that at the time, and it was a privilege to see the world that so many never have the opportunity to see. Those are good memories, as they brought out the best in Papa. He was always the gracious host and teacher on these tours. And once again, we had the attention of the students. Even family vacations were good times. We traveled most of the United States and Canada by car throughout our childhood. We were poor in possessions, but rich in experiences.

To be left at home was a treat, too, being free of adult stress placed on the children. Because Mom was sleeping most of the time, she eventually lost her job at the school. She didn't know if we came or went. For us, Papa being away meant us being allowed to be children. We explored the land with the babies and imagined other worlds. When Papa left, we would ask Mom how long he would be gone. The question that followed was, "When will he leave again?"

As I took on womanly features and developed physically, my family began to say I looked very much like my Grandma Shultz. It is true. I even had her personality. She was very nurturing, and I took on this role with my brothers. From the time Martin was born (I was ten) and would cry to be fed in the night, I rose from my bed, took him into mine, fed him, rocked him, and returned him to his crib. I loved him like he was my own baby. He gave back so much more to me then and in years to come. He only thought I was his security blanket at the time. In reality, he was mine—my diversion from the truth of what was unraveling in my own little world.

Papa began to look at me like I was Martin's mom. When Papa was home, he was the main cook in our house. Now he took me under his wing and taught me everything he knew in the kitchen. I felt special. It was positive attention. He was being kind. It was a far cry from the belt beatings and cruel put downs I'd received from him in the past. I got out of doing the dishes because I helped cook and took care of the baby. He began to tell me how special I was. He told me I was just like his mom. She was the sweetest lady. Both of our parents were raised in good homes, well taken care of. No abuse. To be compared to Grandma Shultz was the greatest compliment.

One night, after dinner, Ann and Kristina were doing clean up. Papa was lounging on the couch and told me to rub his feet. He wore size twelve shoes, and I thought his feet were gross, but I did it anyway. It progressed from that to rubbing his scalp, and then his back. He began to whisper to me, "I will return the favor." I was ten. I had no idea what that was supposed to mean, but I know I felt weird.

Shortly thereafter, our family went fishing nearby with our cousins, the Hafners, Mick, Edie, and their son, Joe. Papa parked the family van on hill above the lake. He told everyone to get their gear, except me. I was going to take care of the sleeping baby in the van. I was sad and felt left out but hoped that soon I would have a turn.

Everyone else went to the lake below. After a while, I saw Papa walking back up the hill. It surely was my turn to go fishing! Papa got in the van and began to tell me how awful his marriage with Mom was. She neglected him. I was the only person in the entire world who understood him and whom he could count on. Martin slept soundly on one of the van seats, oblivious to the events that were about to unfold.

Papa said, "Give me a hug, little girl." I did. Papa pointed to his cheek and said, "Give your Papa a kiss." I did. He pointed to his mouth. I froze, eyes wide. My innocence began to peel off of me as I realized something just wasn't right. I was too young to fully understand what was happening, but old enough to feel uncomfortable. I debated in my mind what was going to happen if I said "no". I was scared he would hit me and go into one of his rages. I chose to shake my head but was otherwise paralyzed. The family returned quickly and I was saved ... that time.

After dinner that night, as I rubbed his head, feet, and back, he didn't say anything. I felt foolish, like I had imagined the whole thing. I shared a room with Ann and Kristina. Ann and I shared a bunk bed. Kristina slept on a twin bed across the room from us. I was sleeping on the top bunk that night. Ann and I alternated every couple of weeks from top to bottom bunk. Before we would fall off to sleep, the three of us would engage in girl talk. That night, Papa came into our room. He carried on a conversation with the three of us as if it was a night like any other. As he spoke, his hand reached under my covers and began to rub my back. I felt very strange. He motioned on my body to roll over, and when I did, he began to touch my breasts. Suddenly, I froze as I had in the van. Why was he doing this? I couldn't move. I couldn't speak. He whispered in my ear, " You like this, don't you?" I did not answer. I was too afraid. What if I said "no"? What would he do?

Night after night, he began to come into our room. It didn't matter if the baby was sleeping next to me. My mother never once came in to check on us or the baby, or to ask him why he was in there with us. He would touch me everywhere. It sickened me. Yet, still I could never move or speak. It was as if I was paralyzed. I never even told him to stop, so I began to shame myself with self-accusation that what was happening was my fault. I had to have caused this! Why didn't I yell for Mom? Why didn't I tell someone?

Suddenly, my new normal was anything but normal! Papa began to send the family fishing without us, explaining that, "Heidi doesn't like to fish." Even though I had only fished maybe once or twice, I did begin to hate it because of what it reminded me of, because I didn't get to go! I had to stay and endure whatever this was!

He began to tell me what was wrong with my body; what I needed to work on. Strangely enough, my mother did the same thing. By the time I was a teenager, I was five-foot-six inches tall, a good four inches taller than Ann. She weighed 90-95 pounds. I was probably 115-120, but mentally I had to be at least 200.

There was no place to hide. Nowhere was safe. Not school, not home. I had no close friends, except for Diana, who was the daughter of one of Papa's older students. We attended different schools. I had my siblings but couldn't tell them my dirty little secret. I was alone, living inside my own mind, which was deteriorating. My grades fell in school. I became an average student. I simply couldn't process information. My parents praised my sisters, the straight-A students. I was called "stupid" and "fat".

At the age of twelve, my world was crushed. Within the year, Diana, my only friend, suffered a brain hemorrhage and died! At that moment, I realized that kids can actually die, too!

The following year, Grandma Shultz had an unexpected heart attack and was gone. She was 65. She was my world! At this point, I felt such despair and hopelessness. Who would love me now? Papa had the nerve to come to me the night she died. I wanted to scream as he told me how much I reminded him of her and how I was his right arm. I wanted to throw up.

One night when he was in our room carrying on a conversation with my sisters with his hands on me on the top bunk, my sister Ann playfully moved her hand like a spider up the wall to the top bunk to tease me. Feeling her hand, I grabbed it and squeezed, hoping she would get the message somehow and stop him. Being a kid, she yelled, "What are you doing? Let go of my hand!" Strangely enough, from that point on, I had recurring nightmares about giant spiders crawling around me, on me, or hanging from the ceiling coming at me, for many years of my life. When it happens, I wake up screaming incoherent words. As a married woman now, I know of countless times my husband has 'killed' the imaginary spiders for me so I would settle back to sleep. Sometimes I remember waking from these nightmares. Sometimes, I don't.

I also had choking nightmares. During my college years, anytime I stayed somewhere other than my apartment, I would wake up shaking and crying in a corner in the fetal position. I would end up in various places in the houses, holding my throat, or calling out to Joe to save me. It was very frightening. I sleepwalked. Once I even drove my car in the night, asleep for several miles on the highway before a semi shone its lights in my rearview window! Another time in Oklahoma, a friend found me in a T-shirt and underpants walking on our street. It was joked about, but I knew it revolved around trauma. When my father passed away in April of 2014, those nightmares went with him. Thank God!

I often worried if anyone would believe me if I ever told that story. You have to know, my father was a well-respected man, both in business and within his family. I never reported him, as I didn't want our family to be split, and I feared the possibility of being taken away and placed in a much worse place, among strangers. As of this writing in 2019, I was finally validated when my sister Kristina found some letters Papa had written to Mom. One was written the year I told Mom about what he had done. He acknowledged what he had done and told her he would carry the guilt for the rest of his life. He was sorry and referred to me as their most compassionate, loving child. His only wish was that she didn't go around telling all of their friends. I never knew she did. He absolved me from all guilt in that letter.

Chapter 21
Getting Active in the Church:
Acts of Kindness

While living in Rocheport, Papa began taking us to Midway Methodist Church, not far from our house. We got involved in a youth group there and got to know some of the kids we attended school with a little better. Some actually became lifelong friends, not the monsters I had perceived them all to be on my first day of school. Although I haven't seen that little girl, Sherri Wise, since we were kids, I reconnected with her on Facebook. I have intended to write her and let her know what an impact she had on my life. Having raised a child with mental illness, I can tell you the smallest act of kindness can go a long way in someone's day or life. Her kindness lasted a lifetime for me.

Through her Facebook posts, I can see that she has continued to be a shining light in many people's lives. In our group, I got to know Eddie and Tracy, two boys who died way too young in adulthood. Eddie dated both a close friend of mine and one of my cousins later on. Tracy and I remained friends and reconnected at high school reunions over the years. I knew Tim, who continues to be a friend even though we live states away.

One of the times I remember so well (and believe was a turning point for the poor Shultz kids) was a spur-of-the-moment event that occurred following an MYF (Methodist Youth Foundation) meeting.

One of Papa's students, a young man named Rick Skrivan, showed up to pick up us girls. We had no idea he was coming. Rick came from a well-to-do family, yet you wouldn't know it. He was laid back, wore his beautiful straight blond hair long, and tattered blue jeans were his style. He was a bit wild in college and had a ton of fun, but was the most down-to-earth guy you could ever meet. He had a big heart and we loved him like a brother. He and Jeff Berbrick showered us with attention—much needed attention—which they may or may not have known we needed so much.

So, Rick showed up in this really nice, black Mercury Cougar with a sunroof opened on the top. Everyone turned to look at the car and asked aloud in wonder, "Who is that?" This gorgeous man stepped out. He was about four years older than I was, so naturally the girls' mouths were hanging open.

We said, "Oh, that's our brother," then ran into his open arms for a hug and climbed into his car! We stood and waved out of the sunroof as Rick drove us away. Almost instantly, we all felt ourselves rise a notch in the others' eyes. Once again, a seemingly small act of kindness by Rick. He continues to be a wonderful friend and a part of our family. I apologize to him now, as he will be shocked after reading this to learn of certain dirty little family secrets. Hopefully, he will be as forgiving as I am today by the end of this read.

My purpose is not to hurt anyone, but to gain understanding of how mental illness affects people in various ways. What are the triggers, the behaviors, the fallouts among the families and friends? How can we change this? How can these things be prevented?

I apologize to Jeff as well, as he looked up to our Papa as a father figure. Jeff is nine years older than I am. I had the biggest crush on him as a teen. I thought he was the most adorable man I had ever laid eyes on. He had curly dark hair and a mustache (mustaches were big in those days), and eyes that twinkled when he smiled. He had a cute New Jersey accent. He really was my rock as I moved from adolescence through my teens and later in my early years of college.

I never knew if he picked up on how shy and reclusive I was back then. It doesn't matter; the time and attention he gave to me set me up for future confidence and some amount of pride in myself. I can remember countless times my parents had a party. All the college students would be doing their thing. I would be off alone somewhere and Jeff would somehow find me. We would sit and talk for hours. He really and truly cared.

When I think of the seeming coincidences Dr. Mary Neal speaks about that are not really coincidences, I think of these people. Whether they played a small or major role in my life or development, they all helped shape me into who I am. I try to remember these people or even total strangers who have smiled at me as if to say, "I understand; I know your pain." That way when I pass a stranger, a homeless person, or someone with a mental illness or any other kind of illness, I can pass along what was given to me.

To smile or say hello, to sincerely ask how someone is doing, can make all the difference in the world to that person, who now knows that at least one single person cared about them.

Today, I often remind myself of this when I am faced with a person who is different from me, whether they struggle in health (mental or physical) or have a different financial status. We have to remember that we are all connected to one another, and one person's love and compassion can make a difference and change the world, one person at a time.

Chapter 22
Out of the Country

When I was 16 years old, my parents had regained enough financial stability to buy a house once again. We moved from the country into Columbia, Missouri. We moved on New Year's Eve, an icy, freezing cold day. Papa was on a cruise tour in the Caribbean with Kristina and one of his groups. Mom, Ann, and I did the entire move ourselves. On our first night in the new house, the electricity went out, and we smelled gas and had to call the fire department! We wrapped ourselves in blankets and played games and ate by candlelight.

In spite of her issues with drinking, Mom was actually pretty fun during our teenage years. We played a lot of music and games together, and she made an attempt to be our friend. Well, if we couldn't have a mom, that was the next best thing. Our friends in high school (yes, we did eventually have friends!) actually thought she was pretty cool. They thought Papa was, too. On the plus side, he took us traveling a lot. He was always at his best when traveling.

I was sixteen when the sexual abuse ended. Papa was away on tour and Mom was getting her drunk on for the night. I was downstairs in the basement in the room I shared with Ann. Ann was out with friends for the evening. Mom came down to talk to me, martini in hand. She told me she was concerned about my behavior.

My behavior? I thought. I knew I was struggling with my grades in school. I had difficulty with concentration due to my own PTSD. I was full of anxiety and panic attacks that I never shared with anyone. I was terrified of everything, from being in public alone, to driving, to walking the halls of school. I had trouble sleeping at night. There was

105

no one there for me during that time. Programs were not set up in the schools or elsewhere like they are today. I just kept to myself for the most part and did what I had to just to get by. My behavior was shyness, not acting out. Not drugs or alcohol. So, what the hell was she talking about?

Somehow, one of my sisters thought I was being promiscuous, and Mom confronted me with this. I actually laughed out loud at the thought. At 16, I couldn't fathom the idea of sleeping with a man … ever! The thought disgusted me, and I told her so. I told her that something had happened to me, and I had no interest in such things. Immediate concern almost sobered her up for a second. She pondered over who this man might be. She decided it had to be Jeff because he spent so much time with me. I assured her he was nothing but honorable. She said he wasn't in trouble. She would get him help. "It is not Jeff!" I screamed. "It is Papa!"

Silence.

Mom drained her glass. She walked to the bar that was on the other side of the open basement room. She refilled the glass.

"Well, that will never happen again!" she said. "Son of a bitch is out of here! I am done!" She went on a rant about the countless affairs he'd had since day one of their marriage; her hurt, her pain. Not once did we ever discuss my pain. Never was counseling or any form of help offered to me. We were done.

Regardless of what she said, Mom never did leave Papa. I heard them yelling in their bedroom above the basement. I couldn't understand what was being said, but I heard my name being uttered several times. For the next two years until I moved out, I feared him coming back into my room and punishing me for telling Mom what he'd done. But his anger and issues had by that time shifted more towards my younger brothers. I became more protective of them and my younger sister, as I feared something happening to her, as well.

I knew that Ann had escaped it as we talked more during our teenage years. She was more in disbelief. She knew how violent he could be, but what I told her was beyond her comprehension. I later learned I had been the only one who endured that kind of abuse, and I was thankful that my siblings had not.

Chapter 23
High School Ends, College Begins

I had a few good friends during junior high and high school whom I could rely on and have fun with. A few remain friends to this day: Elise Rugolo, Christine Jones (Amihere), and Clay Cottingham, to name a few. I have even gained friends or gotten to know others better thanks to Facebook, even those who I figured thought me a dork back then. (Well, I was!)

I graduated from high school in 1980. I had a boyfriend I will call "James" my senior year and first year in college. He was physically abusive to me. I was literally thrown down a flight of stairs twice and had my head banged against various walls, but as he proclaimed, he never "hit" me. I finally ended that relationship with the support of some great college friends, who encourage me and supported me.

When I went to college, I dove into psychology courses, trying to understand what had happened to me and why I was the way I was. Studying and learning on my own was a sort of therapy for me. I gained a lot of insight into my parents' behavior, as well.

I lived in the dormitory at Columbia College. My roommate during the first year was Ann. One day, Papa asked me to lunch. I felt uncomfortable dining alone with him, but never knew how to tell him "no". We went to Katy Station in Columbia. He told me how proud he was of me. I was terrified as to where this was leading. He then drove me to their house. I felt the panic coming on. We were alone. He went into the bathroom—to shave of all things, late in the afternoon.

He called me to him. My legs heavy and slow, I went to the open bathroom. He said, "Heidi, you need to know that what happened was not your fault. It was mine. I am sorry. I don't know why I did it, and it will never happen again." He hugged me and took me back to the dorm.

Relief swept over me. We never discussed it again. He seemed relieved of his guilt, but I never got over my shame. I had been changed forever inside. While he did apologize, my relationship with him was permanently damaged, as was my brain. During the years to come, he would spend the rest of his life trying to make it up to me. He was a wonderful grandfather to our children and actually a good father in my adult life to come. So, I faked it at every family get-together. There was love and happiness, but I could never be alone with him or leave my children alone with him. I still had my fears and anxiety. As a mother, I could take no chances.

While in college, I decided to start anew. No one knew me from my younger years as the shy, dorky girl. I worked in a clothing store, built up my wardrobe, improved my image, and actually gained some popularity, the likes of which I had never experienced before. I did some partying.

I never tried drugs, but I did drink a bit and got a bit reckless as far as men were concerned. It's something I am not proud of, but now I understand it as a behavioral symptom of the abuse I had endured: a coping skill that gave me the feeling that somehow I was in control. I could control this! I also allowed myself to become very thin; my weight was something else I could control. I went through relationships that did me no good. My first lover, "L", discarded me quickly, saying that I needed more experience. I lived with the next one, "D" for six years. He had no affection towards me at all, which was something I desperately needed. He was kind, though, and I dealt with the loneliness for as long as I could. I loved him very much, but knew that inside he would never feel about me the way I did. So, I left.

The next one, "B", was a friend I worked with at the *Columbia Missourian*. He was a perfect gentleman in every way but was clingy and insecure, and I saw these as red flags, fearing he would change and become like "James" was. There were other dates along the way, but nothing significant until I met Joe, the love of my life.

I moved out of Mom and Papa's house at eighteen and lived in the dorms for the first two years I attended Columbia College. Papa taught there until I was twenty. They moved with our brothers and youngest sister, Kristina, to Topeka, Kansas, to start a new travel school, called Bryan's Travel. I moved back into their house in Columbia, worked full time, attended Mizzou, and made their house payment. I took in boarders to help cover the payments. I did not drive, due to my anxiety and phobias. I feared anything on wheels. I feared going anywhere alone. Grocery stores were a nightmare that took me a long time to face alone.

I was still working at *The Missourian* and was promoted to supervisor in the mail room. My boss, Bob Ludeman, looked out for me and really helped me through a lot. Eventually, he moved up into the circulation department and needed a district manager. He offered me the job. Taking it meant I needed to drive because I was to be in the field a lot. I forced myself to do it, and it changed my life and opened many doors for me. Even though today I still have trouble in unfamiliar places, large arenas like football stadiums and such, I have no problem going into a store, library, etc.

My husband Joe is well aware of my issues and makes sure to never leave me alone in a situation that makes me uncomfortable or scared. At a football game, no matter how close a bathroom is, he always walks me there and waits outside. I become easily confused and unaware of my surroundings. It is frightening. I am the same way going somewhere in a car. Thank God for GPS, or I'd never find my way home! I always say I am direction dyslexic!

My sister Kristina ran away from home and went back to Columbia. She was a senior in high school, so she stayed with me and the roommates, and also worked full time.

Our parents returned two years later. Both of us moved out and into our own apartments with our then-boyfriends. I continued to slowly make it through school as I worked full time, helped the boyfriend graduate, then left him, and moved into an apartment of my own. I finally learned to be by myself and cope with it.

After a breakup with "B" following that move, I moved back into my parents' home. I was 25. "B" was a great friend to me during my relationship with "D" and after our breakup. I was too broken to deal with having a relationship with anyone. I just wanted to be alone. I was feeling okay about that decision. I was closing in on 26 when Joe came along.

Chapter 24
Joe

Joe was born in 1959 in Memphis, Tennessee, to a poor, uneducated woman named Dorothy Hames. She was Cherokee, which was a shock to us, as Joe had a light complexion and was freckled with reddish blond hair and blue eyes. Dorothy told us he looked just like his birth father, although we never met or searched for him, as she begged us not to. She had been 21 and he'd been 31. He was well-to-do and ashamed of their union. We suspect that he was married but will never know.

Joe's birth mother was placed in a home for unwed mothers in Memphis. Joe was taken away from her promptly at birth and placed in St. Peter's Catholic Orphanage. There, he was cared for by nuns.

Dorothy lived in Ringgold, Georgia, on the border of Chattanooga, Tennessee. I later met her when our kids were little. She previously had two sons, whom we have never met. Following Joe, she had two daughters. We met one briefly, when meeting Dorothy.

As I mentioned earlier, Joe was born with a severe case of clubfoot. It was suspected that he would never walk. He was adopted at the age of nine months by Clifford and LaVonne Custin who lived in Murfreesboro, Tennessee. As the story was told to me, back in those days, you could shop for a child much like you were shopping for a puppy.

You'd walk through the orphanage and look at the children and decide which one might be a good fit for you. Joe was passed up many times due to his disability. His adoptive parents had one biological son named Steve before they adopted Joe. Steve was seven when Joe was chosen and said that Joe was the one he wanted, even though his parents were looking for a girl at the time. (This worked out later, though, when they adopted a girl named Debbie who hadn't yet been born when Joe was adopted.) Apparently, the nuns were not too happy to give Joe up. He was eight months old and they had grown pretty fond of him.

Joe had a pleasant childhood in Tennessee and later in Normal, Illinois, when his father was transferred there with State Farm. He went through Catholic schools up until high school, when he became a bit wild, he says. If you knew my Joe, you would never guess that! He is very bright and responsible and is a hard worker. But back then, he played in a band, partied hard, and slacked in school.

After high school, he tried the college thing, but it didn't work out for him (the first time). At the same time, he was working at State Farm in the custodial department. He was always a hard worker, beginning with a paper route as a child. He always found something to do from that point on. He joined the Air Force. His parents were not happy about this decision, although he says that looking back, it was the best thing he could have done. He feels he became the shame of his mother. She was very tough on him growing up, and I'd have to say, throughout most of his adult years, as well.

Joe spent four years in the Air Force working as an airplane mechanic, something he thoroughly enjoyed, as airplanes were such a fascination to him. When he came home from the military, he joined his parents, who then lived in Columbia, Missouri. He went back to State Farm and worked in the mail room while he went back to school and earned a business degree with honors!

While Joe was in the military, he was dating a young woman. One night while at her apartment in Shreveport, Louisiana, a man came to the door asking for help. Back in those days, we didn't have cell phones to call for help. Being the nice man he is, one who would literally give the shirt off his back, Joe let him in.

His nightmare began when that man pulled out a gun and brandished it at him and the young woman. Then the man tied Joe up, binding his hands and feet behind him so tightly that the blood circulation was cut off. The man began giving orders to the woman, and when Joe refused to order the young woman to do what the man had instructed her to do, he was pistol whipped him in the head, The man threw her body on top of Joe and then raped her. After many hours of torture, the man threw a blanket over them and said, "Bye-bye." Joe said his thought at that time was, "This is going to hurt." He believed that they were about to be shot.

The man was later caught and sentenced to twenty years in prison. It was discovered that he had also raped an older woman and a child. My husband has lived with the scars and trauma of this event, which was the first trigger for his PTSD and depression.

When Joe and I met, our wounds were still fresh from our traumas, but we didn't have a name for the things we were dealing with. We met in 1988, and no one spoke of mental illness back then. I am pretty sure I had never even heard of Schizophrenia, Bipolarity, or PTSD, and I most certainly had not heard of Borderline Personality Disorder. I had probably heard of depression without fully understanding what that even meant. To me, it was something someone had because they were sad about something but could snap out of in time. It never occurred to me that Joe and I were dealing with Post Traumatic Stress and depression.

We talked for hours on end about our experiences. Even today, we do this periodically with each other. It is cathartic and helps us deal with the pain of the past as it affects us in ways even today.

So, if we examine our histories, our parents, and ourselves, we can see patterns of mental illness emerge. We know that Joe's birth mother was illiterate and poor and smoked heavily, but we learned very little else about her. Had she smoked during her pregnancy? Did she have good prenatal health care? What impact did that have on Joe? We do know that Joe has a half-brother who was drug addicted and physically abusive to his mother and a half-sister.

Was there a gene for mental illness in Joe's birth line? Possibly. Joe's adoptive mother dealt with depression for many years. Did that environment impact Joe's brain?

My father was in the military and probably suffered from PTSD. We have been told by his sister that he wasn't abusive or the way he was until after the war. He had been scarred. Would he have been different if he hadn't gone through these experiences? Did the war trigger this side of his brain? Or was he predisposed to mental illness, and did it get passed on to me (and other siblings who also have children with mental illness)?

My mother drank and smoked while carrying all five of us children. Did this impact our development and mental health? She broke her neck at eighteen after living an idyllic childhood and mentally remained in the era prior to her accident forever after because she couldn't feel happiness beyond that time. Did she suffer from PTSD and depression? Probably.

We never considered these things in our lives because that was the norm for us. We all thought we were "normal", but I don't now.

Moving down the family line, did our mental health affect our own children? Did we hide our own issues well, or did we pass them on through our own emotions, behaviors, or genetics? These are the questions we will always have. What caused Adam to have Schizophrenia?

What caused Stephanie to have anxiety and depression? We

know what triggered her PTSD, but where did all of this begin? Sadly, our daughter will never have children of her own as a precaution against passing on mental illness or an autoimmune disorder like Juvenile Diabetes. Who knows? Maybe in the future, we can look at a brain, or someone's DNA, and know for certain if this will manifest or be able to be prevented by a medical procedure.

Chapter 25
Joe and Heidi

I enjoyed living at home that last year before I met Joe. I was with my youngest siblings, Jimmy, then 18, and Martin, 14. They were the light of my life, and I loved them dearly. Being separated when they moved away was heartbreaking. Somehow, I felt I could keep an eye on them and protect them from harm, but in reality, it was the other way around. They both towered over me by then and protected me!

Martin had a girlfriend whose mother, Janet, became friends with me. She and I went out often and had the greatest laughs and fun. We celebrated her birthday on Friday, April 29, 1988. The next night I was getting ready for bed, took my contacts out, and began to clean them. She called and asked if I would like to go out dancing again. I told her I was tired and didn't really feel like it, couldn't see too well without my contacts, blah, blah, blah. "I will buy the drinks," she said. So, I went.

Janet was dancing and in the mood for fun, while I was standing on the sidelines watching her. A couple of guys hit on me. I really wasn't into being there that night until I got a tap on the shoulder. This handsome, blond, blue-eyed man asked me to dance. I couldn't say no. After the dance, we talked and talked. It turns out he was dragged out the same night by a roommate who offered to pay for drinks if he would accompany him out. It was fate. But when I left for a moment to use the restroom and returned, he was gone …

The following Monday, I was sitting at my desk staring at an open page of the phone directory, thinking he said he worked for All-state. His name was Joe. Hmmmm. Columns upon columns of listings.

The switchboard operator's office was right next to mine, so fortunately she knew me when a call came in, not asking for a manager, but for Heidi Shultz. It was Joe! (He worked for State Farm, not Allstate). "I am not sure if you remember me?" he began.

Joe took me to the Red Lobster restaurant that next Thursday. I was so nervous. My parents' living room was filled with people. Aunt Jane and Uncle Don were visiting. Mom was drinking and smoking a cigarette, Papa, a cigar, because in those days people smoked anywhere! I didn't smoke so I was worried it might offend Joe. Also, right by the front door was a hole in the carpet big enough for a toddler to lie in!

Joe arrived in an old International Scout. He was nervous that I would judge him because of it and had worked for hours cleaning it up for me. I climbed into the passenger seat and silently peeked at his profile several times. The weirdest thought came to me: I am going to marry this man! A total stranger!

We met April 30, 1988. Early December of that year, we decided that we would marry. We set the date for September of 1989. I got pregnant on New Year's Day. We had decided to start trying since I was recently off the pill, thinking it would take a long time. He would be 30 when we married, and I would be 27. We wanted kids right away.

We moved the date up to March 4, 1989. Joe's parents were less than thrilled with us (it was not like we were 16!), but mine were. No more fears of me becoming an old maid! Cliff and LaVonne's response is still laughable to this day, but at the time, it was very hurtful. They were very devout Catholics, and in their opinion, you simply did not have sex before marriage.

But in those days, with my generation, there was something wrong with you if you didn't. We went to visit them to let them know.

Joe told them with great happiness and enthusiasm. LaVonne literally collapsed on the couch with her hand thrown over her forehead. So dramatic. "Cllliiiffff!" she wailed. "Are you going to say something???" Cliff was pacing the room, arms crossed over his chest. "There is nothing to say!" he retorted.

With that, I said, "Joe, I will be in the car. I am not listening to this."

As I was leaving, LaVonne said, "What will we tell our friends?" She was so concerned about her image. Abortion was completely out of the question, and I think she would have agreed with that. So what was done was done. Move forward! There was much talk and speculation about how short this marriage was going to be. As of this writing, we have been married for over thirty years! At any rate, Cliff got over it and ended up being the greatest father-in-law I could have hoped for. LaVonne never forgave me, though, and our relationship was rocky for many years to come.

Joe was in Personal Lines Underwriting with State Farm at the time. State Farm opened a new regional office in Tulsa, and Joe moved there in July of 1989. I followed in October after finally finishing my degree and giving birth to our firstborn, Stephanie, on September 25, 1989. She was due on the 26th, so Joe said he would take that week off. I told him babies will come when they wish, and he retorted, "The doctor said the 26th." I cracked up and hoped she would be on time.

Tulsa was a six-hour drive! She was born about forty minutes prior to the 26th. Close enough! Joe simply said, "I told you so."

We made the trek to Tulsa when Stephanie was ten days old. Joe drove his little Toyota pickup truck, and I drove my little Nissan. Stephanie rode with Daddy to ease my nerves. Every now and then, he would stop on the side of the road so I could feed her! What a trip! At one point he drove with her in his arms so I could have some quiet time, something we would never do today!

Chapter 26
Our Little Family

And so began the lives of Joe and Heidi in Tulsa, Oklahoma. Initially, we lived in the apartment Joe rented until we arrived. We chose a neighborhood in Broken Arrow to build our first house, a small ranch style with three bedrooms, perfect for our little family. We moved in January of 1990. Right about that time, I found out I was pregnant again. We were so excited!

During my second trimester, about four-and-a-half months along, I went in for a checkup with my ob-gyn. She didn't hear a heartbeat so I was sent to ultrasound. Apparently the baby's brain had stopped developing, and she had died. My doctor was young and so was I. She scheduled me to have surgery two weeks later!

I was asked many times during those two weeks, as people patted my belly, when my baby was due. I remember blankly staring the first one down and numbly saying, "My baby is dead." One friend asked me when I had miscarried, and I replied, "I didn't. Surgery is next week." She was a nurse and said that was really dangerous; that I should have been in surgery right away. So, then I got it into my head that the baby must be alive, and they wanted to take her out because there was something wrong with her brain!

Going into surgery prep the following week, I questioned the anesthesiologist before he put me under. "I want to keep her. I don't care if there is something wrong with her brain. I love her! I will take care of her." Little did I know, how true that statement would be in my future.

He coldly looked at me like I was a lunatic and replied, "Your baby is dead." Then I was out. I woke up to emptiness. I just wanted my Stephanie. I needed to hold her and feel like everything was going to be okay.

Losing that baby was traumatic, but it opened the door for Adam to be born. I was pregnant with the second baby about two months after giving birth to Stephanie, and then with Adam very quickly following the loss of that baby. So, Stephanie and Adam were only seventeen months apart.

Adam was due on Joe's birthday, February 22. I mentioned to Joe, "You do know it was a fluke that Stephanie was born so close to her due date?" But he still believed the doctor was right on target and that Adam would arrive on his birthday.

My pregnancy with Adam was difficult. I was sick through over half of the pregnancy and gained only seventeen pounds total. Adam didn't arrive on the 22nd. A week later, I still hadn't gone into labor. My doctor set a date to induce labor. She chose March 4. I said that was our anniversary, so she agreed to do it on the fifth.

Well, babies have a way of showing up when they choose. Adam came into the world on March 4 after all! Happy anniversary, Mom and Dad! He was the best gift anyone could have hoped for. Since I had gained so little weight, we were shocked when he arrived weighing nine pounds, four ounces! He had a bowel movement in the birth canal and breathed it into his lungs. Like his sister, he was swiftly taken away.

Having lost the second baby, I was in a panic. In the meantime, there were medical students who wanted to see who had given birth to this huge baby. They were in shock to walk in to see this little woman in the bed. "You had the big baby?"

Adam was returned to me a while later. I felt so relieved. He appeared to be a healthy baby boy! I'm not sure who was more excited: Joe to have a son, me to have a healthy girl and boy, or Stephanie to have a baby brother. She immediately laid claim to him: her baby, her boy, her Adam Boy, "Amboy", as we continued to call him that for years to come. Later it became A.B. It confused some people, as his middle name is Patrick. His Aunt Debbie always called him A.P. and we'd chuckle and not say anything, as that became her personal nickname for him.

We brought Adam home and laid him on the couch. Stephanie climbed up and leaned over him, beaming, and said, "Eyes," placing two little fingers in his eyes. He cried so hard—and she did, too, not realizing that it would hurt the baby. Joe and I joked about his welcome home for years to come.

Poor Stephanie was booted out of her bed so young. In her room we had a queen size waveless waterbed (they were popular in those days). We had one in our room, too. Looking back, I am horrified to think of this, but we moved her from the crib to that tall, huge bed. We placed pillows around her, and amazingly, she never fell out! We were so naive. Adam shared the same room and slept in the crib.

When Adam became big enough for a bed, Joe built a fabulous bunk bed with a double size on the lower bunk and a twin size on top. The kids loved that bed. They were so ornery. We would hear them laughing hysterically, and that usually meant they were up to no good. One time we went into the room. Adam was around four and Steph was five. She was shrieking, "Adam, do it again!" and going into fits of laughter. There he was, standing on the top bunk, stark naked, swinging his penis around. It was shortly after that that we moved Adam into the third bedroom. They were so upset to be split apart like that. You would think they were twins!

Of course eventually, they came to love having their own space and became territorial of their own rooms and belongings like any siblings. But they always remained close, kept secrets, and had private codes and language between the two of them.

When they were young, they laughed a lot. They were the happiest children. For some reason, that bothered some people. I remember two situations I could not wrap my mind around. One, we were visiting my youngest sister, Kristina, in Kansas City. She was married to her first husband, Dwayne, who is now deceased. They lived in an apartment. Her two little girls, Brittney and Jessica, were playing in their bedroom with Stephanie and Adam, and the giggles filled the place.

Kristina told me in hushed tones that we needed to get them to stop so it wouldn't upset Dwayne. I couldn't for the life of me understand how the laughter of children filling a home would upset anyone, but out of respect, we asked them to calm it down. Years later, she divorced him due to abuse and threats of killing her. That explained why she wanted the kids to be calm.

Once—only once—my children were invited to spend a week one summer with their paternal grandparents. Their cousins spent many weeks several summers with them, and we couldn't understand why ours were not invited back. First of all, I recall shopping at JCPenney for brand new clothes for the week. Their Mimi opened the suitcase and told my daughter that she was embarrassed to dress them in those crappy clothes. She went to garage sales and bought them replacements! Years later, she told us our children were not invited back because they laughed too much. Did they? Or did she just have it out for me from the start? She wasn't going to treat me or my children equal to her other grandchildren. It made me sad, but thankful to live six hours away. Oh, how I prayed for laughter and a return of happiness as the years went on. I savor the memories of those carefree giggles today.

Following Adam, I became pregnant again. During the fifth month, once again the baby's brain stopped developing, and I had another D&C to remove the fetus. A year later, a fifth pregnancy resulted in a miscarriage during the first trimester. We decided to stop trying. No longer did we think a big family was worth my health. The pregnancies with Stephanie and Adam, having larger babies in my small body, had caused my bladder to fall. I'd had surgery for that at thirty.

Chapter 27
Joe's Promotion

During the summer of 2008, Joe was offered a job with State Farm Insurance in the Kansas City area. It was a promotion. It was closer to Columbia, where both of our parents resided, along with two siblings. All of my siblings live in Missouri. Joe's sister lives in Illinois and comes to Columbia often. The move made sense in many ways, although it was heartbreaking to leave twenty years of memories and friends behind.

Joe felt it would give the kids a push in the right direction. Stephanie was 18 and Adam was 17. We made it clear to them that if they wished to live on their own in the town they called home, that was fine. If they chose to move with us, that was fine, too. A new environment in a new state could give Adam what he needed away from drugs and such, right? But both felt they would stay in Oklahoma.

Joe moved in July of 2008 into a one-bedroom apartment in Lenexa, Kansas, as his territory was on the Kansas side of Kansas City. We sold our home and the kids and I moved into the small house I now used as my preschool. Movers put most of our things in storage in Lenexa. Joe took what he needed for the year, and I took what I needed. I stayed in Oklahoma for another year. We had many reasons for this, among them that I had just enrolled students for the upcoming school year and felt a dedication to those families to honor those contracts.

Aside from that, I was terrified to leave our children behind, as they had both said, "I am not leaving!" At this time in our lives, I firmly believed Adam was very sick mentally, while Joe felt he needed to get motivated and become an adult.

Stephanie had graduated a semester early, and Adam, who had dropped out of high school, went into the service center and took his GED, passing easily. He later told us he was high on cocaine when he took the exam. He had not participated in class since the eighth or ninth grade, so we were baffled as to how he accomplished that. That being said, we have since learned in working with other families this is not uncommon with the mentally ill. It seems like most say something along the lines of, "I just don't understand it. He/she is so smart, like off the charts intelligent. Why can't they just get it together?" Why do we think that if someone has a mental illness they are less intelligent? From my experience, people with mental illness that I've known are some of the brightest people I have ever met! Adam could outsmart you in any argument. It was really frustrating!

In June of that summer, we went as a family to Branson, Missouri, with the Custin clan and celebrated both graduates. I was happy that they honored my two this way and felt they both needed that love boost.

When Joe moved, Adam was working at Sonic and Stephanie worked at a Cinemark movie theatre. In Adam's world—the world of the person with a mental illness—jobs came and went. He was certain he would stick this one out because he was not moving to Kansas City! As usual, the job lasted two weeks. He just walked out.

During that same time period, Stephanie was going to Tulsa Community College. She had a high enough GPA to receive the first two years free of charge, except for books. That first semester was tough on all of us. Stephanie became very ill and was hospitalized. Being in college, she partied like many of us do. Unfortunately, it affected her blood sugars and she went into ketoacidosis, a life-threatening condition that develops when the cells in the body are unable to get the sugar they need for energy because there is not enough insulin.

When the sugar cannot get into the cells, it stays in the blood. The kidneys filter some of the sugar from the blood and remove it from the body through urine. Because the cells cannot receive sugar for energy, the body begins to break down fat and muscle for energy. When this happens, ketones (fatty acids) are produced and enter the bloodstream, causing the chemical imbalance ketoacidosis. It can be caused by not having enough insulin, having a severe infection, or other illness, dehydration (which she had), or a combination of these things. It can be very scary. Thankfully, I had my incredible assistants, Keli O'Neal, Tess Ogden, Jessica Cook, and Mikalynn Robb to step in for me as I tended to Stephanie.

During the same time, Adam, still determined to make it on his own, moved out of the house. He moved into a house a few miles away with a man named Joe. He was probably in his late twenties, living in his parents' home while they were missionaries in another country. He took in all sorts of young people who had issues with drugs and or mental illness. He seemed like a nice man, but I couldn't help but wonder what was in it for him.

The place was a pit. I stopped by often to check on Adam. Young folk lay strewn around the place, smoking pot and cigarettes. Adam was turned down for job after job application, so young Joe gave him the responsibility of keeping the house clean. He did a pretty good job of it, all things considered.

I brought food to the house every week. The kids began to look forward to my weekly visits. I did not show judgment. I joked around with them. I just wanted to make sure Adam was safe and fed. I couldn't control everything he did, but at least he had access to food.

Two serious incidents occurred at Joe's house while Adam lived there. The first one was a fight. Apparently, the boys were taking some Xanax one night, along with alcohol. Adam and another boy, James E., whom he referred to as a friend, began messing around in the front yard. I think what started in fun turned into a fight. They were wrestling around, pushing, shoving, and hitting one another.

The other boy fell and hit his head on a rock. He was cut pretty badly and went to the hospital for stitches and a concussion. I am sure Adam was in psychosis during this time, a bad combination mixed with drugs and alcohol. But the boys became friends once again the following day as if nothing happened.

The second incident ended with Adam being injured. Joe had a very old, large dog, who was blind and deaf. She was a sweetheart but had to be approached gently or would startle due to her condition. Adam was stumbling around, high on something, and he tripped over her. She bit him on the mouth. Her teeth went clear through the skin above his upper lip. He called me to take him to the doctor to get it sewn up. He did not want to report the dog, acknowledging fault in the incident. It seemed to me he didn't care what happened to himself. He was careless in his actions, taking drugs and taking chances without thinking about the possible consequences.

One day, I received a phone call from the Broken Arrow Police Department saying there had been an accident and that I needed to come to the intersection of 71st and Elm Streets, not far up the road from our house. All I heard was that he had been hit by a car. I was shaking as I approached the scene lit up with police lights and two kids sitting on the ground. Adam had jumped out in front of a car thinking it would kill him. It had swerved to avoid hitting him. He had landed on the top of the car, doing a bit of damage to the it, but luckily, he came out with only some bruising and bumps on him, no broken bones or head injuries! The driver of the car had had a child in a car seat in the back seat and his wife in the front. Amazingly, he did not press charges and simply left. I couldn't believe it! The girl Adam was with (I will call her S.M.) relates the story this way but admits she did not remember all the details, as they were both high at the time. She does not recall him actually being hit by the car, but I have the doctor receipts and injury reports. Anyway, she tells the story (along with her story of meeting Adam and what he was like as a friend) as such:

"I had the first opportunity to meet Adam in 2007. At the time I was having problems with my mom, where she would erupt into violent episodes and kick me out with nowhere to go. So, this girl I was friends with, Erin, who I would confide in, had a boyfriend who lived a mile away from my house.

"So, I went and stayed for a while. The first night, I met Harley, Cary, Lauren, Danielle, KC, and Adam. We were smoking the medicine for our souls, which is marijuana, and the kids whose place we were at gave us a line of cocaine or so. Adam was sitting on this chair, the only sofa in this place. He had a nice smile and giggled quite a bit, and we were all having fun and getting along at our rebellious teenage hangout for the night. Adam was in the chair, looking so comfortable just embracing the time with everyone, enjoying the moment. He really stood out to me as a special kind of person—no ego, just an all-around person with no judgment, easy to talk with and relate with, always down for adventure. Every now and then we would take ecstasy pills, which seemed to be everywhere in Tulsa at the time. We would go riding around in a friend's car, and usually we ended up at James' house, where his room was lit up with neon lights and posters reflecting on that. It was very therapeutic in a way, just us laughing and being silly [sic].

"A couple of years later, we were in the same group often. We would have pretty deep talks about regular teenage emotional stuff, surrounded by just wanting to have fun and whatnot. I never saw Adam act out too much until after this one night in like 2008. (I believe it was the night of the fight.) The next day he was telling me about this girl, whose name I'd rather not mention (M.T). He'd been with her awhile and really had a lot of love for her at the time. She said she didn't want to be with him anymore and basically left him with a cold heart, but I could tell he was in pain. I told him I would walk him home because he was acting a little odd. Then he straight bolted out in front of a car on this road we were walking on. Thankfully, the car swerved. After, I held him on the sidewalk, telling him, 'It's going to be alright. Calm down, man.' The cops came and took him (he actually left by ambulance and I followed in my car). I was taken in another police car, as there was a warrant out on me for running away."

This being another attempt at suicide, Adam had to spend a few days at Laureate. At this point, Adam came back home to me. He had been out for about three months. In some ways, I was relieved to have him back with me. In other ways, it was difficult because when he was with the young man, Joe, he stayed put, and I knew where to find him. Living with me, he would wander off, and I was in the dark about where he would be. I had a few places in mind, but he would not answer his phone, and if he was missing a couple of days, I would panic and go searching for him. If he stayed put, I was in constant worry over what would come out of his mouth in front of one of the children's parents or a child.

In March of 2009, Adam turned 18, relieving my husband and me of any legal responsibility for his actions. That part was a good thing, but the bad part was that now the Health Insurance Portability and Accountability Act laws stepped in, saying we could no longer have access to Adam's medical records or history unless he signed a waiver allowing us access. In the case of a mentally ill child, this is very difficult. Such as was in Adam's case, he did not believe there was anything wrong with him for a long time. It was all Mom and Dad's doing. We were the ones with a problem.

In the preschool house, I had a pull-out couch in the room we used for naps. I slept on this that year. Early in the morning, I would fold it up, make sure the house was in order, and get ready to greet the children. One of the rooms that had been Stephanie's when we lived there before had a futon in it. Stephanie and Adam slept in there. It was always a mess with food wrappers strewn everywhere, bottles, cans, dishes, and clothes. The kids slept most of the day, so that worked for me. By naptime, however, I had to boot them out and clean up the room so I could put a child in there in a porta- crib.

At this point, Stephanie had quit college. Due to her illness, she had been absent too long and felt helpless to bring up her grades. She still worked at Cinemark that first semester, but I was told she quit during the second one. I just figured she had changed her mind at that point to move with me because she had been a dedicated employee since she was around fifteen. I employed her part time. But what she tells me today is a different story. She says she was into the drug and alcohol scene just like her brother. She was fighting her own demons, but most of the focus was on Adam, as he escalated and frequently was suicidal.

She tells me she and another employee were outside the building smoking pot and someone caught them. When confronted by the manager, the other person lied and denied it and was fired on the spot. Stephanie told the truth and was placed on a probationary period. She felt it was only a matter of time until they would let her go, so she simply did not return to the job. Stephanie has given me permission to tell this part of the story because it all plays into how mental illness affects everyone in the family and close friends. When your loved one is ill, everyone else is, too, in some way or another.

When I booted my own kids out of the room for naptime for the little ones, Adam often left the house for the day and possibly the night as well. I never knew what would happen to him. I displayed a happy, fun face and personality for the little ones and parents, but inside, I lived in terror every minute of every day. At night I barely slept, listening for sounds of Adam coming home, hoping and praying he had lived through the night.

Just as S.M. tells in her story, Adam did end up at his friend James' house a lot. That became my first place to look for him, and sometimes he would call from that house to be picked up. One morning, I received a call to pick him up. He got into the car smelling like hard liquor. It was so strong, I could smell it coming out of his pores. It made me feel nauseated as I am sensitive to strong smells. Fortunately, it was one of those nice days you could drive with the windows down, so I did just that. Adam was calm, though, and didn't slur his words or appear intoxicated.

He spoke clearly and intelligently, and the conversation that followed was so strange, yet he made it sound like it was the most normal, reasonable thing to be telling me. He told me of this table in James' house that had a lamp on it. People set their keys, wallets, etc. down on this table, and the table absorbed the items. I asked him if it was some kind of magic trick. He was so serious as he told me he had set a $20 bill on the table, and it had eaten it! He could see through the table and see the money inside. "This is for real, Mom!" he said earnestly. "One guy lost a whole set of keys!" He really believed this! It was so bizarre!

Another night that year, he was at a different friend's house with a group of kids. They were all hanging out in the garage when someone said he needed to make a run to QuikTrip for cigarettes and asked who wanted to go with him. Some kids jumped into the car. Adam chose not to but then suddenly decided he wanted to go. He ran to the car yelling, but no one heard him. He grabbed the handle of the back door just as the car was pulling away and was dragged for a moment before falling face first to the pavement. According to testimony, he walked back to the remaining group in the garage, and people began backing away, some telling him he needed to go to the hospital. He went to the bathroom and looked into the mirror. His chin looked like hamburger. He vomited at the sight. He then lay down, feeling no pain at the time, and slept.

Around nine the next morning, Adam called me, screaming in pain, begging me to take him to a doctor. I told myself (again!) to be calm no matter what I would be seeing. I was scared. If he was in a panic, it had to be bad. He got into the car, and I seriously nearly passed out. My stomach lurched, but I had to get him help. I could not believe he had made it through the night like that. On the way to Urgent Care, he kicked the dashboard and screamed obscenities all the way there. I was in an agitated state and so was he. I held back what I really wanted to say. I worried about him. I worried he was going to break the dash or the window as he began kicking that, as well.

Stitching up that chin was tricky, the doctor told us. There was no straight cut, just a mangled chin. Along with the scars from the dog bite, Adam now had a jagged scar under and on his chin.

At one point, Adam became obsessed with the movie *Donnie Darko* starring Jake Gyllenhaal. At the time, he began to watch this he was around sixteen or seventeen, but he watched it over and over for a few years. We just thought it was this bizarre dark movie. Jake and Adam looked so similar, it was eerie. Watching scenes from that movie now, I am amazed at Gyllenhaal's acting ability. He portrayed the part of a young man with Schizophrenia so well, the mannerisms, thoughts, etc. Adam acted very much like this person Gyllenhaal portrayed. I listened to the theme song recently (very recently), and the lyrics really hit me. Adam watched this movie over and over and listened to "Mad World" over and over because he identified with this young man. Wish I would have had the insight to see this early on. The words could have revealed so much to us.

I was dealing with all this drama in Broken Arrow, and one night, Joe's mom decided to call me to let me know what a loser she thought I was. Like I hadn't already known all those years that she felt that way. She told me I was a loser as a mother and a wife. She spent a good hour telling me what a low life I was, and the kicker was telling me how I had caused Adam's illness. I tried to remain calm. I asked her how she possibly knew what kind of mother I was. She had kept my kids once in their entire life for only a week, and she'd visited us maybe twice during our twenty years in Oklahoma. "How do you know what I have done or not done?" I asked. She tried to turn me against Joe. Joe feels this and Joe feels that. Who does that? In tears, I finally told her I had to go and hung up.

I called my friend Carol Ogden, who lived down the street, and she came over right away. She assured me that I was one of the best moms and wives she knew and told me never to listen to such nonsense. I knew that, but it still hurt.

I took a trip to Columbia for a University of Missouri football game against Georgia. Steve and Connie joined us, and I got to hear it from Connie, who had heard this and that from LaVonne. I asked if I could tell my side of the story. It seems they were all up in arms because I had stayed in Oklahoma a year. LaVonne had told everyone that I was never going to K.C. Connie and I talked through the evening. We compared notes on the things our mother-in-law had said about each of us behind our backs. The only thing LaVonne had accomplished through those antics was bringing Connie and me closer than ever before.

In December of 2008, I drove to Kansas City to see Joe for a few days before celebrating Christmas with our kids in Broken Arrow. When we returned from Missouri and walked into the Preschool House, our temporary home, the place was a pit! Booze bottles, beer cans, trash strewn everywhere. We walked through the rooms of the house and found various young people in drunken or drugged-up states. Someone heard us, and suddenly a group of people fled into the field behind our house. I went throughout the house checking on things. I had decorated for the holidays.

The classroom in the garage area was trashed, along with some treasured ornaments and Christmas decor. Many of those were smashed or broken. It was heartbreaking thinking that Adam had so little love and respect for me that he could do something like this.

In April of 2009, Joe called to let me know his dad was having surgery in Harlingen, Texas, where they lived during the winters. He headed down there to help care for him. That weekend I was in Lebanon, Missouri, visiting my sister Kristina, when I received a call from Joe late at night. One of the first families I'd had in my daycare during the early nineties were the Finnegans. Jim Finnegan had been Joe's roommate when we first met. He had married Jeanne and they'd had two children, Kaitlyn and Kevin. Kaitlyn and Adam were born seven weeks apart. I have the most adorable pictures of the two of them.

Joe said that Kaitlyn had been murdered by a "friend", who had lost his cool and shot her. I rushed back to Tulsa to see Jim and Jeanne and attend services. When I got to their house, Jeanne rushed to me in an embrace. She knew that Adam had made multiple attempts on his life, and we were both weary. As we hugged, she said, "This is not better. This is not better." It was heartbreaking! I had to attend the services alone, as Joe was still caring for his dad.

I was using the van, and Joe had taken our pickup truck to Kansas City. He had a company car, so he didn't need either except to travel to see us. Fortunately, during the summer I did not need a van for transporting kids to school, so Adam borrowed the van to take Stephanie to Burger King. After passing through a stop light, there was a median to his left. He wasn't paying attention and drove right over it as he turned left into the restaurant's parking lot. Not realizing he had knocked out the transmission, he continued on through the drive-through. The car was leaking fuel, draining itself. It was destroyed. Adam could not get the van past the payment window, and sat there for several minutes, until the manager came out and helped him push it out of the way so other customers could order.

Joe came down and assessed the damage to the van. The repairs would cost more than the van itself. Good-bye, van. So, I drove Joe back to Lenexa and brought the pickup back with me. A single cab Chevy truck. This was becoming the year from hell! I couldn't wait to get to Kansas City at this point. I was exhausted from worry and fear. I was missing Joe and his strength.

Since summer had come, the school year kids left. Now I had my summer group, and much to accomplish, packing and moving things to K.C. On weekends, I would load stuff into the truck and tote it to Joe's apartment. He had every square inch of space full of boxes by the time we actually moved. It looked like hoarders lived there!

When Joe had moved, I had kept not only took the kids, but all of our pets as well. We had our two dogs, Alaska and Nellie, and Fred the cat. During the spring of 2009, one of my preschool kids' mom called me on a stormy day to let me know that there was a dog in my trash outside. I had a ton of trash back there, from diapers to food waste and random things I'd tossed trying to organize for the move. As I was getting drenched while putting trash back into bags, this tiny dog leapt out of nowhere onto my shoulder. I couldn't be angry as I took this pitiful thing into my house. He was a chihuahua mix. My dogs were huge compared to him, and the cat doubled him in size. I thought, "This is all I need right now! Another responsibility!" We tried to find where he had come from, but to no avail. So our menagerie just became larger!

We named him Jack. I figured Joe would flip out, so I took Jack on a road trip to K.C. on one of my moving weekends. Joe had not been thrilled when I'd talked to him on the phone about it, but as soon as Jack saw Joe, he jumped into his arms like a long lost friend. It was all over then!

As sick as Adam became as time went on, these animals were a Godsend. He was calm around them. They seemed to give him some security. He would sit outside with them for long periods of time, hug on them, and talk to them.

Chapter 28
The Move

The summer was coming to an end. We still had some furniture to move, along with the animals. I was worried about the cat. He was getting up there in years and had only lived in that little house. Even when we'd moved into the second home, Fred had stayed in the preschool house. My nephew Chris had moved to Tulsa when we bought the second house and lived with us for awhile. He moved into his own place when Joe was transferred. He took Fred in for a while, intending to keep him until we had a permanent residence. We ended up renting for three years, but got Fred back a few months later because of Chris' allergies. We rented a house on State Line Road on the Missouri side of the street. Before it was available, we all crammed into that one-bedroom apartment filled with boxes for one month, animals and all! We looked like the Beverly Hillbillies!

The move itself was traumatizing. Stephanie was seeing someone new, a man named James. Adam said he had seen James at the QuikTrip in Broken Arrow with Stephanie, and he'd been pulling her hair and slamming her up against the building. Stephanie said it wasn't true (although years later she admitted that the hair pulling part had been true). We were thinking, "We're moving, so she will never see him again anyway."

Adam was staying up until the last minute in Oklahoma. One of my girls who worked for me wanted to take over the preschool, so she and her husband lived in the house for a few months (it didn't work out). We told Adam he couldn't stay there. He reluctantly climbed into the pickup truck with me, loaded down with stuff.

Joe drove his motorcycle with Stephanie on the back. It was only a four-hour drive, yet it seemed like forever. I stressed over watching Joe and Stephanie on the little Harley Sportster in front of me. I stressed over having Adam in my passenger seat. He was in high psychosis that day.

In spite of the fact that he finally agreed to go with us, his body language and his words on the drive said otherwise. He kept trying to start arguments along the way. He was agitated and so was I. He kept trying to push me into fighting with him. The drive was stressful enough without this, and at some point, I did start raising my voice. Adam threatened to jump out of the truck about halfway to Kansas City. I was driving with one arm on the steering wheel and the other arm ready to grab his arm at any moment to keep him in the from jumping out of the truck. I would have felt better if he had agreed to wear a seatbelt, but that was not happening.

We finally made it to Lenexa, Kansas. It was late in the evening, as we had gotten a late start to begin with. I parked the pickup truck, which was piled high with stuff, underneath a parking shelter at the apartment. We went into the apartment and threw a mattress on the small living room floor, which took up every bit of space between the couch and a widescreen TV. The kids slept on the couch and the mattress with three dogs sprawled around them. Exhausted, Joe and I fell into bed. We had a lot to do the next morning, unloading the truck and working on the search for a house to live in.

The next morning, Adam was in a very high state of psychosis (although we didn't know what psychosis was at the time). All of us were tense. Joe was trying to get the kids motivated to help around the apartment and get things a little more organized. Adam wasn't having any of it. He and Joe got into an argument, and Joe pushed him out of the apartment. Adam said that he didn't want to live there anyway, so Joe told him to go on home then, meaning Oklahoma.

So Adam left barefooted, walking down the highway. Later, a police officer stopped him and picked him up. He brought him back to us. Joe was just plain mad, and—typical me—I was just plain scared. Any and every time Adam left us, for whatever reason, it created a gnawing feeling of dread in the pit of my stomach. I never knew at any given time he walked out the door whether it would be the last time I ever saw him. I certainly didn't want it to end with a disagreement between us. I didn't want it to end at all; no matter how frustrated or angry we felt, we still loved him.

We lived in that apartment in Lenexa, Kansas, for an entire month. We finally found a nice-sized house on State Line Road on the Missouri side. It was a ranch style, very spacious, with three bedrooms, a living room, a dining room, and a breakfast nook set off of the kitchen. It had all wood flooring, except for the kitchen, nook, and bathrooms, which were tiled. The nook was big enough for office space for Joe, since he worked from home now. He had a window facing State Line Road.

Adam's room was between the dining room and the living room, but at the same time, it was at the back of the house. The backyard was huge and filled with trees. We felt this was a good haven for Adam, and we knew that the dogs would love exploring back there, too. Stephanie's room was down a long hallway at the back of the house.

Ours was at the front, down the other end of the hallway. We couldn't believe our good fortune at finding such a house in the city. After we had lived in Kansas City for awhile, we began to call it "the city of trees". The house was built in the 1950s. It also had a huge unfinished basement, so we could unload the storage unit we had been

141

using for the past year and put what didn't fit into the house down there until we found someplace more permanent.

Mikalynn and her then-husband Chris (the couple renting our Oklahoma house) drove up with a trailer and Joe had the pickup truck. We recruited family to help, too. Brother Martin and his family, sister, Kristina, and then-husband, Mark, with their pickup truck, and nephew, Tad, to name a few. There was a Chiefs' game that weekend, so we tied that into the deal. So, the move began! We had the apartment and storage unit to unload, plus cleaning up the apartment and organizing in the house. The women cleaned the apartment and organized, and the men loaded and transported everything. Adam even participated!

On one trip, the pickup truck was loaded down with stuff, with mattresses on top. Adam and Tad were in the back when one of the mattresses came loose and flew onto I-435 in crazy, busy, rush hour traffic. Joe stopped the truck and the boys ran out to get the mattress, securing it once more. Everyone agreed it was a good thing I had not been there to witness that. I know I would have stressed out the situation even further with my panic! We were so thankful for all the help everyone gave to us that day. The next day, we enjoyed our football game together, which wrapped up the weekend on a calmer note.

Chapter 29
The First Year in K.C.

We moved into our house on State Line on the last day of August. Joe was working hard. I had been working since mid-August as a nanny in Shawnee, Kansas. With Adam so ill and having to close down my business in Oklahoma, I didn't have the heart to start over. I had run that business for twenty years. I began my search for a job during the summer and had a job offer as a lead teacher with the five-year-old children at a prestigious private school, which offered infant care through kindergarten. I was also offered the nanny job, which paid better than the teaching job. I figured I could use a little less pressure after what we had gone through in Oklahoma with family and business. So, I took the nanny job with one infant. What a change after a house full of children!

The baby was Tyler Wilkens, a good-natured child, easy to care for. He was six months old when we met, and we hit it off immediately. He was eight months when I started caring for him. I noticed when he tried to stand, he would always be on tippy toes and fall backwards. His feet simply would not flatten out. As I mentioned earlier, a brother of mine was born like this, and my husband has club feet.

Brooklynn, a child I cared for back in Oklahoma, also had that problem. So I became concerned and told his parents, Monica and Ted. I was worried it would upset them, but they were thankful. He needed casts and physical rehabilitation to help fix the issue. I was a participant in his rehab and felt thankful to be a part of his recovery. Having worked with so many children before, with special needs children among them, this was right up my alley. It gave me some purpose and a distraction from the problems at home, as this child kept me very busy.

Later, we would learn that Tyler also had several food allergies, along with environmental allergies, so I became his teacher during the early years, as well. I had saved my curriculum materials, art supplies, manipulatives, and even some educational toys. Ty and I had a lot of good times learning and playing together. Even though he is older now, I still continue to spend a little time with him during summers today. He has grown into a very active, intelligent boy. He has no issues with his feet and participates in sports! He is a great conversationalist and a compassionate young boy. In many ways, this child helped me through some very difficult years.

Stephanie got a job in October 2009, just down the street from our rental on State Line at Panera Bread Company. She eventually became a trainer there. One day, James, the man Steph had been seeing in Oklahoma, just showed up at our house with a "Hi, Mom! How are you doing?", which took me aback, as I had never met him before. I am not sure what happened after that. Was it our distraction with Adam? Did we not believe what Adam had told us about James because Adam was delusional so much of the time that we believed he was just causing trouble?

All I know is that gradually James moved in and none of us did anything about it. He was a smooth-talking man, appearing to be a sweetheart. He was helpful around the house—a clean freak—which appealed to me. He took Stephanie everywhere she needed to be. Adam even seemed to like him over time. We just didn't question it, or why we let a man live in our house with our daughter. She was of age. We could have just asked both of them to move out, but we didn't.

Adam was spiraling out of control with his self-medication of drugs and alcohol. He was in psychosis, ranting and raving through the house, in and out the back door and the front door. We took Adam to Research Psychiatric Hospital for help. Since we had had previous suicide attempts and hospitalizations, he was admitted by our word. Documentation proved that when in this state, he could easily become suicidal. He was put on a 72-hour hold but came home as usual after a not long enough stay. Here is the reality when you have an adult child with mental illness, and you have to hospitalize them due to psychosis or suicide attempts or threat of suicide. First, you have to convince them that they need treatment (unless they make a suicide attempt). If you cannot, you call a crisis intervention trained (C.I.T.) officer to take them for you. Of course, during this time period, we knew nothing about C.I.T.

If you know nothing about it and you get another police officer, they might take them to jail due to obvious drug use or "behavior". If you are lucky, they are transported to a psychiatric hospital for help. The intake counselor then decides if they need to stay. If the patient can convince the person on staff that they are fine, they are released back home. They are also asked questions about their safety, such has, "Do you feel safe with your parents?"

I love this one! Ask someone with psychosis if they feel safe at home? I will let you in on a secret. First of all, they have psychosis, not a lack of intelligence, and can be very manipulative in the right set of circumstances. So, of course, they will say, "Yes! I feel unsafe. I am fine. They are just trying to put me away." (Evil parents that we are.) Or they will state that they are not a danger to themselves or others, and if we as the parents cannot prove that they are, they are sent home.

We received a stay every time Adam got arrested because of the long history that began at fourteen when he was a minor, and we kept a good file as proof. Even if you get that stay, it is often a holding period of 48-72 hours for observation and a new regimen of medications. Then they are sent out with a doctor appointment and a follow-up a month or so later. If you are lucky, they are kept a week but still spit back out without a hope or prayer before you can know if the new medications are effective. If they have undesirable side effects or no immediate relief, the patient often gives up and ceases to take their medications. If they self-medicate on drugs or alcohol, they usually return to that for their comfort. This cycle can continue over and over again.

If you let your family and friends know what is going on, you get talked about behind your back or shunned. No one can possibly know the trials and hard work that a family member goes through to get help for their loved one unless they walk in your shoes. No one! Yet horrible things are said about and to us. What kind of parent allows their child to behave this way? Why don't you control that child? Or discipline them? Or insist on longer hospital stays until they get well?

People who never witnessed the "kind of parents" that we were always assumed the worst. Nobody picked up on the fact that I helped raise over a hundred children, and those parents knew what was going on and never judged me. They trusted me! No one noticed how well adjusted most of those children were, who grew up, went to college, and became successful in their careers and parenting. None of the good shines through when your child has a mental illness and acts out accordingly. So, as parents we end up secluding ourselves and we stop sharing our troubles. People are not willing to listen and support, so why bother? During this time period, we still did not have an accurate diagnosis, so we did enough judging ourselves on our own.

Adam decided to get a tattoo on his forearm. It filled the entire area from his elbow to his wrist on his right arm. It was dark black, the entire thing. A dark man in a dark suit with a dark hat, ominous looking. I asked Adam what it was. His reply: "Dead Man Walking."

Chapter 30
Stephanie, Adam, and James on State Line

Adam became more and more agitated with James living with us. Some of the things he said were so outrageous you couldn't tell the truth from a lie sometimes. Like I said, James was helpful around the house and polite to Joe and me. All of us went out from time to time and had great times, so I was surprised one day when Adam told me that James was hitting Stephanie. I was in disbelief. I wasn't sure if it was true or if he was trying to get James to leave because he had nobody of his own and was jealous of Stephanie. I simply didn't know. So, I got Stephanie alone and confronted her. She denied all of it. She was very believable, and I decided to believe her over Adam because he "wasn't right in the head". I will regret that decision for as long as I live.

Stephanie worked double shifts sometimes, which meant coming home around 10 p.m. and returning to work the next morning at 5 a.m. Most of the time, she worked evenings and slept late, then watched the big screen television in the living room, which was turned up loudly. It annoyed Adam, who had trouble sleeping at night and was trying to sleep during the day. It annoyed Joe, who was working from home, but we didn't say anything. So much had happened in our family, we never wanted to rock the boat and create any unnecessary disturbances in our home.

Not every day and night were nightmares. There were times I remember Adam sitting outside behind the house with the dogs. The yard on State Line Road was large and filled with trees, like our own little forest. The dogs loved it back there and spent lots of time out there. So did Adam. He sat out there often, smoking his cigarettes or

147

marijuana and talking to himself or the dogs. I feel like that was his only retreat of peace and solitude on that street. It was a busy street; cars raced past our house at all hours of the day and night. We heard police chases on both the Kansas and Missouri sides. Joe and I ran a fan at night to drown out the noises and eventually became accustomed to it.

Chapter 31
2010-2011

Adam turned nineteen in 2010. We were hoping that along with getting a bit older, he would show some signs of maturity, yet he only worsened. He had charges on the Kansas side of the city after being pulled over for a traffic violation and having drug paraphernalia found on him. Strangely enough, he was not arrested. In Missouri, he was driving down State Line Road to pick up his sister one night from work with dogs in the truck, speeding.

It was only a mile drive, yet he got pulled over. The police officer saw the drugs, gave him a ticket, and told him to go home. He never got arrested, and we couldn't believe it! He had court dates to deal with the charges, but he never was arrested! To this day, he never faced the courts in Kansas but never drove in that state again to be safe.

Adam got a job at the Subway right next to Panera. He actually worked there a few months, which is a record in our world. He bought a cheap car and owned it a brief time before he was pulled over and the car was impounded. He bought a second car, but the same scenario played out.

During the fall of 2010, we went home for my mom's birthday. I believe it was her 75th. The kids and James came with us. Nieces and nephews, brothers and sisters—a huge family get together. Everything was going pretty well. Even my kids seemed to be having a good time. Sometime during the early evening, Adam was sitting on the picnic table behind the back of the house on the patio by the basement door. He seemed upset. Joe went and sat with him and gently asked if everything was okay. He told him how much he loved him and how he was there for him. Something snapped inside Adam (we would later learn this is psychosis), and he spat in Joe's face, telling him he hated him. Joe slapped him. Adam became very angry and came at his dad. Our then-brother-in-law, Mark, a large man, came up behind Adam, wrapping his arms around him to calm him down. Joe left the scene and called 911.

Not only did police arrive, but also a firetruck and an ambulance. Sirens blared. It was scary and humiliating. Adam had a tin with marijuana in it and dropped it on the ground. He was taken to the hospital to be evaluated. We were assured he would be staying overnight for observation. What we didn't expect was that he wanted assault charges to be pressed against his dad. Nobody faulted Joe. It was a reflex reaction to being spat in the face. The officer made a deal with Joe. He was not allowed to see Adam for 72 hours.

The next morning, I called the hospital to check on Adam. I was told he was unresponsive during the night but seemed to be coming around that morning. Unresponsive? What? He was fine when he was taken there, so what happened? They said he was brought in unresponsive at five that morning.

Someone had found him in their car with a drug overdose. I told them that made no sense because he had been taken in around seven the previous evening. Apparently, he told them he was a legal adult, and they had to release him, so they did! He didn't know Columbia. He wandered around until he found a Walmart parking lot, went inside, and stole tons of over-the-counter cough medicine and took it. Well, that got us our hold! The hard way.

Joe returned to Kansas City as he was helpless to do anything in Columbia. I stayed. Popi (Joe's dad) came to the hospital to give me support. My cousin Gary was there in the room with Adam counseling him. He is a pastor at The Church of the Revolution in Columbia. He and Adam had a special relationship and Adam trusted him. Gary came out and told me that Adam was a believer and had worried about his destiny beyond death, as a Catholic priest had earlier told him he would go to hell if he took his own life. Gary assured him that he was okay and that God loved him.

Later that day, Adam was transported to the University Hospital and placed in their psych ward. Popi took me everywhere I needed to go to get a 72-hour hold on him. I had to have an affidavit.

We made a couple of trips to the court before everything was in place. I had to write up all the documentation and reasons I felt he was a danger to himself. My sarcastic side (in my head) said, "Duh, he just attempted suicide in a Walmart parking lot in someone else's car!" I had a lot to write after the years of suicide attempts and many hospital stays to back me up with documents. They kept him of course.

Papa, my father, took me there to visit him. He was much calmer, and after a week, they released him and we took him home. At this point, his dad was able to see him, too. They made up when we got home, but for some reason, Adam always acted as if his dad was the devil. We later learned this is typical of psychosis, that the ones you are closest to are the ones you trust the least. If you think about it, it makes sense. We are the parents. We make decisions that affect our children, for better or for worse. We were the ones who kept "putting him away". Therefore, we were the enemy. Never mind that we were trying to keep him safe. In his mind, he didn't see it that way.

Over the years, we had family tell us he would never have behaved like that in their house. It was our fault. We didn't know how to parent. We believed them, not knowing for so long that Adam had a brain disorder that caused the behavior. In January of 2011, when he was almost twenty, my parents offered to take him in. Papa felt that after the autumn before, they had built up a rapport, and he would be fine with them. We were too close to the situation, they said. They felt he needed a fresh start. Get a job there, save some money. They assured me they would turn him around.

He wanted to go. I didn't want him to go, but he was an adult, so I didn't have any say in the matter. He got a job at Taco Bell on Providence near Columbia, where my folks lived. Papa drove a cab. Sometimes Adam rode in the cab; sometimes he walked. He loved it there, talking enthusiastically about it over the phone. He was still being treated for depression and anxiety, and I hoped he was following through on his medications. Mom said she reminded him daily. The deal was that he would get a paycheck, give Mom some for staying there, and bank the rest.

Unfortunately, it didn't go down that way. Mom said she needed the money, and she spent everything that Adam brought in. He became increasingly agitated and spent more and more time after work hanging out with the guys who would give him pot to smoke. He stayed up through the night and slept until he had to go to work during the afternoon.

My parents got sick of him really quickly. I provided food for him, so they wouldn't have to feed him. Papa told him that just looking at him made him sick; he couldn't believe he was his grandson—he was disgusting. They told me this too, and said he would be coming home soon. I made plans to get him in two weeks as he had to give notice at his job.

Apparently, he gave notice and it ticked off the boss, so he told him to go ahead and leave. He spent several days in the basement of my folks' house where he lived. They never knew he had lost the job. Then one Saturday night, he took too many of his pills, called me Sunday morning, and with slurred words, said I needed to come save him.

I drove like a bat out of hell, parked in the neighbor's drive, and walked around the back of the house and into the basement to get him. That driveway was below my mom's office. She sat there and never noticed what I was doing. I loaded trash bags full of his belongings, then him into the car. I half-carried him out as he could barely walk. He was starving, and I am sure he was drugged up as well. He cried all the way home. We were so hurt and angry. It took two days before they noticed he was gone. We had words over the phone, and it took a while to repair that relationship. He had lived with them for two months and kept a job nearly the entire time.

I will say that all has been forgiven for my parents' behavior. Like us and so many people, they didn't understand what they were dealing with. In order to forgive ourselves, we must forgive the others in our lives, who ultimately did or said the things they said because of their love for us and frustration over something they could not fix for us any more than we could. None of us understood mental illness because it was foreign to us until it landed in our laps.

When he came home, things were okay for a while. After all, I had rescued him, and Joe had given them a piece of his mind for the treatment of our son, so for a moment we were heroes.

That March, Adam turned twenty. His behavior became more and more erratic. He was agitated all the time. He had new friends in the city we knew nothing about, but who sent him home high as a kite every time they were out. That summer he was at an apartment complex swimming in the pool "minding his own business" when someone called a police officer to get him and the other guy out of the pool as they didn't live there and were making some people uncomfortable. He actually got into a fight with the officer, and even then, he wasn't

153

arrested! We have no idea how he got out of these situations, but he did!

Chapter 32
National Alliance on Mental Illness and a Diagnosis

One day in the summer of 2011, I was down in the basement going through some boxes we had stored there. I came upon a pamphlet with NAMI written on it, which stood for The National Alliance On Mental Illness. It was from Tulsa. I wondered why I hadn't read it before. I must have picked it up during a visit with Dr. Puls while waiting for Adam in the waiting room. I seem to do that everywhere I go—on trips to offices, or anywhere.

I wondered if Kansas City had a NAMI office and googled it. Sure enough, they did. I was so nervous as I made the call but was really at my wits end wondering how I was going to save my son or help him. We all felt helpless at this point. A young woman named Jen Boyden answered the phone. We talked for a very long time. I was in tears throughout the conversation. She was so calm and soothing to talk to. Little did I know that the connection that day would send me on a different path for years to come!

Jen talked to me about many things that day. She told me to think about attending a support group for families and gave me a referral. She also told me about a class called Family to Family that families go to for twelve weeks, one night a week, free of charge.

The program teaches families about what their loved one is going through and how to communicate with them. They define all the different types of mental illnesses and talk about medications and much more. I told Joe about it. He was just trying to work, get bills paid, and keep us afloat as we swam in medical bills. We realized that in all our years of marriage (at this point, 22 years), we had not escaped a hospitalization during any given year, and sometimes had more than one. The expenses were high.

So, I attended a family support group in July alone and found it very beneficial. "Wow, I am not alone!" was the first thought that came to my mind. We all looked different, but we all had mentally ill family members. Some were sons, some were daughters, some were spouses, and some were even parents! I could not imagine trying to raise a parent because any parent that behaved like Adam surely couldn't raise a child. For the first time in many years, I felt I belonged somewhere!

In August, Stephanie and James came with me. She felt the same. She even related to someone in that room on a personal level, a lady we would later take classes with and have in our own support group and befriend, Pam. She later became a support group facilitator and Family to Family teacher herself. After that, Joe decided to go to a support group meeting. He went in September, and it was enough to convince him to take the Family to Family class with me that also began that month.

Jen Boyden taught Family to Family with a young lady named Laura Denkler. Through NAMI, Joe and I would become lifelong friends with both of these fine women. During the first class, we all got to know each other, sharing our stories of our loved ones. I was amazed at how similar some of our stories were, down to the characteristics and behaviors of our loved ones, the self-medicating, and their casting the blame on their closest family members.

During the second class, we dove into the various mental illnesses and the diagnostic criteria for each one. Joe and I looked at each other in shock as we reviewed Schizophrenia and recognized for the first time in six years that, although Adam might be depressed and have anxiety, the main diagnosis for him was definitely Schizophrenia.

Criterion A: Two or more of the following symptoms for at least one month:

- Delusions
- Hallucinations
- Disorganized speech
- Grossly disorganized or catatonic behavior
- Negative symptoms such as: Alogia (decreased speech) avolition (lack of motivation), flat or blunted affect (emotional responses), inappropriate affect (such as crying, laughing or yelling inappropriately), inability to relate to others
- Note: Criterion A does not require a second set of symptoms if there are bizarre delusions, auditory hallucinations of a voice providing running commentary, or two or more voices talking to each other.

Criterion B: Social and occupational dysfunction

Criterion C: Some symptoms must persist for six months or more

Criterion D: Schizoaffective disorder, depressive disorders and bipolar disorders with psychotic features have been ruled out

Criterion E: Disturbance is not attributable to physiological effects of substances or another medical condition

Criterion F: Symptoms are independent and additional to any existing Autism Spectrum Disorder

Phases of Schizophrenia

A. Prodromal Phase (may build slowly over years). Negative symptoms often start in this phase.

Behaviors: Social withdrawal, decline to function, less attention to hygiene, odd, peculiar behaviors, developing unusual rituals

Thinking: Suspicious, superstitious, illogical or odd beliefs

Senses: Odd sensory experiences such as illusions (misinterpretation of a sensation such as seeing a shadow and thinking it is a monster or believing that you are hearing words in the midst of a radio station)

B. Acute Phase: Must be at least one month long. May continue negative symptoms from prodrome but may become more anxious, irritable and angry (showing more intense effect than in other phases)

Behaviors: Grossly Disorganized Behavior, In rare cases, catatonic rigidity (bizarre body postures, mutism) or catatonic excitement (intense agitation)

Thinking: Grossly Disorganized Speech, Delusions

Senses: Hallucinations

C. Residual Phase: Can last years. Negative symptoms are often the most disabling symptoms during this phase. May develop depression.

Behaviors: Similar to prodrome but may have a lower level of functioning. Some disorganized behavior may persist.

Thinking: Cognitive deficits often persist. Delusions many persist but are less intense than the acute phase

Senses: Hallucinations may persist but are less intense than in the acute phase

Both Joe and I were looking at all the mental illnesses and symptoms that were listed, yet both of us had our handouts opened up to this same page, and were both staring at the words. Then it hit both of us like a ton of bricks: our son had Schizophrenia! We were frightened at this realization, yet at the same time relieved to define what was going on. For the first time, I felt like Joe and I were on the same page. We both now believed Adam had a mental illness. He was not a bad boy or person. He was someone living with mental illness. Maybe after having this explained to him, Adam would open up and get the appropriate treatment.

Adam did end up in Research Psychiatric Hospital during the fall of 2011. He had a wonderful counselor, Aimee Johnson, and this was when and where we finally received an official diagnosis: Paranoid Schizophrenia. We let the family know and of course got many common answers back. For instance: "You know he caused the Schizophrenia when he took the drugs." (Interpretation: You are to blame because you allowed this to happen.) There were no reassuring words, such as, "You realize now that is why he self-medicated; to relieve himself of the horrible voices in his mind."

We wrapped up the Family to Family class in December of 2011. Following the end of the class, I had a hysterectomy. I was dealing with a lot of hemorrhaging and discovered I was carrying around a twelve-pound fibroid tumor! I was worried about my recovery with Adam in the house. I was amazed at the compassion he showed me during that time. I saw glimpses of my old Adam in there. He wanted to feed me and made sure I was comfortable on the couch in the living room. It made me realize that he was still a human being needing to be wanted and needed.

It was during this phase that he briefly took on a job at Subway down the street next to Panera where his sister worked. He did the best he could for as long as he could. His bosses didn't know about his mental illness and didn't like some of the things that came out of his mouth (they tend to be inappropriate sometimes). He was very paranoid that customers and employees were talking about him behind his back. His delusions were becoming greater.

It was apparent he saw and heard things the rest of us didn't. (That had really begun at 14 when he would insist there was a dinosaur named Ted in his world who came out of the walls. He even drew pictures of him. I always thought it was the drugs.) He began missing days of work. Some days he simply could not get out of bed. He lost his job like so many before. I felt so sad for him. He really wanted to contribute to society and be like everyone else.

Chapter 33
Advocacy

In January 2012, Joe and I began facilitating a support group for families. We were officially trained in October of 2012 but started early so we would not lose the people we had bonded with in our Family to Family class. (We still meet at Research Psychiatric Hospital in Kansas City, although I go solo to support group and Joe teaches Family to Family.) These folks were the seeds that were planted to begin a beautiful thing for all of us: a connection and understanding we never knew existed before NAMI.

Through our Family to Family class, we learned how to better communicate with Adam and de-escalate behaviors that come with psychotic episodes. Adam also could see we truly cared about what was happening with him since we not only took a class to better understand him, but we continued to offer support to him and others through our family support group.

Our personal relationship improved with Adam. He had opened up to his psychiatrist and was officially diagnosed with Schizophrenia. Life was still very difficult, but we all worked at trying to make Adam more comfortable and at showing understanding.

Adam couldn't sleep at night. He paced in and out of the house yelling at the voices in his head. His room was in total disarray. Food wrappers, cans, and other trash lay strewn on every inch of floor space and in his closet. Clothes—clean or dirty—were everywhere. His windows were covered with dark blankets he had tacked to the wall. The mirror in his adjoining bathroom was shattered. He had hit it with his fist, disgusted with his own face reflected in it. The walls had streaks of various colors—mostly brownish—from drinks, we think. We never did learn if he threw them at the wall in anger or frustration or if he bumped into the walls and spilled.

Adam's appearance mimicked the appearance of his surroundings. He grew his hair long and rarely washed it. It lay matted on his head. His face in psychosis was the face of a madman, much like you would see in the movies. On a calmer day, he looked uncared for and dirty, like a homeless man. By all outward appearances, you would never guess he came from a family who took hygiene very seriously, or that we took care of his basic needs of shelter, food, medical maintenance, etc. He often wore the same clothes for days. It took the bravery of one of us to suggest a shower and change of clothes without pushing the psychotic buttons.

Adam slept during the day while his dad worked from home. During this time, Stephanie sometimes worked days and sometimes evenings at Panera. James would pick her up at night around 9:15, and they would head to bed. When she was home during the day, she would watch television in the living room, which happened to be right outside Adam's bedroom. Since he slept during this time, the television's sound agitated him.

One particular Friday night, Stephanie worked a back-to-back shift. She came in late that evening and had to be back at work around 5 a.m. We had been trained to keep the peace during an event of psychosis, but we were put to the test that night.

Joe and I were in bed. Adam was in the living room watching television. It was at a reasonable level of sound … until Stephanie and James walked through the door. Adam turned up the sound full blast.

As I mentioned above, Joe and I had become accustomed to using a fan on State Line due to the loud traffic, our snoring dogs, and the occasional outbursts from Adam. We had to sleep as much as we possibly could to better take care of him and ourselves.

That night, Adam turned the volume up so loud that we could hear it over our white noise. He waited until Steph was in her room with the door closed. Then, with boots on, he stomped up and down the halls and throughout the house, speaking loudly. The floors were all wood, so it made quite a commotion. Then he loudly opened and slammed the front door and resumed the routine over and over. Then he would sit down and laugh loudly at whatever he was watching. "Ha! Ha! Ha! That is so funny!" he would call out.

Steph and James were down a long hallway from our bedroom. Steph began texting me from her room to ours. "Mom," she begged. "Please make him stop. I have to work early in the morning."

It was easy (this time) for her dad and me to deal with because we didn't work on Saturdays, and we knew we could sleep later. Unfortunately, as we told his sister, confronting him would probably escalate the situation. Soon she and James were in our room, begging us to put a stop to it. It would almost have been comical if the cause of the situation hadn't been so sad. I felt like all of them were children coming to tattle on one another. Adam had just turned 21 and Stephanie was 22. James was around 30. I reminded them both of what our role was, and that we had to just ride it out. To confront him would certainly make things worse. So, they went back to their room, and Adam followed them, trying to force his way into the room. An argument started and they eventually pushed him back out of the room. Finally, at around 3 a.m. Adam became tired and went to bed. Joe and I went to sleep and Stephanie probably didn't sleep at all.

The point that Adam had been trying to make was that the family kept him from getting sleep during the day, so now he was going to prevent us from sleeping at night. It would be easy to say, "Now, wait a minute! We sleep when we are supposed to. Why don't you?" But that is the nature of Schizophrenia and other mental illnesses.

With his mental illness, the voices never let him sleep when he needed to. With most mental illnesses (according to what I've heard from other families' input in our support group) anything, including racing thoughts, anxiety, actual fear of the dark, or visual, audible, or tactile hallucinations can keep folks from sleeping. That night I found myself wishing Stephanie had taken Family to Family, as it had really helped us to have empathy over the situation. We even had a giggle or two that night, which I am certain beat yelling at him and feeling frustration.

During one of our class sessions, we had an exercise in empathy and understanding. The class was divided in half. Half of the class left the room. We were each given a line or phrase to say over and over again. The rest of the class was seated around the table with one appointed teacher. Each student had a piece of paper and pencil, and the teacher gave instructions on particular shapes to draw and where on the paper to draw them.

Those of us who had a script stood behind someone in the class and loudly repeated our phrase. Over and over again we spoke. Some of us were given negative phrases a nurse might say about a patient. Others had ugly things a voice in one's head might say. Several people turned around and looked at us in agitation, and some in anger, even though they knew this was just an exercise; an experiment. They were frustrated because they couldn't follow the directions, simple simple as they were.

At the end of the exercise, we looked at all the drawings, and no two were alike. No one could follow instructions. This exercise left us all exhausted and some of us in tears. This was not a long exercise, and we realized this is what our loved ones experienced 24 hours a day, with no breather in between. Because of this exercise, Joe and I were able to make it through the night with understanding and a touch of humor.

We have a list of principles in NAMI, and one of them is: We embrace humor as healthy. If we didn't laugh at some of the situations we were faced with, life would be even more challenging than it already was. And boy, was life challenging. Soon we would learn how much more challenging it would become. The year 2012 was one of the toughest years we would face, and this episode was early in the year!

NAMI Principles of Support:
1. We will see the individual first, not the illness.
2. We recognize mental illnesses are brain disorders.
3. We aim for better coping skills.
4. We find strength in sharing experiences.
5. We reject stigma in ourselves and others.
6. We won't judge anyone's pain as less than our own.
7. We forgive ourselves and reject guilt.
8. We embrace humor as healthy.
9. We accept we cannot resolve all problems.
10. We expect a better future in a realistic way.
11. We will never give up hope!

Later in our support group, Joe added two more principles (an inside joke with our own group through conversations and stories of dealing with our loved ones):

12. The most brilliant thing I ever said was nothing.

13. There is NO normal.

Chapter 34
A Life-Changing Moment

In May of 2012, I turned 50. Joe gave me a card with a Harley Davidson picture on the front. Inside it said, "Happy Birthday. For your 50th year I am having a new house built for you just down the street from Gail's Harley Davidson." We needed some good news in our world. We would finally be establishing roots in the Kansas City area in Grandview, Missouri. Aside from the people we had met through NAMI and work, we hadn't really established relationships since our move from Broken Arrow. Our lives were tied up from work and keeping an eye on our son, trying to keep him safe. Our NAMI friends were pretty much in the same boat with their loved ones, so aside from NAMI classes and events, we didn't get to see them much. So, we had hope of making some new lifelong friends on our home turf.

Joe, Adam, and I excitedly visited our spot of land almost daily, discussing where each room would be, and we watched it grow from a dream into a real home. James and Stephanie moved into an apartment in June of 2012. After three years on State Line, our home was finished and ready to close on July 20. Just before closing, Stephanie and Adam announced that he would be moving in with her and James. She felt we were closing in on Adam and not allowing him to grow.

Adam had a new excitement about doing something new. We didn't encourage or discourage him but secretly enjoyed the idea of having a break and some time to ourselves—something we'd never had in all our 23 years of marriage. I had been pregnant with Stephanie when we got married. Joe had moved to Tulsa while I finished college and had our baby. Then I had moved with our daughter in tow. At the same time, we looked forward to being empty nesters (I know that sounds weird, but in our world, you might never get to experience that.)

Joe and I settled into our new home. We had three bedrooms, our room, Adam's room or guest room (we let him know the option was always there for him), and the third bedroom became Joe's office since he still worked from home.

We lived apart from Adam for one month. While we enjoyed our newfound freedom, we still worried night and day about our son. Stephanie was letting us know how he was doing pretty regularly. Though we applaud her efforts to be this big sister and help him, he was wearing on her. She had felt that with a space of his own, he would respect it, but nothing changed. He smoked cigarettes in the apartment even though that was clearly against her rules, then marijuana. Then he would yell from the balcony to dealers and strangers to find out if they would sell him anything. Steph was at a loss and her patience was wearing thin. She was working and he was not. He had been put on disability during that past year, so he did contribute to the rent and bills, but Steph soon found out it wasn't worth ruining their close relationship.

All of it came to a head one night when Stephanie came home from work with James and Adam was smoking pot in the apartment. She got upset, and he became agitated. He was going into psychosis and they (not having the training we did) didn't know how to handle it. He said something sarcastic to James, and the next thing we knew, Steph was calling us to tell us that James had left the apartment after putting Adam's head through a wall.

It was certainly not the way we would have handled it, though we thought James was a nice guy and figured he had just snapped—one guy to another, having a fight. We told the police that Adam was in psychosis and he spent the night in jail. We later learned that James didn't just snap that night. He had been abusing our daughter from day one, back in 2009. I recalled that day Adam actually warned us of this on State Line, but thinking he was jealous that she had a relationship, we had pushed those thoughts away, believing they were hallucinations. After all, he said horrible things about his own father that were not true. So, it is sad that we had not believed him.

Following his release the next day, we took Adam home with us to the room we had called his all along. He was pretty good about following house rules. As our dear friend Becky from family support group says, "When you have a mentally ill child, you lower the bar." Another inside joke. Basically, it means that in a "normal" (there is that word again!) situation with a child, certain basic expectations are put in place. You go to school. You do your homework. You clean up after yourself. You get a job. You go to college. You honor curfew. You don't smoke. On and on. Life is different for those like us. If they make it through high school, that is a plus! If you can get them to at least put their dirty dishes in the sink, hurray! If they get a job and last there a month, that is saying something! If they smoke and you can get them to do it outside, it is a win-win situation.

Adam had clothes strewn around his room, as usual. He did put his trash in a can. I put a large one in his room near his bed! He smoked outside. Butts were everywhere, but they were outside, and on a good day, he would collect them and put them in an empty water bottle. Usually, his dad cleaned those up after him and didn't say anything because that was the most brilliant thing he ever said! We gave him the bathroom near his room, and much of the time he showered!

We had downsized considerably from our big house in Broken Arrow, and Adam seemed to feel safer there. Joe and I still live there, and it is cozy. Although we reside in a neighborhood, it sits outside Grandview and is surrounded with wooded areas. Deer frequent our backyard. It is peaceful, and it became a gentle haven for Adam. Away from the traffic noises on State Line and feeling understanding since we had become involved in NAMI, he seemed to calm down quite a bit. If he was up all night, at least his room was on one side of the house and ours was on the other. We have a front porch and a back deck, and although there were nights of pacing as usual, he did enjoy staying out front or back for chunks of time. Joe and I continued using the fan at night, so that helped some.

Since Adam was fourteen, he'd had at least one suicide attempt a year, usually during the fall months, so as summer moved into fall, we were both hopeful with his new home, he would escape that in 2012. But we were fearful due to his history. In our group we call it "watchful waiting". You hope for the best, but you are always on high alert, just waiting for the other shoe to fall.

As fall was approaching, as usual Adam became very agitated and nearing a psychotic break. Keeping him medicated was a challenge. He did not like how they made him feel, yet it was okay to self-medicate with an illegal drug to feel "normal". It was frustrating to watch, and we slept very little. Joe, who was working from home, tried to get him out of the house and into the real world as much as possible. If he had a meeting, he would sometimes take Adam with him, and they would do lunch or something. Adam was always respectful to our friends or people we worked for or with. We were the recipients of his ongoing outbursts, which is typical, as we were the ones he loved most and his safety net.

Bizarre thoughts were going through Adam's mind. For a while, he thought Brad Pitt and Angelina Jolie were his parents (strangely enough, Todd and Alice, another couple from group, told us their son thought they were his parents, too, and he had gone all the way to California to find them!). The next thing we knew, his Facebook profile name had changed to Adam Thatcher because he believed Margaret Thatcher was his mother. It was Waldo at some point, too!

We all made friends with our next-door neighbors, John and T. They moved in one week after we did. Adam loved them as much as we did, and we all began to hang out for dinner or just visit at each other's houses. John and Adam had this banter of jokes that flew back and forth, and Adam enjoyed that because John treated him just like anyone else. It was a friendship we felt would stand the test of time. Joe and I took John and T on a trip back home to Tulsa's Oktoberfest that year. We introduced them to our long-time friends in Oklahoma. Our neighbors there jokingly referred to John and T as "the replacements". But no one could ever replace our Broken Arrow friends. We just looked at it this way: we were very blessed to experience this twice in our lives. Finally, we had found a home and new friends, and life was becoming bearable.

Even though Adam was dealing with daily psychosis, we felt he was settling into our new home. He seemed comfortable with his room and the peace and quiet of the neighborhood. He spent a lot of time on the back deck, which overlooked the trail and a small wooded area, as well as the front porch, with no houses across the street and more woods. He usually had both dogs outside with him.

Adam began to get help from ReDiscover, a mental health facility in the area. He had a psychiatrist who prescribed his medicines and a clinical case worker, Nick, who saw Adam both at ReDiscover and did home visits. We felt Adam was making progress.

171

As fall 2012 approached, Adam seemed to become sicker. He trusted Nick, whom he dearly loved and bonded with. Nick was able to get Adam to do things no one else could. He was a young man Adam could relate to. They went out for coffee and walks, and Nick worked with him on life skills. He made sure Adam made it to his appointments. We all felt Nick was the answer to our prayers. He had been working with Adam for some time—since State Line—and we were lucky to keep him after the move. He really made a difference in the quality of Adam's life.

Nick was as concerned as we were that Adam was changing for the worse. We all watched him as well as we could with our busy work schedules. In early November, Adam admitted to us that the voices were stronger and crueler than ever, and he asked for help! We felt this was a milestone, as usually his cry for help was a suicide attempt. We had him admitted to Research Psychiatric Hospital in Kansas City.

At Research, Adam was assigned to a caseworker named Aimee. Aimee and Adam bonded immediately, which is a rare thing. Usually, these caseworkers seem very clinical. I understand this, as they daily deal with so many patients that getting too close to any of them can have devastating consequences. We were happy, though, because we felt she could reach him, and with the privacy laws, we couldn't get far ourselves. She even got him to agree to allow us information about his case. Someone told me during that stay, that he was the worst case of Schizophrenia they had ever seen in twenty years of experience! That left me with feelings of no hope (We will never give up hope! NAMI principle number 11). Aimee had a grandmother who had Schizophrenia and was still living! That gave me back some hope.

Adam stayed for about a week and seemed a bit renewed, with an improved attitude and new medications. We hoped for the best. That same week, on November 8, we went to our first NAMI awards banquet. Adam did not attend, but some of our family did. Joe's sister Debbie came from Illinois, and my sister Kristina from Columbia. Joe and I received the Family Award for our work that year. We let Adam know that he had been a big part of that and really talked a lot about hope and a better future.

Things seemed unusually calm that month. Adam had met a girl at Research. She lived in Olathe, Kansas. I will call her "K". She came from a nice family. I know her mom was a teacher, and she had sisters who were triplets. We were thankful that Adam had a friend, and we drove the miles to take him to her house for social activity. That gave us hope! Little did we know, that she would be like a match that lit the flame to a series of events—both bad and good—that knocked the wind out of all of us!

November 25 was a day no different from any other day. It was a Sunday. Adam had just spent time with K and was in good spirits. Joe and I were wrapping up the weekend and preparing for the work week. I got up early to go to work. At that time, I worked in Shawnee, so I had a forty-minute drive in the morning. I checked into bed early. Joe worked in his office in the hall across from Adam's room. At the time, we had this tall, queen-sized bed in Adam's room. He was sitting on the floor next to a wall on his laptop, blocked from view by the bed.

At some point, Joe decided to go in and check on him and say goodnight. Adam was sitting cross-legged, with his torso leaning forward, head hanging over the laptop. Joe asked him if he was okay, and it startled him. Groggily, he said he was tired, and Joe suggested he get in bed where he would be more comfortable. Adam did. Before Joe left the room, Adam said, "I love you, Dad." These are words we both longed to hear for so long, as with his illness, that was difficult for him to say. Monday morning, as usual, I peeked in on our son. He was sleeping peacefully in his bed on his back. It was a habit to look in on him and make sure he was home and alive. This was our world. When Joe got up, he did the same thing.

It was an unusual day because both Joe and I worked late that night, away from home. We came home at different times, and both of us looked in on Adam, who was still sleeping on his back. We both figured he had been up at some time during the day, eaten food or whatever, and gone back to bed. Two nights of rest were very unusual, but he'd had such a rough time that month and lots of activity with his new friend, alternating with nightly pacing, so we looked at it like it was a good thing, sleeping at night versus the day! That meant sleep for us, too!

On Tuesday, November 27, I got up to go to work as usual. I checked in on Adam. He was sleeping in the same position as had been in the night before, on his back. When he walked, he always stood straight, walked a straight path like a ritual and never moved his head, staring straight ahead. The thought crossed my mind that perhaps he even sleeps that way, body rigid, on his back, not moving his head. It was a passing thought. I left for Shawnee.

At around 9 a.m., Joe decided to wake Adam and offer him breakfast. Neither of us had spoken to him since Sunday night. Shortly after nine, I received a call no mother ever wants to get. Joe was crying and I couldn't understand a word he was saying, but I knew in my heart that Adam was either dead or dying.

"Is he gone?" I yelled.

"I don't know!" Joe cried. "The paramedics are loading him into the ambulance right now. They are taking him to St. Joseph Hospital on State Line." That was halfway from Shawnee, where I worked, to home. I told him I would meet him there. In shock and panic, I called my friend Sarah Boyce. She and I had playdates with her son, Tarin and Tyler, the boy I was nanny to. I am not sure what I said, but it seemed she was there in less than a minute. I remember apologizing because Tyler was still in his pajamas. She basically said, "I got this! Just go!" We hugged quickly, and off I went.

On the way to St. Joseph Hospital, I called my friend Lorna Hesskamp in Louisiana. Her daughter, Kelie, had just had a baby girl. I made her talk to me about the baby the whole way. "Just keep talking," I told her. I needed her to distract me from my terrified thoughts and to keep me calm so I didn't drive recklessly. My adrenaline was working overtime. I don't remember anything she said to me, but it kept me focused on the road.

As I entered the parking lot to the emergency room, I saw the Grandview ambulance. It arrived in front of me. I had to park in a far lot, so by the time I ran back to the building, Adam was already inside. I desperately wanted to see his face and body.

Joe and I waited fearfully. We notified family in other parts of Missouri, Illinois, and Georgia. At some point, Joe and I were asked to go to a private room in the back of the emergency waiting room. We knew the news was not good if they were doing this. Perhaps Adam had died, and they didn't want to make a scene in front of other patients or their families. We didn't know.

Our Columbia family arrived first, from two hours away, my brother Martin and sister Kristina. It seemed like they were there immediately. Time floated in and out. We couldn't seem to keep track of it or our bearings. We felt like we were in a time warp. It was like an out-of-body experience. He had made so many suicide attempts before and had always survived, I thought, so how could this be happening to our indestructible son? Before we knew it, Ann was there from St. Louis, and Suzanne, my brother Jimmy's wife arrived from Southern Missouri. Then Joe's sister Debbie, who had driven seven hours from Illinois, showed up. Later, Joe's brother Steve flew in from Atlanta, Georgia. As people filtered in, we knew this was for real.

Doctors came into the room we were in to deliver the preliminary news. There was no brain wave activity in Adam's brain. The frontal lobe was gone. His organs, such as his kidney and liver, were shutting down. He was being moved to Intensive Care and placed on life support. I felt numb, sick to my stomach, confused, scared. Were we really going to lose our only son this time? For real this time? It was too much to process.

Our family was awesome. They stayed by our side for days and nights. Literally! The neurologist confirmed that Adam was dying and that there was nothing they could do for him. We called more friends and family and made the decision to pull life support. It was November 28, 2012, my father's 80th birthday. We were supposed to be having a party celebrating his birthday, but instead we were making the decision to allow our son to die. As we waited for the big event to go down, tons of people showed up. It was so overwhelming to know we were loved by so many! To know that Adam was loved by so many yet had never comprehended that. How sad!

Jim and Jeanne Finnegan, our long-time friends who had lost their daughter to murder in 2009, arrived. At one point, Joe was on the verge of a mental breakdown, and they and Steve got a doctor to admit him for treatment for extreme anxiety. It was horrible to watch my rock crumble like that!

NAMI people came by the dozens! Adam's case worker, Nick, showed up. He looked so forlorn, his head down, beaten. He had never lost a patient before and felt responsible. Joe and I went to him, suddenly mustering the strength to comfort someone else who was involved in Adam's life. Joe told him it wasn't his fault. It was no one's fault—just this insidious disease that had taken over his brain. Our hearts ached for Nick and for everyone who loved him and played a role in his life or ours.

My cousin Gary, who is a pastor at the Revolution Church in Columbia, couldn't be there in person, but he prayed with us over the phone. Other family who couldn't make it did the same thing. The night of the 28th, we prepared to remove life support. We filled the room with people, old and new friends, NAMI folk, and our family. I felt so sad that Addie and Alex, the children of my youngest brother Martin and his wife Angie, were there. They were given the choice to stay or leave, and they had wanted to stay. They were so young. My parents were there as well.

I had a song to play before they pulled Adam off of life support. My cousin Donna had sent it to me months before, knowing we were struggling with Adam. I had played that song, "He's my Son" by Mark Schultz (ironic, because that is my maiden name) day after day as I prayed for his healing. I pulled it up on my phone and laid it on his stomach. The room was silent as the song played.

With the exception of soft crying around the room, we were all in silence for a moment. Then we all held hands and prayed. We were blessed to have a St. Joseph priest, Father Anthony, on staff at the hospital with us. He gave us so much guidance and peace throughout the entire process and prayed with us many times. Our neurologist, Dr. Southwell, was also with us. He had told us he was a Christian first, a doctor second. Our main ICU nurse, Tess Fekas, stayed by our side. She was so patient with Joe and me, explaining the process over and over, no matter how many times we asked. She prayed with us, too. The staff was amazing! Joe, Stephanie, and I were by his bedside, surrounded by these lovely people. Joe went down on his knees and knelt at Adam's side to pray. I was so touched by his love for our son. We were informed that he might not pass immediately. Sometimes it could take days.

Adam was extubated. Joe and I collapsed, but he was caught by Steve and I by Ann. We had no idea that they'd been there behind us. I will never forget that moment or their support. Adam did not pass that night.

The next day, November 29, Adam was moved to a general room on the main floor. It seemed cold and callous, but when death is imminent, it is no longer necessary to remain in intensive care. He was given no fluids, no monitors. If he looked uncomfortable in any way, we were allowed to give him morphine. There is an irony to that. You see, on Adam's pillow, Joe had found three pills that turned out to be morphine pills. On his phone, I found a photo he had taken of many morphine pills laid out in the shape of a heart. I counted them. There were 100 of them! He had made it through 97! How could someone live through that?

We just waited. Several of us stayed at the hospital day and night. Joe's siblings, Steve and Debbie. My siblings, Ann, Kristina, Martin, and brother Jimmy's wife, Suzanne. Her daughters, Kataryna and Ahreanna, came for a while, too but stayed at our house. Steve stayed with them one night.

Adam had several visitors during those days. My nanny family, Monica Wilkens, Ted Wilkens, Tyler Wilkens, and his maternal grandparents, Jerry and JoAnne Ausburn, came from Arkansas. They took care of Tyler for me while I was unable to. Monica brought food for everyone. Sarah Boyce came from Shawnee. Friends from Oklahoma who had moved to the Kansas City area some years before we had came. Susie Green and her boys, Bryce and John, were there. Bryce and Adam had been childhood friends. Those boys were torn up. They hadn't been around Adam since before the onset of his illness, and it was a shock to see him like that. John had some healing stones that he asked if he could place in Adam's hand. We allowed that. Susie stayed around above and beyond that time. We will be forever grateful. Many of his childhood friends who couldn't make the trip called to offer their support. Many of Adam's cousins called. Our family, especially the Shultz side, is huge and spread out.

Cousin Bev came but couldn't set foot in the room. It was the same room in which her mother, my Great Aunt Lois, had passed away, years before. She has always been a great support for us. We call her "the card cousin". She loves to send cards, lots of them, to let you know she is praying for and thinking about you. She brought the most sinful, delicious cake her daughter-in-law, Ceri, had made for us. Many people from NAMI brought food, too. We never went hungry. It was comfort food, and we definitely fed our pain.

November 30 rolled around. Adam was still with us. We began to think about arrangements for a funeral and burial. I chose the child-hood friends who would be the pallbearers. Alex Foster, his very best friend since he was three. Joe's brother, Steve, and sister Debbie took care of all the arrangements so we wouldn't have to leave the hospital. They picked out a casket and a cemetery plot.

That night we went to a nearby establishment, Ugly Joe's, and ate bar food and drank pitchers of beer. We had been ordered out of the hospital, and Debbie stayed with him. Later, Martin snuck beer into the room, and we toasted our son. Our nurse even joined us for a drink after her shift. Steve wasn't too happy about that decision, but we were sad and weary and needed a release. We told stories about Adam and even laughed a little.

The sleeping arrangements were not exactly comfy. Joe and I shared a twin bed. Debbie slept in a chair. I think Martin, Kristina, Ann, and Suzanne shared a couch. Every now and then one of them would sleep at the house and bring back fresh clothing for us. Steve slept on the floor in the waiting room. He was too tall for the seating. Most of the time he paced, though. His brother, Joe, was heavy on his mind.

That night something happened that we still joke about today. We were told of signs Adam would show just before death, certain changes in the sounds of his breathing, a coughing sound, etc. Well, he did that on the night of November 30. Everyone said I levitated from the twin bed to his bedside. Even so, Kristina beat me to it and got up in his face saying, "Adam, go to the light!" like we were in a movie. But he did not die that night.

The morning of December 1, hospice showed up to make arrangements, since the dying process was taking longer than expected. After speaking with them, Joe and I went back to the room with Adam. We were expecting my brother, Jimmy, who worked in a North Dakota oil field for several weeks at a time, to then go home to southern Missouri for a couple of weeks. He wasn't allowed the time off until those two weeks rolled around. He stopped by to pay his respects and say goodbye to his nephew. This was a Saturday, and our neurologist was gone for the weekend. There was a female one on staff who did not have the best bedside manner. She was annoyed with questions other members of the ICU staff were so patient with. We asked about things like tears coming out of his eyes when certain people spoke to him or squeezing our hands. She'd tell us they were just reflexes.

Any way, Jimmy was at Adam's bedside. He said, "Adam, I don't know if you can hear me or not, but this is your Uncle Jimmy. I just wanted to say goodbye and tell you I love you and I hope to see you on the other side one day." I was in the room with him, and both of us heard Adam speak!

"Yeah, yeah," he muttered. "How you doing?"

"Did you hear that?" Jimmy exclaimed.

Oh my God, he was alive and talking! The impossible had happened! I asked Joe to get the neurologist on call. She was not very happy with us. She told us we were imagining things. She went into the room, and Adam was unresponsive to all her tests. Joe, Jimmy, and I insisted that he had really spoken. Joe demanded he be put back on fluids. She argued that we would just have to go through the whole process over again. But he was alive and talking! To us that meant there was a chance. She said it was impossible: there was no brain activity. There was no frontal lobe to control speaking or anything else. So, the three of us had imagined it? She left. We sat with him, begging him to speak and respond again.

Later in the day, Kristina said, "Adam, why do you always respond to the guys with tears, squeezing hands, talking? What about me? What am I? Chopped liver? Haven't we had some heart-to-heart talks over the years?"

Adam responded again! "Yeah, we have," he said.

We ran to get the doctor again. Once again, there was no response from Adam once the doctor arrived. I am certain she thought we were all lunatics! This time, Joe insisted on fluids. She was angry-but put in the order anyway.

Still later that afternoon, a nurse came in to check on things. This time, Adam opened his eyes and said to the nurse, "I am hungry.

Can I have a piece of cheese?" She was freaking out! Now we had a medical professional on our side! At that same moment, hospice came in with some paperwork she had forgotten to have us sign. She looked bewildered and said, "Oh, I guess you don't need this anymore!" and she left!

Things really started rolling at that point. You couldn't stop Adam from talking!

Chapter 35
The Miracle

When Adam woke up from his coma, we all went a little crazy. I recall running down the halls yelling, "He's alive! He's alive!"

His friend, Alex, finally returned my call at that very moment, crying. He told me that of course he would be a pallbearer, and I yelled, "No! He woke up! He is alive! It's a miracle!"

We began to make calls and spread the good news. The doctors all agreed this was impossible, but there he was, communicating with everyone. His body was not in great shape due to the trauma. He had suffered at least one stroke to the left side of his body, but he was alive!

As he began speaking, we realized how much of a miracle this was! Not only had he beaten the odds, but he had crossed over to the other side and had seen the face of God! It was the first thing he told us. "I saw God, and He was beautiful! He told me, 'You are my son. It is not your time to go yet. You have things to do.' Heaven was so beautiful. The colors were so bright and amazing. And the love! So much love. More love than I ever felt in my entire life! God loves us all! He loves us all the same. He loves ME!"

He looked at me and said, "Mom, I met my brothers in heaven. They are fine." I was stunned because I had lost three babies before him: two surgically. Doctors had disposed of them, never telling me their genders. I knew that Stephanie was a girl. I knew Adam was a boy. I'd been certain the others were all girls. I'd even named them, Amy, Jennifer, and Rachel. I told him this and he said, "One of them is a girl. The other two are boys."

"Well, what do I name them now?" I asked.

"Alex, Maxwell, and Shelby," he responded. I had to chuckle because those were the names of his childhood best friend and siblings, the Fosters.

Adam looked right at Debbie and said, "I can't figure out who that little girl with the blond hair is. She was carrying a red balloon and she looked like you, Aunt Debbie." Debbie fled the room in tears. I went after her. She had lost her first child, Stefanie, whom our daughter was named after, at birth. She told me no one knew this, but she always pictured Stefanie carrying a red balloon in her hand! She had never told a soul, so how could Adam possibly know this?

Adam looked at his dad, his poor dad who had taken the brunt of his illness. For so long, the voices had told him that his dad was evil and many other ugly things about him. He looked at Joe with so much love in his eyes and said, "You remind me of God. You are beautiful. I love you." I choked up over that one.

As day turned to night, Adam became angry that he had to come back. I heard him mumble, "I should have used a gun." I felt panicky inside. I had hoped the traumatic brain injury (TBI) had erased the Schizophrenia, but apparently it hadn't. Of course, he had gone to a magnificent world in which he felt no pain or sorrow, only love and beauty, and he had to return to his hell on earth. Who wouldn't be angry?

Adam was agitated all night long. I had already lost many nights' sleep, but I climbed into bed with him to prevent him from pulling out the IV tubes. Everyone else was exhausted, too. Some went to the house since they felt he was out of danger.

It was a long night. He was given sedatives and still fought the night. I was scared. This was a major attempt on his life that should have taken him. Would his near-death experience save him? Could it override the voices in his head? All night I pondered where we would go from here. He needed physical therapy to help him walk and recover from the stroke. He certainly wasn't ready to come home, and we were not equipped to care for him. He needed round-the-clock care. What we needed was another miracle!

Chapter 36
The Aftermath of the Coma

December 2 was a new day. Adam seemed to have a better attitude. I felt like he was angry with me this time around, maybe because I had fought to keep him down all night. This time Dad was definitely the hero. I now understood the hurt Joe must have felt for so long. All of the night before Adam had been belligerent and confused. He said really bizarre things. He kept trying to pull the catheter out, and thought it was the missing foreskin on his penis. Somewhat comical, but gross. That day brought many visitors.

John and T from next door came over. My parents came. That was very interesting because when I had called my Mom on November 27 to let her know that Adam was going to die, her response had been, "Well, what did you expect?" in a very sarcastic tone. I am sure the idea of traveling here and not being able to drink her booze for a night was very upsetting, but really? Who says something like that to her daughter who is getting ready to lose a child? I was really upset and told Joe about it in the family waiting room at the time. Well, apparently during Adam's near-death experience, he had watched all this taking place from another realm. When my mom walked into his room, he was sprawled out sideways, his head over one side rail and his feet dangling over the other. Mom said, "Well, hello there, you little stinker!"

Adam responded with his middle finger and said, "F*** you, Grandma!"

She laughed and sat down at the foot of his bed! I'm not sure why she thought that was funny!

Mom began to tell Debbie a joke none of us could hear, except the punchline had the word "bitch" in it. Adam heard "bitch" and yelled, "Grandma! Did you just call me a bitch?"

She laughed again and said, "No, Adam. I was telling a joke. Are you angry with me?"

"Yes," he replied. "I heard what you told my mom, and you just don't care!" I was stunned into silence.

My friend, Sarah Boyce, came to visit Adam, and he gave her a huge grin and said, "How about you, me, and the family? One big orgy?"

"Uh, I don't think so, Adam," Sarah replied. "Don't think my husband Ryan would like that too much."

Oh, my, we have a long way to go, I thought. Thank goodness it was Sarah, who could see that for what it was, laugh about it, and let it roll off her shoulders!

On the third day, the nurses began working on getting Adam up and walking. He was very unsteady and dragged his left foot. He was given a walker for support and walked the halls to gain strength and coordination. He was very determined, and it showed.

Inside, his body was slowly on the mend. His kidneys and liver previously showed deterioration, but they were healing. Amazing! He was placed on all kinds of medications for psychosis, anxiety, internal stomach issues, blood pressure (the experience left him with high blood pressure), and more. The doctors and nurses did a phenomenal job of monitoring his progress. He was given a "sitter", a person who stays in the room 24/7 to make sure he was safe. He was still a suicide risk. This also meant Joe and I could leave for pockets of time to work on future arrangements.

Our friend, Susie Green, also spent many hours with Adam. He had trusted and loved her from his early childhood days on, so this gave us a lot of peace. She is a very Christ-centered woman, and we were horrified at some of the things he said to her. He brought up the fact that Bryce and John Green had come to visit him while he was in the coma.

He had known that they were there! But he had to add that he thought it was a shame that John would never get any p**** in his whole life because he had red hair. Susie just shot comments right back at him like it was nothing. We all knew it was a combination of an anoxic brain injury and Schizophrenia causing these words to pop out of his mouth, but to a mother, it was very embarrassing!

Joe and I began the search for a good rehabilitation center. We started close to home and asked for recommendations. Many of the places we visited were nursing homes for the elderly, and we were not comfortable placing him there, thinking he would lose hope. We went to Columbia and checked out Rusk Rehabilitation Center and were very impressed. We were set to go there after a lengthy search, only to be shot down later.

We were told there and many other places around the state that they couldn't take him until the psychosis was under control! What? So, his body was just going to deteriorate and we couldn't help him because he had mental illness? We felt the sting of stigma in the worst way. We hadn't gotten the psychosis under control for seven years so far. What made them think that would happen quickly, if ever? We were told by the hospital that on day seven (the time up to which insurance would cover him), he would be going home with us. He could barely walk and still had thoughts of suicide. How in the world could we possibly keep him safe?

From the day Adam was admitted on November 27, we began to take notes and post on Facebook asking for prayers. The following are taken from this time:

My first Facebook post, on 11/27/2012:

Begging for prayers for Adam!!!! He is in St. Joseph Hospital in Kansas City, Mo. Unconscious. Intubated. Kidneys shutting down. He is dying. Please pray for a miracle.

Notes written on 12/01/2012, after Adam woke up (with Steph and James):

"Hi, Adam. It's Stephanie."

"I know!"

"It's James."

"Hi, J-j-mes (couldn't say his name).

To Steph: "I love you so much." As he said this, Adam was looking at her as if his vision was blurred.

Steph: "Can you see me?"

"Yes, you have something on your face." (A mouth ring.)

With prompting, he squeezed her hand, then moved around.

Adam: "Do you know what happened?"

Steph: "Do you know where you are?"

Adam: "No."

Steph: "Hospital. What's my name?"

Adam: "Stephanie Elizabeth Custin."

Steph: "You know I'm your sister?"

Adam: "Yeah."

Excerpt from a lengthy talk with Aunt Kristina:

Adam just looked at her.

Kristina said, "Adam, it's Aunt Kristina. I'll be quiet and leave you alone."

Adam's response, "Uhh ... okay."

189

Adam wanted to watch television:

Mom: "Do you like Disney?"

Adam: "F*** no!"

Mom: "What do you want to watch?"

Adam: "Channel 37." (I change it to 37.)

Adam: "They are just murdering people. Let's go back to Disney."

Aunt Debbie was settling down for the night near Adam:

He gazed at her with such love.

She had to get up, emotional. She had been tending to his lips with lip balm every day and night, and was affectionately known as "the Lip Nazi".

10:40 p.m. (The night I had to sleep in the bed with him and hold him down to prevent him from pulling out his catheter and IV's:

"I want to smoke some weed."

Later: "I am showing you I have full control of my brain."

Mom: "Did you know you have a brain injury?"

Adam: "Yeah. I knew that. Everybody told me that."

11:25 p.m.: "Can I have some ice chips? Now can I have some cheese?"

He said many things. It was a shock to me that he could even speak at all, much less comprehend anything. Some of the things he said were inappropriate, some were funny, and some were touching.

Notes from 12/04/2012:

December 3rd Joe and I went home to sleep and get some much-needed rest. We came in on the 4th. Adam told me I needed to read the Zen Koan, "A Cup of Tea", a story about a blind cricket. The moral of the story is, "You cannot catch what you cannot see." I thought he was rambling on about nonsense. I looked it up and it was for real. I was amazed at his memory.

Adam said he had asked for Dad and me all night. He said he had not seen us for six days! I reminded him that we had been here all week; that we had just spent the night at home. He hugged me and asked me if he could gently touch my nose. I let him, and then he gently caressed my cheek and said my aura flowed from my face and it was beautiful.

More notes:

Adam talked a lot about John Green, Susie's youngest son:

"He came with Susie to visit me and she came many times. And then he brought the other guy (who happened to be one of Adam's best childhood friends).

"Bryce"? I asked.

"Yeah, yeah. I see in John the man I could have been. It's awesome."

Note: John was here with his mom while Adam was in the coma. Bryce came then, too.

"Aunt Suzanne loves me for who I am. We talked for hours." (They had talked all night on the third, when Joe and I had gone home to sleep.)

From physical therapist:

Adam stood with help for the first time.

Sat on his own for the first time.

From Occupational Therapist:

Adam washed his face.

Adam to Mom:

"God laid out a map for me of what I have to do."

I asked him what it said.

"He gave me a map and explained things to me, but it's complicated."
Adam had been put on Zyprexa for the psychosis.

Notes passed from me to Joe on 12/05/2012:
Heidi: "No one else heard this a few minutes ago. He said, 'If I had shot myself in the head instead, I'd have made it.'"
Joe: "I heard it. Will be months upon months of therapy. Zyprexa is driving him insane!"
Moments later:
Heidi: "His eyes are closed. Is he finally sleeping?"

The month prior to the overdose, Steve and Connie came to visit us. They had an eye-opening experience witnessing Adam in psychosis. I remember Steve saying, "Honestly, I never believed all the things you said about Adam until I witnessed it myself. You can't make this stuff up. No actor in the world could play this role as good as he is, and quite frankly, why would someone do something like this for attention for years and years?"

I wish that everyone in my family had the opportunity that they did to see this for themselves, instead of making assumptions about us without knowledge and truth. During this trip, Steve told Adam one night that he was going to ride a bike on the trail the following day. He asked Adam if he would be accompanying him. They had bonded very well. Adam said he would but then backed out the next morning. When Adam awoke from the coma and saw Steve, he gave him a sarcastic smile and said, "I should have gone on the damn bike ride! That's why you are here, right? To give me some s*** about that?" We all got a good laugh out of that one.

Adam's brain was so confused trying to reroute and organize his thoughts. He had had a stroke on the left side of his brain, and a symptom of that was the replacing of one word with another one that didn't make sense to the rest of us. He believed the catheter that was in place was foreskin on his penis and constantly tried to remove it. To no avail, I explained that his foreskin had been removed at birth.

It was scary, and some of the things he said were downright embarrassing but comical, too. He was obsessed with his penis and lost all modestly. Wearing only the hospital gown, he would toss the front of it aside, revealing himself to anyone who entered the room. It was exhausting just trying to keep him covered! Nurses would come in on shift, and he would flirt with them and ask if they came to see his penis.

One attractive, tall blond nurse we had not seen before came in to see Adam. Most would ignore his comments, but this gal was a hoot with her snappy comebacks. As she entered the room, Adam announced that she was one hot tamale cicada. (What???) Adam asked if she came in to see his penis with the "foreskin" on it. She quickly responded with, "Adam, the nurses are fighting over which one gets to care for you. We drew straws and ... lucky me, I won!" He just knowingly smiled. It was times like those that I'd look at Joe and say, "Your son."

We have a good friend from our NAMI family support group, Becky, who was also by our side during this ordeal. She is brilliant and insightful—a major contributor to mental health discussions. She has a son with Bipolarity, and through her own life experiences and much personal research, she has helped many people, including Joe and me, to cope with this life sentence we have been dealt.

Many come to our group initially believing we are going to fix their loved one. It is sometimes a shock to them when they find out that there is no cure, no fix to this dreadful illness. But there is hope for the future and for our loved ones to find a way to navigate around their illness and live a full life. She was the one in our support group who spoke about the lowering of the bar.

I love the way Becky puts things into perspective. It is helpful and alleviates some of the parenting guilt, knowing that you are not alone and that we are all playing this same game. We witnessed similar behaviors, just with different players.

Becky came to visit on December 6. She was one of our great prayer warriors. Quoting from *Star Wars*, she said, "The life force within this one is strong."

She was right on! And strong-willed he was! He also announced that day that he was going back to Tulsa when he got out, which was the worst-case scenario. He also told us he would be joining the Army. Of course, we knew with his medical/mental history, this would not be happening, and if he tried, he would be so very disappointed.

Chapter 37
Finding the Contract with God

While Adam was still in the hospital and we went home, I searched through his belongings, looking for clues or answers. I came across a form, handwritten by Adam, which was entitled "Contract With God".

Adam believed that he had lived several lives before his present one, and that he had died tragically in every one of those lives. He believed he would die tragically in this one, too, but had decided to create this contract with God because he believed God wanted him to leave life early because he wasn't "getting it right" over and over again. He was making this deal with God, saying he would leave this life as a young man, too, if God would send him back the way he wanted to be next time.

The following is Adam's contract. I have omitted or reworded some of it because it included inappropriate sexual content. He believed that he was inadequate in every facet of his life, including that part of it. Of course, that was due to the voices in his head telling him these things, and often he would be inappropriate because of that. I recall one visit from my sister Ann in Broken Arrow, during which he saw fit, for example, to come downstairs and prance around totally nude in front of her and speak with her as if he had clothes on. Such was the life of a man living with Schizophrenia! Reading the contract without those words in it, I am certain you will still get the gist of his intentions. I will make comments in parentheses wherever I have an explanation or thought about where he was going with the statement based upon later conversations I had with him.

195

CONTRACT WITH GOD:

I want any contract with you in the future to not be a real contract if I say it's voided. The contracts we've already made are not included in this contract. (Both statements cause me heartbreak because it is clear to me that he wasn't sure if he wanted to go through with a suicide, wavering back and forth over time, creating contracts repeatedly. At the same time, it gives me peace knowing that he believed in God even before he had a near-death experience!)

I want my family to have money, at least $200,000 banked, no more than $1,000,000, but they can have stocks and such. (This shows that he was concerned that he was being a financial burden to us, as well as his love and unselfishness.)

I want to not care about money.

I want to look good. (Sadly, his voices told him constantly how "ugly" he was. He had no idea how good-looking he already was!)

I want to be desirable to a woman.

I want to look a little bit better than M.K. (the woman of his dreams).

I want to be cool.

I want to meet M.K., my soulmate, at the age of 13-14. (I believe he had met her at 15 and maybe thought he could change the course of things if he had met her earlier.)

I want M.K, my soulmate, and I to be best friends until we die.

I want to marry M.K., my soulmate.

I want to be 5'10" to 6'1". (Adam was 5'6" tall and 135-150 pounds, depending on his mindset or health.)

I want everyone to like me for my personality. (I did! And I know many others who did, as well.)

I want to never be famous.

I want to say things people think are smart.

I want to smoke weed.

I want to experiment with drugs. (He already had. Did he want to without consequences this time around?)

I want to love M.K. in a way she likes.

I want M.K. to make her own decisions. (He felt he had ruined her life by his own choices. She had her choices and so did he. If he ruined her life, then who is to blame for ruining his? No one, of course. It just reveals his disorganized thought process.)

I want to want M.K. on earth. (So that she would return, too? Was he thinking that she would die shortly as well, or just when?)

I want M.K. and I to spend as little time in Hell as possible. (Did he believe he wasn't even worthy of going to heaven?)

I want you to put M.K. on earth as soon as you can.

I want M.K. and I to have the best life in Hell that we can.

This contract says I will not be able to see in Hell only. I will be able to see on earth. I will be able to see on earth. You will give me everything I ever wanted.

Then we signed

_____

The things on this contract are all the things I ever wanted.

Adam Custin

_____

Side Note: I have controlled my mind many times in many ugly lives, so you can trust that I won't bother you or brag about this contract, especially after this life. I respect you and your authority. And I respect that you have to keep my contract in effect. This contract is as real as the one I said I didn't sign.
Mental signatures always count. You said so and so did God's God. If you had never signed it you would have never led us on. You said and

believed that you signed it, even if it was putting your mental signature on it. Everyone, even you, knows that it's a real contract. You can't go back on your contract no matter what anyone, including yourself says. You said you signed the contract. You have to obey the contract no matter what you think.

(This ending was confusing to me as to who "you" was referring to. Was it God or Adam himself?)

I also found this page written in his handwriting:

If I have lung cancer, that means that you start over if you kill yourself. We have a "deal" that He will let me into heaven when I die unless I kill myself, because when you kill yourself you start all over. He sends everyone but up to twenty people to hell, so before He tried to convince me he was giving me lung cancer I thought he was going to break our deal. Now if I have lung cancer I know he was going to keep our deal, and the only way He wouldn't have kept our deal is if I killed myself. Otherwise He wouldn't be giving me cancer so I "kill myself". So people, if I can't do anything about it, everyone goes to hell except about twenty people. The only chance you have of not going to hell is to kill yourself so you will hopefully start over. Don't worry for if I don't kill myself, or die of lung cancer, God and I have a deal, that will, if not broken, salvage our souls.

This makes me wonder if he was trying to get lung cancer "accidentally" by smoking so much to get him off the hook. I also wonder what made him believe that most people go to hell. From his perspective, with the constant cruel thoughts that ran through his mind, I guess it shouldn't surprise me that his view of the world we live in is so much more evil than good. I also came across the following writing:

I would want to know that even when people/animals said I sounded gay; that I wouldn't think they were telling the truth if I said something to someone else on earth with the same voice. I would want to know that humans would think that I would sound sarcastic and I wouldn't want to sound that way. Don't sound gayer because I told you that. (I will clarify that when my kids used the word "gay", they meant "stupid"). It's okay to sound bored. You don't sound as boring the longer you sound bored.

God loves his time alone and wants to do whatever He wants. Never make decisions for him because he'll be rude to you. Of course, you don't care, but it might annoy you. I will try to just say nerd or nothing at all while I am in heaven, because undoubtedly He will be rude when I talk because no matter what I always have the dumbest things to say when everything's been said for a thousand years. You do sound geeky in heaven, but it makes everyone happier to call you a geek. Don't try to figure it out! Please, please, please, even God feels better calling you a geek. Everyone on earth feels better calling people geeks.

I wouldn't want to dress like a nerd, just normal or okay, that's fine. Talk to yourself and don't pretend they're listening.

I couldn't tell who the author of that one was: Adam or one of the voices in his head. He clearly believed he couldn't measure up to anyone on earth or in heaven, and that is so sad.

The next one is a letter to Jesus:

You are nothing less than perfect. My love for you ages further than the stars themselves. Nothing can change who you are. You're more important than the universe. I sound like a nerd, but nothing in this body or mind can express my love to you. It is my fault for not listening to every word you've ever said in life and death. Your words are more important than any other man or God, including myself. This is import-ant. You are more important to me than anything could ever be.

Do not defy the Lord, God. Everything happens for a reason. Amen (everything that doesn't defy God).

Jesus, stay in heaven.

Stop and think, a short life in Hell (for others) for a horrible life on earth that every animal is envious of.

God is your father. Nothing good can happen without Him. Those are the most important words in the history of the universe.

God is the reason you feel love. Important. More important than you can comprehend.

I think that last portion of his writing was the part that by far made the most sense.

Rereading that writing, it makes me wonder if this is why God sent him back and gave him the miracle. Adam proclaimed his love for Jesus and talked about defying God. Maybe God was trying to show

Adam that He had heard his cries and wanted to show him how much He loved him by the miracle so he could pass that on to others.

Chapter 38
Continuing the Recovery

Joe and I slept at home again on the sixth of December.

Notes from 12/07/2012:

Adam was so happy to see us arrive today. More coherent than ever before. We had a wonderful conversation and I was thinking, ooh, the meds are working. But then he went backwards. He said, "Mom, the lady with the mole on her face is trying to kill me, along with the black lady who lives with her." He said this with an accent, so I am assuming it was the sitter from last night (she is Jamaican). "Mom, they captured me and locked me in their basement and chased me with knives trying to stab me."

These comments made me question: is this Schizophrenia speaking, a bad dream or traumatic brain injury talking? From one day to the next, we didn't know what we were dealing with. Also, on that day, *Adam used a walker twice today in the halls. Second time he really booked it!* I do recall that he dragged his left foot when he walked, due to the stroke.

Notes from 12/10/2012:

Adam said, "When you are in heaven you can see your memories like on a movie reel. Where was that house Aunt Suzanne, Aunt Debbie, Aunt Ann, Aunt Kristina, Uncle Steve, Uncle Martin (basically named everyone who was there while he was in coma) lived in?" From wherever he was he saw us all together! I'm guessing the house was the hospital room we resided in together night and day.

Notes from 12/12/2012:

4 p.m. Adam came home today against our wishes. He really should be in a rehabilitation center but no one will take him because he is mentally ill! We came home and Adam seemed confused by his surroundings. This is your home, we told him. He looked around his room, moving very shakily. Then crashed on the couch. He lost control of his bladder and did not wake up. We tried to awaken him. He was lethargic, had a fever, back pain and a rapid heart rate. By midnight we were back in the ER. Doctor said his white blood cell count is high. Possible spinal infection. He will have an MRI tomorrow. He was readmitted.

Notes from 12/13/2012:

MRI of brain was clear. We are stumped.

Notes from 12/14/2012:

Adam is feeling much better today. The social worker is concerned about his memories, not too good. She said, "Adam insisted to me that one of his sitters in the West wing tried to kill him and that he lived with her before going into the hospital." Does not recall living with us. Still insisting he needs marijuana when he leaves the hospital. Adam told Dad not to come to visit him tomorrow because he was trying to get the hospital to keep him. In the past when he had thoughts of Dad like that it progressed into "He reads my mind. I need to die," etc. This is getting scary again.

Following this, Joe and I visited a lawyer and began the process of gaining Adult Guardianship over Adam so we could legally keep him or place him wherever we wished without his permission. At this point, since he was an adult, he could nix any decision we had made thus far due to HIPPA laws, which were put in place in 1996. "The Health Insurance Portability and Accountability Act which was to publicize standards for the electronic exchange, privacy and security of health."

The problem many of us face with HIPPA is that when our loved one is incapable of making an informed decision about his/her health due to a mental illness and we are the caregivers, the ones providing healthcare, food, shelter, transportation, etc., we have no rights in the decision-making process in regards to that person. It is very frustrating. Through Guardianship, we would have that right. This was the prime time to push it through as Adam also had the right to an appointed lawyer and could plead his case, in which event we could be declined if the judge agreed with Adam. Since he was clearly disorganized and we had a thick file on him, we stood a chance at winning. Unfortunately, we found out in our meeting that it would take months before our case even went to court.

Chapter 39
Coming Home

In spite of all the concerns surrounding the past two weeks, we had hope—hope that Adam would take this second chance at life seriously. Hope that his experience with God had changed his plans to die. We were still giddy over the miracle.

December 12, the day we took him home, was a cold winter day. I saw a couple I didn't know approaching our house. I went out and met the new neighbors on the other side of our house, Tim and Lorrie Gordon, who would play a big role in Adam's life and ours from that day on. They were introducing themselves, and I was rambling on about miracles and whether they believed in them or not. They had to think I was a nutcase! "Our son came home today! It is a miracle! He is a miracle! He survived the impossible!" They listened in the cold as I had to tell the story. Amazingly, they didn't walk away. They listened and smiled. We have been friends ever since.

Another neighbor stopped by to tell us about his business and offer us a card for so many free oil changes. I ranted to him, as well. He said he believed in miracles and began to tell us about his faith. I think we purchased a card from him mainly because he listened to our story! I don't think we ever used it!

When we got Adam out of the car, Joe assisted him and I went to open the front door. Our dogs, Alaska and Nellie, were so excited to see him that Nellie nearly knocked him down the stairs. I was trying to get them both to back down. "Nellie! Don't jump on him!" I shouted. He was too fragile for that!

We got him into the house. The first thing he wanted to do was look in his room. "Yes, I remember living here," he said. This was interesting because at the hospital, as soon as he could walk with assistance, he needed to go look in the bathroom mirror. He returned saying, "Yes, that is what I thought I looked like." He had a lot of confusion and mixed memories from various places we had lived to things he had done in life to, yes, even what his perception of who he was and what he looked like.

Observing his return was fascinating, yet frightening at the same time. I was scared we wouldn't be able to sleep that night worrying about him possibly trying to get up by himself if even to simply go to the bathroom. Would he remember to call for help? Would he try to wander outside, fall, or get lost? We were not equipped to deal with this anymore then than before the overdose.

We never made it that far. We had decided to put him on the couch in the living room outside our bedroom with our door open so we would hear him. He fell asleep and slept for a few hours. He woke up soaked in urine and sweat. He was feverish and incoherent. That was our ticket back to St. Joseph Hospital.

Chapter 40
Back to St. Joseph

Adam was admitted once again and stayed about another week. His brain injury prevented his brain from communicating information to his body like how to keep its internal temperature normal, or his blood pressure, blood sugars, etc. under control. I had never heard of such a thing. I knew our brains are very complex but didn't realize it literally sends messages to every part of our body including our organs, and how they regulate these functions. Adam also had a bed sore on his buttocks that probably began in his own bed the fateful night he took those pills. It was huge—big enough to put a tennis ball inside on his thin, frail body. He was five-foot-six, and at this time weighed maybe 125 pounds. How a butt that small could have a sore that deep was beyond me!

I had no idea that bed sores burrowed into one's body like that. He had other spots on him where bed sores had begun to form, but they didn't develop into anything worse than a small mark, like the ones on his ears. He also had a few circles on his scalp where the hair was missing!

No one could ever explain how that might have occurred. Extreme stress on the body was my guess, like with Alopecia, which according to Wikipedia, is also known as spot baldness, a condition in which hair is lost from some areas of the body, often resulting in a few bald spots on the scalp, each about the size of a coin. Psychological stress may result. It is thought to be a systemic autoimmune disorder in which the body attacks its own anagen hair follicles and suppresses or stops hair growth. Adam's were about the size of quarters. It wasn't just hair missing, though. The circles caved in slightly. No one seemed to be too concerned about it, and no one ever confirmed if this was Alopecia or not. To us, it was a mystery.

During that week, both Joe and I heard Adam mumble random things about taking his life. We were really nervous about the approaching date to return home once again. We had tried previously to get him admitted to a psychiatric hospital, but like rehabilitation, they would not take him, because "at the moment" he was not a danger to himself or others. We took notes on the things he would say.

That week we went to Research Psychiatric Hospital with our documentation, including why he was at St. Joseph in the first place. They deemed this serious enough to admit him once St. Joseph released him. Ah, finally we felt we were getting somewhere. Hope, once more! The following is what we put together hoping someone would listen, and they did. I tell people in NAMI family support to document, document, document EVERYTHING! It could very well save a life.

Documentation:
Adam's social worker, Nick Pinnell pleaded our case to no avail. He agrees with us and has spent countless hours with Adam (phone number provided).

Laura Denkler-Social Worker from NAMI (phone number provided) said:
John Dean with ReDiscover where Adam receives treatment said Adam needs a Level II review and the hospital social worker needs to recommend this. Send to the Department of Mental Health, Missouri. With his Medicaid he should be recommended to a lock down long term facility. There is a lock down Level III facility in Kansas City called Ridgewood

at 11515 Troost Ave. 816-943-0101.

From Heidi Custin (mother):
Proof of intent to harm himself-suicide note, Contract with God.

Adam was on 24-hour surveillance on floor 3W at St. Joseph Hospital. Adam almost died due to morphine overdose. Numerous attempts for eight years (included in file).

Adam stated several times, most recently being 12/15/12, that one of the nurses is trying to kill him and he "lived with her" before coming to the hospital. (He lived with us.)

Adam said one night in 3W, "I should have used a gun. Then I wouldn't be putting up with this shit."

Adam said yesterday that he looked forward to going home and smoking weed again. This ALWAYS leads to non-compliance on medications, to voices getting stronger, to suicide attempts. (Refer to documents on hospitalizations due to suicide attempts.)

A girl Adam was with prior to the overdose stated to her mother that Adam offered her pills, too. (She is actually the one who provided the pills.) She refused them, but said he told her he wanted to kill himself. Her name is K.O. (phone number provided).

Adam just called me (12/16/2012). Apparently he was told I provided this information. I requested NOT to be thrown under the bus again. This leads to mistrust and anger on his part and serves no purpose in his getting help. He has already begun the process of manipulation. "The suicide note is so old, Mom. It's almost a month old." (He has been in the hospital three weeks now).

"But, Adam," I said. "You told me yesterday of your intent to do drugs when you return home."

He said, "Weed is not a drug. That's all I do."

I said, "You overdosed on morphine."

Other references, all witnesses (all included contact information):

Angela Shultz (Registered nurse, family member)

Kristina Estes (my sister and mental health advocate, Event Coordinator in School of Health Professions at Columbia University Mo. Dept. of Disability policy studies)

Debbie Custin (Joe's sister and observer)

And then from Joe Custin (father):

To Whom it May Concern:

I am Adam Custin's Father and I believe Adam needs long-term professional mental health care.

Adam was admitted for an overdose of morphine. This admission is yet another of a long line, for the last eight years, of overdoses and attempts on his own life to kill himself.

As Adam's father it would be a travesty not to seek inpatient psychiatric care for the long term.

We have tried everything but nothing has helped with the disorders. We need help now for the long term.

Respectfully,

Joseph Custin

Somewhere around December 15, St. Joseph released Adam to Research Psychiatric Hospital! Proof that documenting and advocating strongly for your loved one opens doors. Don't ever give up. Be a bully if you have to be! This is someone's life you are talking about.

So, we finally had Adam in a safe place while we worked on figuring out where to go from there. Two days following his placement in Research Psychiatric Hospital, Stephanie became very ill with pneumonia, which in turn wreaked havoc with her blood sugars. She was in very serious condition. She did recover, but we felt like we just couldn't catch a break!

Chapter 41
Research Psychiatric Hospital,
Going Downhill on the Rollercoaster Ride

Adam wasn't really thrilled about going to a mental health facility, but we eased his anxiety by explaining that by going there first, finding the right medications to help with his Schizophrenia and anxiety, a rehabilitation center would then accept him and he could get back on the road to physical recovery. He seemed to be okay with that explanation. The last thing we wanted to do was set him off or trigger suicidal thoughts. We simply wanted him to be safe and recover.

Joe and I visited Adam daily at the psych ward. There are rules and specific times you are allowed to visit your loved one, limited to one hour each evening. This caused us concern, as we felt Adam needed the reassurance that we had not abandoned him or locked him away for good. One of his greatest fears was being in a place like that for the rest of his life. We reassured him that we wanted him home with us, and that this would never happen. At the same time, we were terrified for the day he would be back in our care.

After the first day, his previous case worker, Aimee Johnson spotted him there and asked his assigned caseworker if she would trade a patient for Adam since she had already established trust and a relationship with him before his coma in November. She agreed, and Adam remembered her! We all felt a bit of relief.

Adam was in the psychiatric ward for ten days. Each day he seemed to be changing in a negative way, and it wasn't psychosis. He came into the hospital using a cane to walk with. The second day he was using a walker. Aimee explained to us that Adam had fallen a few times, and the walker gave him more support. A few days later, Adam was in a wheelchair. He wasn't talking much and still seemed happy to see us when we visited. Aimee fixed it so we were allowed to visit him anytime outside of visiting hours, given the fact that he was a special case.

We were concerned about the fact that Adam wasn't walking anymore. But no one else seemed to be too concerned about it since he'd had a traumatic brain injury. On Christmas Eve, he was in a new wheelchair with his head held in place.

On Christmas evening we brought Adam a special treat. We were only allowed to bring prepackaged items. He had been begging to have some chocolate cheesecake prepared by his Aunt Ann, my sister. So we snuck it in inside a large Ritz Cracker box. No one was the wiser. He sat and stared. He did not eat his dinner. He did let me spoon feed him a couple of bites of the chocolate cheesecake. I saw love in his eyes. I saw fear. He was trapped in there. He did not—or could not—speak.

We felt desperate that we were losing him again. Joe spoke to the staff, and no one seemed concerned. We became frustrated. One aide in particular told us to leave, that visiting hours were through. We told him that we had special permission. He was sure we were lying, and when he went to check the records, he discovered that it was the truth. He didn't apologize, just huffed off. Joe asked to have a meeting with someone in charge. We did, and he insisted that Adam be taken back to St. Joseph. When they refused, he said he would call 911. So, they gave in and sent him there. We went home to sleep a few hours, as this went long into the night. We understood it was Christmas but felt this was an emergency.

To top it all off, when Joe, Stephanie, and I got back to the car to go home, we saw that someone had broken into it. Stephanie's and my purse and my cell phone had been stolen! We were not allowed to bring those items into the psych ward, so we had left them in the car.

Joe was really upset. He said, "I must have left the car unlocked! No windows are broken. It is all my fault!" It really just showed the state of mind all of us were in. We were in panic mode to begin with and not thinking of normal things like locking the car or possibly putting the purses in the trunk, out of sight. The worst thing for me were all the memories and lost photos, videos, and voicemails from Adam which I had saved.

The next morning, we called St. Joseph to see what room Adam had been placed in. They said he had been returned to Research Psychiatric Hospital. We were shocked! Apparently, when he'd been wheeled into St. Joseph, Adam finally spoke. One line: "Lucifer won't let me move." They said it was psychosis, not paralysis or for any medical reason—it was all mental.

We headed back to Research Psychiatric Hospital. The night before we had given Adam new clothes for Christmas, mostly sweaters to keep him warm. He was wearing one when we got there. He had been placed in a glass room for observation due to the circumstances. When we arrived on the morning of the 26th, Adam was lying in the bed in the fetal position, soaked in his urine, and no one knew. His clothes were strewn carelessly on the floor. Knowing Adam was immobile, we knew he hadn't done this. As I gathered his things to take them home, sobbing in the corner of the room, Joe lovingly undressed Adam, cleaned him up, dried him off, and changed his clothing.

We alerted the staff, and finally someone said he needed medical attention. He was moved to the medical side of Research Hospital. Adam was not in a coma, but at the same time, he was not responsive.

He breathed on his own, but mentally he was in another place, far from us. Sometimes his eyes were closed. Other times they were open and staring blankly. He did not move. He received the best care from doctors and nurses there. He had what they called a "sitter" in his room 24/7 to ensure his safety.

Adam had many visitors, some regularly. Social worker Aimee Johnson came in after her shifts to read to Adam from books on Buddhism, a subject that fascinated him. He had shared this similar interest with Aimee the previous November during his stay at Research Psych. Our friend Susie Green stayed with him many days and hours. Our friend Liz Muleski from our NAMI support group came in and sat with Adam on Thursday evenings to give us a break. All of these people played such an important role in our lives and our sanity during this time—something we will forever be grateful for.

Aimee took a shot and invited Lama Chuck from a Buddhist temple in Kansas City. Lama is a title given to a high priest, a teacher of the Dharma in Tibetan Buddhism, a monk who has achieved the highest level of spiritual development. So far, a Catholic priest and my cousin Gary from a non-denominational Christian church had prayed over Adam. So, why not? Lama Chuck was one of the kindest, most gentle human beings we had ever encountered in our lives. Adam had a gentle soul, too. No wonder he could relate to the gentleness of Buddhism. Lama Chuck prayed over Adam, too.

There was a rehabilitation center that rented space in Research Medical Center. Adam was transferred there, on the same floor so he didn't have to be moved too far. While there he became increasingly weaker, still not moving, eating, or communicating.

He had surgery to insert a feeding tube into his stomach. We were so concerned about bed sores since he had the huge one on his buttocks that we made sure Adam was moved often to prevent further sores or making the previous one worse. I couldn't see how that was possible, however; by now it had many tunnels running from it. Doctors said he could get an infection from that and die. What if he didn't wake up? What if he remained a vegetable for the rest of his life? Joe and I researched places for Adam to live whenever this place decided to make us leave. This was a place for recovery, and he was not improving.

Once again, many visitors came. Liz, Susie, and Aimee continued to visit. Adam's cousins, Derek and Lauren came, cousins Brittney and Byron, and Stephanie spent a lot of time there, along with her childhood friend Megan Born and her then-boyfriend Kevin, a childhood friend and fellow scouter with Adam. Megan was studying to be a nurse at the time. She washed Adam's hair and he smiled! Many others from support group stopped by. Our neighbors, John and T came often. Our friends, Brad and Tracy Young, whom we have known since we met in Columbia many years before, came. They have always been a part of our lives, and beyond this time would come to play a very important role in them.

The room was small and a divider ran through the middle of it. Adam had a roommate on the other side of it. He spoke a lot and seemed to be on the mend. I felt jealous that his visitors could engage with him as we watched Adam wither away.

Adam had new brain scans, which showed water on his brain. The places that were damaged in the coma scans were filled with water. It was scary, but one doctor gave us hope, saying he could recover from this. One thing we have never given up, and that is hope!

At night we turned the television on to *The Voice* or *American Idol* as we had watched those as a family. Over time, Adam seemed to make facial expressions. Hope continued. We kept a journal in his room so anyone who visited could write about the visit or if they saw any changes. The comments also gave us hope.

RECORDED COMMENTS and progress and Meadowbrook following this time:

1/4/2013, 9:30 a.m.:
Uncle Jimmy visited along with Dad. Adam followed Uncle Jimmy with his eyes as he moved throughout the room. Uncle Jimmy said he moved his left leg a little bit.

1/4/2013, 4:43 p.m.:
Aimee wrote me a text: "I asked Adam to blink for me when I had an answer right and he blinked multiple times. I asked him if his favorite was Zen Quotes or Zen Tao and he blinked for Zen Tao. He yawned twice and chewed on a piece of skin on his lip."

Lama Chuck came to visit Adam and shared his faith with us. Buddhism interests Adam and you could see in his breathing and eye movements he was listening.

Mom, 6:45 p.m. Adam made a low sound in his throat when I arrived and watched my movements. He moved his left leg!

1/05/13 Mom and Dad: John and T visited.

Adam moved his left leg several times. Eyes like slits but you can see his eyes tracking our voices and faces. We all worked on his hands, arms, legs and feet. Joe washed his feet. They get stinky in the boots they put him in. John had everybody cracking up. Lots of laughter.

Derek and Lauren visited in the afternoon: Adam seemed to open his eyes a lot to say hi to Derek.

1/06/13 Vanessa Welchen and Saundra Morman came to visit: We prayed for Adam. He was asleep, did not move. Just before we left Adam moved his left foot, jerky way. He snores real good! Love ya!

1/07/13 Mom arrived at 5:45. Adam has been snoring hard. Did several huge gasps for air. It scared me. His legs are not in the boots, knees are bent to the right. Occasionally his legs jerk or he moves his left arm slightly and I think he is about to wake up. He swallows too and moves his lips up and down as if he is talking, but no sound comes out. After 35 minutes and thinking I'd get no response (and getting teary eyed) Adam tried to thrust his chest forward. His right arm was straight, hand facing down on mine and I asked him to squeeze. Well, he pressed down his arm and hand hard on mine! He moved his face! His foot! His leg! Left hand! Aunt Ann called and I put her on speaker and he tried to move toward her voice.

Dad came in: Adam started "showing off" moving hands and right foot. He specifically asked me to watch the Alabama Notre Dame National Championship. (That is a lie! Wrote Mom. He can't even talk.)

Aunt Debbie talked to Adam over speaker phone. Told him to keep up the good work, that she loves him. Adam showed Aunt Debbie how much he can move today. Left hand, right hand, right foot, left shoulder.

Amazing!

Side Note: keep in mind when we talk about movements, they are very small, but to us it meant hope for recovery and made us feel he could hear and see us even if he could not communicate.

1/09/13, 3:50 p.m. Aimee Leanos (Johnson): Adam kicked his legs. I said, "Adam, I can see you kicking your legs". Then he kicked again! His eyes opened a small bit two times, one time they opened to the sound of my voice, second time when he was kicking his legs. Adam slept the rest of the time.

To Adam, I keep you in my prayers. I ask your guardian angels to keep a good eye on you while you heal. See you soon, Aimee

Dad: WE LOVE YOU, ADAM! Hey, Adam, it's Mom and Dad. You're sleeping right now. You blinked your eyes but still sleeping. Your room-mate left today. You have the room to yourself for now.

1/10/13 HI Adam! It's Aunt Kristina and Derek. We just came by to say hi. We are en route to the airport to pick up Brittney, Byron, and Jude. We miss you! Get well soon! Love you!
P.S. He slept the whole time. Breathed heavier when we spoke to him. He did give us a smile.

Aimee: Adam opened his eyes then his eyeballs moved from left to right and looked at me!

6:25, Mom and Dad: Adam is wide awake tonight and watching us.

Adam breathes hard through his nose in response-trying to communicate. He smiled at Dad! Made our whole week! Dad just told Adam Aunt Debbie was coming next weekend and he smiled big!

1/11/13 Mom: Dad washed Adam's hair tonight. Adam's eyes closed while he massaged his head-so relaxed. He is alert tonight-eyes open. Some foot movement, too.

1/12/13 Don, a pastor and man who took Joe's NAMI Family to Family class: I visited Adam today at 10:20 a.m. He was sleeping and I was unable to wake him. I prayed for him and will come again soon. May your hearts and minds rest in confidence that God is very much concerned about this precious young man.

Aimee: I went to touch his forehead and he blinked when my hand got close.

Mom: Aimee was here reading to Adam when Mom and Dad arrived. I took over. He appeared to listen. We brought in a mirror so Adam could see himself. I believe he was attentive. Dad is massaging his feet. He put a cross around his neck and I put one in his hand. May the Lord put his blessings upon you my sweet boy!

1/13/13 Stephanie: Hey, Adam. I'm here with Mom and Dad. You have been opening your eyes off and on. I took a video of you on my phone. I'll watch it every time I miss you or think about you. Every moment with you, I cherish. Love you Adam.

Mom: Hair washing day! Steph recorded it on her phone. Very sweet. I love you, Adam! Love, Mom

Dad: Adam is showing off now! Stephanie got him to move left foot, then right, then left, then right with verbal directions! Stephie worked a miracle today! We love you, Adam!

1/15/13 Dad: Mom and Dad here to see you today, Adam. We spent lots of time on Sunday and skipped Monday. We missed you a lot! Happy to see you today. We've been praying for you. God loves you. Your family loves you! Lots of prayers everywhere! Love, Mom and Dad

Since Adam had been moving and tracking so much at this time, Joe and I spent hours and days of researching and visiting rehabilitation centers for when he came out of this state. It would take him communicating with us verbally to show that he was ready. Some of the places were nursing homes. Most of them were. It was heartbreaking to think of our twenty-one year old son in care with the elderly. Would it depress him? Would he even be motivated to heal? Reality told us he might be in this somewhat vegetative state for the rest of his life, so we might not have a choice but to find permanent care. Some of the representatives from the nursing homes came to visit, too.

1/17/13 Paula from Harrison Health Care. Adam blinked his eyes when asked if he was in pain. He also coughed. We asked him to blink if he knew we were here and he did.

My name is Rhonda McKinney from Golden Years in Harrisonville. I visited with Adam today. I understand that you are looking to take him to a different facility for rehab. Please take a look at the brochures and if you have any questions, please feel free to call. I will be praying for you. Rhonda

1/18/13 Dad: Dad came to see you. Mom has a cold and cannot come up. You look great! We miss you and love you like crazy! Doctor said you told him "Hi" today! You look very relaxed and in control. We're continuing to pray for you. (Any time we visited Adam we had to wear gowns, masks and gloves. Any infection—even a minor cold—put him in danger. The day Adam said "Hi" was the first time he had spoken since December 25th at St. Joseph Hospital, when he had told them, "Lucifer told me not to move.")

1/18/13 Aimee: you tracked my phone with your eyes. I hope you liked the skate videos. (Adam was an avid skateboarder prior to his overdose.)

1/19/13 Megan Born and Kevin Wallace came to visit. (Megan was in nursing school and had been close friends with Stephanie since Kindergarten in school and church. She was also in my Girl Scout troop and traveled a few times with our family. Kevin went to Boy Scouts with Adam and was a former classmate.)
Megan: I washed Adam's hair and put lotion on his arms and talked about the old days and Boy Scouts. (Megan also showed us an easier way to wash Adam's hair with a bedpan! She laid his head back in it and used the closed area for the water. Brilliant!)

Mom: Today has been a blessed day! Kevin Wallace and Megan Born, childhood friends of Adam, came. He laughed and cried and smiled! Tonight Aunt Ann called and he had tears in his eyes. She talked to him a long time giving him encouragement. He mumbled, "I love you" to her. Amazing! And Adam, we ALL love you! Love, MOM

1/20/13 Adam told me "I love you" Warms my mommy heart! (Cousins Brittney, Byron and Jude came to visit that same day. Jude was a newborn baby and couldn't go in the room, so I got some much-needed baby cuddle time in the waiting room while they visited. They wrote: just stopped by to see Adam. He looks good and we will continue to pray for him. California is only a call away. We love you so much. Stay strong. XOXO Love, Britt, Byron and Jude.)

Aunt Kristina: We miss you, Adam! I know you are trying to talk. Love you and get well soon!

Hey, Adam! Dad again. Love you huge! You're doing great. Keep up the good work!

Sondra and Vanessa here. Adam was awake when we came in at 2:05 p.m. He just stared at the television. Looked like he was crying, had tears coming down. Cissie had prayer.

1/21/13 Hi, Adam! It's Mom! I really enjoyed our visit today. Adam spoke to three people today on speaker phone. I couldn't make out the words. He speaks in a quiet voice and struggles to make words. He spoke with Connor Ellard, McKenzie Teague and Nathan Michaud, all from Tulsa. He spoke most to Nate, but showed recognition to all.

Adam grimaced in pain while being moved. Hate to see him in pain, but glad to see him feel and make the brain/body connection.

Adam also squeezed my hand three different times! Such improvement! Such a blessing! I love you, my sweet son, and continue to pray for your recovery!

1/22/13 Hi Adam, it is Liz Muleski. I visited with you this evening and watched Gone in 60 Seconds. Your nurse came in and asked me where your IV was. I said I didn't know and she was surprised until I explained I was not your mom. You are running fever tonight—100 degrees. The nurse, Rose, gave you Tylenol. You laughed when I told you about Erika's tattoo and how she spelled her name wrong. Stay strong. (Liz continued to visit Adam on Thursday nights when we had NAMI support group, and every other Thursday so Joe and I could have some down time. She and Adam grew very close.)

1/23/13 Dad: Mom and Dad anxious to see Adam. Most definite smile when we walked into the room. For the first time ever Adam said, "Hi" to Dad and said a few paragraphs (not sure what it was). Big squeeze on the hand. Dad sure is happy to hear Adam's voice. Mom then took over. Loved, hugged, squeezed and hogged you all to herself! It's okay, Adam. You're doing great! We're so proud of you!

Mom: Adam ran a fever again tonight. Nurse gave him Tylenol through his feeding tube. Joe and I did the body shift and removal of the boots at 7 p.m. Joe tried to straighten his left leg and he abruptly pulled it back. Concerned about pain. We all watched American Idol together, something we did at home the last three seasons. Adam was alert for most of it.

While Adam was healing in the recovery unit in Research

Hospital, we obviously experienced our highs and lows. He had been placed on a feeding tube early on because he wasn't getting enough nourishment through IV feedings. The bed sore on his bottom had to be treated a few times a day. His brain couldn't communicate to his body to regulate temperature, blood pressure, and many other internal issues, in addition to the physical body. It was difficult to see him just lay there and atrophy. He would draw his hands up under his chin and pull up his legs, too, constantly. We spent as much time as we could massaging his arms, fingers, legs, and feet to prevent this. He was fighting so hard. We had to make this work.

We both worked full time. Joe worked from home, so he did his office work at every hospital Adam was in. What a Godsend! I worked in Shawnee and went straight to wherever he was after work and spent weekends with him, too. We both did that, and Stephanie did as much as was possible for her as well. She worked evenings and weekends much of the time.

Chapter 42
Meadowbrook Rehab Hospital

We finally found a place to move Adam that we all loved and was not a nursing home—The Meadowbrook Rehab Hospital, in Gardner Kansas. One side of the building was set up for brain trauma patients. It was perfect, modern, and updated and had all the best equipment and staff you could hope for! Adam had his own room and it was huge! We got to decorate it any way we wanted; we even had permission to put pictures on the wall.

He had a large bathroom to accommodate himself as well as the caregivers, and a huge machine with a hammock-looking thing hanging from it to carry his body in. He had a desk and chair too, for future use. There were lots of places for us to hang out and visit. And it was clean! The nurses, doctors, therapists, and aides were phenomenal! Adam was moved to Meadowbrook on January 24, 2013. We continued to log his journey through the journal:

1/24/2013, Speech Therapy (Beth):
Adam opened his eyes to my voice immediately today. Slight tracking of me to his right and upward. He answered yes and no questions with encouragement and was fairly accurate to personal questions. He counted to five with repetition. His voice was mostly a whisper, but he was able to state his name and several other syllables with a weak voice-sound. He stated his full name with only minimal support to start. He swallowed to my cleaning his mouth with a frozen, lemon, glycerin swab and stated "yes" to my asking whether he liked the flavor. (these swabs are in the freezer in the galley. Just ask at the desk and they can

get you one!) He tried to move his right hand into a fist for me and held his forearm upright with elbow support. We are so excited about his progress! Looking forward to tomorrow! Beth

1/24 PT and OT: Adam is following occasional commands to touch my hand and push his leg down in bed. Whispers his name to me and tells me who "Heidi" is (Mom). Sits at the edge of the bed for five minutes with moderate assistance of two therapists. When asked, "Do you want to sit up?" he said, "Yes." Completes leg exercises with maximum assistance. Anna Marie PT

1/24 Aimee: Do you know who I am? Adam: (mouthed) Yes, Aimee. (Aimee is pronounced the same way as "Amy", but Adam always called her by the French pronunciation, which means "friend". She loved it and said that is what she originally was intended to be called!)

It's Mom. Adam was mumbling when we arrived and frustrated saying, "I should talk better than this." I explained how far he had come. That he couldn't speak for weeks at all! I swabbed his mouth and moisturized his lips and he had a little easier time speaking. Dad trimmed his beard and washed his hair. Looking handsome and ready for visitors this weekend!

1/25 Mom: Adam was very talkative as Aunt Debbie arrived tonight. He recognized her! Adam told everyone "I love you"! Adam told her he knew who she was and said "I love you." Since he stares at me when I say it to him I asked, "Do you love me, too, Adam?" He said, "Yes I love you! Just because I have a brain injury doesn't mean I have to be all lovey dovey and shit." He's back! LOL. I asked, "Does it make you angry when I say that?" He responded with, "Mom, I could never be angry with you ... I don't think." In between lucid thoughts are confused ones. Aunt Debbie was saying something in the background to Dad about a taxi ride and Adam worriedly looked up at me and said, "How am I going to pony up for a taxi?" Aunt Debbie quick on her feet said she would handle it. No worries.

He watched a lady on television and said he wanted to suck on her lips because they were so pretty. Well okay, then. LOL

We spoke of the voices and he said he is having a break from them! They haven't come back since the night he became unresponsive on December 25th! Oh, I hope and pray that is true ... forever! Let that be the part of his brain that ceases to function! Let him live his life in peace and have a chance at happiness! Let him teach others through his experience in a positive way!

1/25 Aunt Debbie is here A.P. You said, "I recognize you." And we had a chat. It was so good to see you again and I miss being here with you. We put up some pictures and a calendar and a clock to make your new room more homey. Keep getting stronger and work hard! Love you A.P. Love, Aunt Debbie

1/26 Austin Wise: I got to see my cousin Adam for the first time since he has been in the hospital. He is doing better these past few days. It definitely does not look like the Adam I saw before, but deep down, he is still the same guy. I love you, Adam. Get your ass better SOON! Love, Cousin Austin

Aunt Debbie: Aunt Debbie played some of her music and you said, "That's some old shit." But you seemed to enjoy her singing and "danc-

ing" around. Aunt Debbie is pretty cool, huh? Love you tons and tons!
2:50 p.m. BP 158/80

Adam had visits all day with Uncle Jimmy and Austin who work in
North Dakota in the oil fields and were passing through on their way
home for two weeks in southern Missouri. Plus Aunt Debbie, Dad and
Mom. He talked a lot today! But was very weak in his voice. He was
running a fever all day. PT and OT came in to assess Adam as they
plan to start intensive therapy Monday. A nurse ran a midline into Ad-
am's arm to get some antibiotics into his system in case of infection.
They upped his calorie intake in the feeding tube, as well. Adam loves
to have his mouth swabbed mostly for the moisture I think. We had
some interesting conversations today. He wanted to know if John Green
turned black. I said no he hadn't. Adam said he was a good guy who he
would like to be like some day.

Adam: I keep seeing James jump off a cliff.
Mom: Why?
Adam: He's a douche bag.
Adam: I think Lorna's a lip Nazi.
Mom: No, that would be Aunt Debbie. Lorna is in Louisiana, but would
love to be here. She misses you, calls and prays daily.
Adam: She's nice.
Mom: Let me swab your mouth. It is so dry. I bet when that gets better
and they help you learn to swallow you can have that orange soda
you've been talking about.
Adam: James Ebel (a friend in Tulsa) can help with swallowing and
chugging because he knows more about it than anyone. (Strange as I
thought that was, James died in 2015 to alcohol poisoning so I now can

see he meant humor in that statement.)

Mom: I am tired. What would you say if I climbed in your bed and took a nap?

Adam: I would say what the @#$%?

Dad: Hi Adam! Love you huge! Dad. Ditto, Mom. You got a pic line in today.

1/27 Aunt Kristina, cousin Jessica and her son, Mason came. They visited along with Aunt Debbie, Dad and Mom.

1/27 Aunt Debbie: You had a shower today and Mom brought some healing oils and she and I massaged your hands and feet. You are more alert and awake today. The nurse said you told her you felt better today. I have to go back home today and I will miss seeing you and talking to you. Have a great first week of PT. You can do it. Stay strong and focused on healing. One day at a time. One hour at a time. One moment at a time. Love you, Aunt Debbie

P.S. your dad stayed out all night and partied with the band. (No, he didn't. LOL. He needed to rest.)

Ambrose family: John, Christian and I came to see you Sunday afternoon. You were wide awake and watched us come in the room. We were really excited to see you! John asked if Uncle Jimmy had come and you said "yes" and I asked if you had a good visit with Megan and Kevin and you said that you had. One nurse came in twice to change your antibiotic and turn off the beeping and one came in to change your position in the bed. I showed you the Lone Ranger theme this man played on a harmonica at Carnegie Hall and you watched the video intently and seemed to enjoy it. We are thinking of you every day and wishing you a speedy recovery! The rehab hospital is beautiful and we loved your room! Good luck with physical therapy this week and God bless you, Adam! John, Tracy, and Christian 3:10-6:25

Hi Adam! Just stopped by today to see if you could meet Mason and see Jessica. You are doing awesome! Keep up the good work! We love you! Aunt Kristina

Adam-We came to see you today and you said it reminded you of old times. You made me smile! You met my son, Mason for the first time today. It was also the first time I have seen you in about a year. I will be back to see you in July and expect you to be able to hold your second cousin, Mason! I have been and will continue to pray! I love you, Adam and I know you are strong enough to get through this! XOXO Jessica

Joyed to see your legs bounce better than last time I saw you! Good luck with therapy this week. You'll pull through. Stay strong and we'll try to get back up to see you next weekend. Cousin Derek

It's Mom again. You have had a busy day with visitors today even though we moved you further away from home. It is amazing how you have reached out to so many. You are so loved! We really enjoy hanging out in your new place. Lots of space and GREAT caregivers! I have faith you will grow here! Love, Mom

Hey Adam, it's Dad. Was great spending time with you today. Love you huge!

1/28 Sarah and Maria here from OT. Saw Adam at 8:45. Adam answered basic questions we asked of him including where he was from, parents, sisters, etc. Adam answered appropriately. We worked on range of motion of his upper extremities assessed needs. Had him sit on edge of bed with our assistance. Very cooperative and sweet young man!

1/28 First day of rehab and Adam said it was painful. I sympathized with him and said it will be painful for a while. His legs were laid straight for the first time in a long time. Been running fevers late afternoon and nights.

Aunt Debbie gave Adam a teddy bear he calls Ted. He believes Ted smokes pot all day.

He thinks rehab physical therapist called him a bitch. He must have imagined that one. LOL.

I witnessed great manners with nurse, Lisa:

Lisa: Hi, Adam! How are you?

Adam: I'm good! How are you?

Lisa: I'm fine Adam. Thanks for asking.

Adam: You're welcome.

Adam wanted a pizza and a 100 gallon jug of Gatorade. Still on feeding tube. Then asked for chicken strips and white gravy-what he ate every day at St. Joseph. Adam believes Dad plays guitar and sings (very well) in a country band. Well, he does play guitar! Having an anoxic brain injury, having had a stroke and going from no frontal lobe activity in the brain and dead to alive, it is no wonder there is confusion and I am amazed at what he does know and can do! Adam talked about his first day of OT and said it was silly because they asked him stupid questions he knew the answers to already. I explained they needed to ask ques-

tions to establish a starting point, that not everyone is in the same place with a TBI.

Dad: Adam moved his right arm and touched his face! First time to reach up! Praise God! Love you huge! Adam turned his head to the left! (He had only been turning to the right). Adam wants some Gatorade!

1/29/13 Mom: Didn't see Adam tonight. Liz came on a Tuesday night. She texted: Had a lovely visit with Adam. We talked the whole two hours I was there! He said I could come every Tuesday night if it's okay with you guys. Adam had a fever. He said he felt okay and they gave him Tylenol. The difference in him in one week is truly amazing! Last week he did not talk at all! And his kindness and gentle spirit are inspirational. I truly enjoy spending time with Adam and am glad to do it. Forget the Gatorade. He wants a beer! Adam asked me to pull his arm to straighten it. We got pretty far before he said it hurt. I told him about my daughter, Erika a little and he said, "I bet she is good on the inside." I almost cried. He is so right.

1/30/13 PT: Adam participated really well with physical therapy. We got his legs mostly straight when he was in bed and he was able to wiggle his toes on his right foot and reached a little when we helped him roll to his left! He was a pleasure to work with and thanked us when we told him he was doing well!

Dad: Hey, Adam. It's Dad. Spent about four hours hanging out today. You are amazing! Sat up in bed and in a chair, and you moved your arms, did great on recognizing animals and symbols. Keep up the great work! You talked with Mom and Stephanie over speaker phone. You are amazing! Love, Dad

Mom: Third day of rehab Adam sat up in bed and can lift his left arm! Brushed his own teeth and sat in a chair! God is working! So thankful for so much progress on the third day of therapy! Spoke with him on speaker phone. Dad was with him. Voice was strained, but understandable. He was so proud. Said he wants to go to NAMI awards dinner next time and show how good he is doing. Adam remembered we got the family of the year award last November for 2012. This is so awesome and unbelievable! I cried tears of joy today! Prayers of thanks! Adam said hopefully I can give you a hug soon and not break your head. Hehe.

1/31 Hey, Adam! It's Dad! Walked into your room this afternoon to see you wearing t shirt and shorts. First time to wear clothes in over two months! How awesome! Also, today you got to drink water and eat ice chips! Woohoo! You look great. You were very talkative and we had a great conversation. Keep up the great work. You got a haircut today. Love you huge! Dad

2/1 Hi, Adam! Lots of time today, we had fun! Love you, Mom and Dad

2/2 Saturday, We have hung out most of the day. Dad keeps making Mom mad-hehe. Glad I got to spend some time with you, Stephanie

2/2 Adam talked a ton today! He said he remembers his time with God. "He is glorious!" He told me suicide is not the way. He wants to help others feel good about themselves. We want to attend the next NAMI meeting. I love this young man! Mom

2/3 Adam is craving brownies and Blue Bell Ice Cream and wants Megan Born to sneak it in! We called her and she said she just had some Blue Bell Ice Cream with cookie dough in it! He also wants to go to Quick Trip with one of the nurses. He cracks me up. He is joking around with Dad a lot. Love it! They are going to watch the Super Bowl together tonight.

2/4 Adam can read!!! Just found out. He was reading the "motivational pieces" (his words) off the pictures Aunt Debbie hung on the wall. Excellent! Communicating a lot tonight!
Grandma and Grandpa Shultz came to visit tonight and Joe played his guitar and sang. Great time! Love you!

2/05 Liz came tonight. She said, "We had such a lovely visit. He told me he walked today and was very excited about it (he made that up but I guess wanted Liz to be proud of him-she already is). He also said Joe is an awesome guitar player and you should hear him sometime."

2/06 Mom: Adam is talking up a storm about many people and events-Dad/guitar. Megan/bringing Reese's Pieces. Steph/ Chocolate donuts, Aunt Ann/cheesecake, Dad/gigantic chocolate cake. (Big joke about that. When we eat out and a waiter or waitress asks if we would like anything else, Dad makes a huge circle with his arms and says chocolate cake. They either say they will make one or seem embarrassed and say they don't have that. LOL. These memories are blowing me away. He has confusion still with the TBI, but has many short term and long term memories. Amazing!) Someone is to bring chocolate ice cream cake and I am to order pizzas. He is craving chocolate like crazy! I can't wait until he can eat regular food again! We are all looking for-

ward to it! Getting swallow test done at KU soon. Moved to room 506 today because Adam is becoming more mobile and this way he can be closer to the nurses' station.

Adam counted by fours and fives today!

2/08 Mom: I had the day off today so I spent the whole day with Adam. Boy, is he in rare form today! Sassy and frustrated because he cannot have real food or walk on his own. Showing his fighting spirit. Way to go! I got to observe P.T. It was awesome! He moved all of his limbs, did stomach crunches and sat on the edge of the bed! Exciting! Got to witness PENS (Pattern Electrical Nerve Stimulation). Love you Adam Boy! Mom

2/09 Stephanie: I am here with Mom and Dad. You wrote a letter to Tad today and it was hilarious! You had us all cracking up! I had a great time today. I will be back tomorrow and I am bringing James with me. Adam has a great sense of humor.

A couple of side notes here. Tad is Adam and Stephanie's first cousin, Ann's son. He is the same age as Steph (23 at the time of this writing). Tad also lives with mental illness and ended up in jail for some time. He is trying to get help while there and is turning his life around. He wrote letters to Adam that were quite inspirational. He is an artist and drew beautiful Christian pictures for Adam, too. James wanted to see Adam to apologize for the incident at their apartment during July 2012 and seek his forgiveness.

2/10 Went to visit Adam. He looks better than the last time I saw him. It was nice to visit him. Of course the first conversation we have is about poop. Adam, keep getting better and we will try to visit you when we can. I'll keep praying for you. Stephanie

When Adam was trying to figure out language in the beginning of his journey back to good health, he sometimes said nonsense words. When he needed his diaper changed, he would say, "Uh-oh. I had a butt fumble." Too funny.

2/10 Adam has been a ton of fun today. I was worried the voices might be back, but nurse explained the made up stuff, and bizarre thoughts can also be the traumatic brain injury. She agreed he is going beyond what is expected in this kind of case. But, oh, the stories he tells! He keeps on insisting he had a crotch rocket in the closet and one of us stole it. (Joe rides a Harley and Uncle Mark has a crotch rocket so he is probably confusing things. And maybe desires a motorcycle to belong to the family boys club) Can't wait for another week of rehab to begin. Still talking about getting food to eat. Swallow test is two weeks from tomorrow! Hope he can hang in there!

2/11 Mom: Today Adam began his third week of therapy. He has come so far in such a short amount of time. Each week brings something new in his progress. Though for tragic reasons, this is the most rewarding and exciting thing I have been witness to in my entire life. What a miracle! We talked about what he did today. He said he went to the gym. He worked bike pedals from his wheelchair. He said, "It was very hard!" He said speech therapist had him categorize things such as deceased presidents, parts of a car, living presidents, flowers, trees, etc. and repeat over and over again to try and get him to remember and write stuff down. Still wanting to head to Quik Trip.

2/12 Mom: Dad came in to visit Adam today. When he walked in, Adam was lying on his side, his body trapped between the mattress and rails. He said all he could focus on were those huge, blue eyes, that really stood out on that small, 97 pound frame (they jumped out at you like that when he was a baby, too). They eye on top was looking up at him when he walked in. "Uh, Dad, I think I'm in trouble. Can you get the nurse?"

"Adam, what happened?"

"I was going to go to Quik Trip to the creation station and got stuck!" LOL. He was really fixated on going there! I kept wondering where he came up with this creation station. Finally he told me it was this new place inside where you could order all sorts of really great food. Went to one to see for myself and sure enough it was true. I asked him how he knew since he had been in the hospital for so long. He said he had been watching the commercials on tv! This poor man was craving the taste of food for so long and all he could do was watch people eat and imagine it from tv! We were really careful not to eat around him. It seemed too cruel.

Liz visited during the evening. He said she asked lots of questions about the movie he was watching and told stories about her girls when they were in speech therapy when they were in kindergarten.

2/13 Mom here. Adam looks great tonight. Excited about getting a haircut tomorrow.

2/14 Dad was here. Adam got to eat soft foods tonight!

2/15 Dad, Mom and Susie Green came to visit. Adam is done with the sling!!! (the contraption that carries him around) and the special wheelchair! He is now in a new one he can manipulate with his own hands!!!

2/16 Adam requested I bring his computer today. I am nervous about it because I am protective and I don't want him seeking out dangerous people or seeing their names somewhere and be reminded who he can contact for drugs or whatever. In January, Stephanie found the girl who gave him the pills on Facebook, wrote her and threatened her to never contact Adam again. I went through his phone contacts and deleted drug contacts or anyone suspicious. I know he is an adult, but we have come so far. I will risk nothing to keep my son alive. I knew who the drug contacts were by the code names he gave them, names related to a pill or something. At the same time, I was excited to even see if he could navigate a computer or use his fingers to manipulate the keys. So, I brought it in. He can remember passwords and can use it proficiently. Amazing!

2/17 John and T, Mom and Dad spent the day with Adam today. He can now manipulate the wheelchair with his feet, as well as his arms! Adam got the catheter removed last night and knows when he has to use the bathroom. We have had wonderful conversations today. Joe played guitar for Adam. I brought a five pound hand weight and he worked his arms. Then we went outside and he walked his feet along with the wheelchair. First time outside! Adam leaned forward in his wheelchair before we arrived and fell out. He was not hurt. He has foam mats all over his floor. Motivated for sure! Looking forward to beginning week four of rehab tomorrow! Can't wait to see what awaits us this week!

2/18 Mom: I came in to find that Adam himself had written in the journal. I couldn't read what he wrote, but he made an attempt! This is what he wrote: Hey, Guys! I had Susie's pie today. The best thing I have eaten in a year, plus! Thank you, Susie! She did bring him a pie. Wish I could have been there to watch him enjoy it!

Adam got to eat a BBQ pork sandwich today! Doctor says he looks great! Coming along quickly! Adam does look great! He is begging me to feed him pudding and does not believe I am not authorized to feed him, only speech therapist until he is okayed. Susie and J and T brought him various varieties of chocolate pudding. It is in his bottom drawer. He said that I think he is "mentally retarded" and can't swallow. I assured him that is not true. He is very bright and showing it more and more. He watches the news and reports it to me daily. Much of it is sad news, but he is accurate on details. He also knows all the commercials. He said he has decided to lease a car because of an ad he saw.
Adam had a BM on the toilet with help today! Woohoo! So Proud of you, Adam! Love you! Mom

2/19 Liz: Adam was in a great mood tonight. We talked about the food he is eating. He said he had polish sausage for dinner. We talked a lot about when he was at St. Joseph hospital. Tonight his knees were really hurting. He wants knee replacements! Liz

2/24 We hadn't seen Adam in five days and it was killing us! One or both of us visited daily since the incident happened. We had a major snowstorm that trapped us at home. Adam wrote in the journal again. This time I could read it (mostly) without his translation. His handwriting is improving. This is what he wrote:

Suzie's pudding is missing along with 16-26 of J and T's puddings. I smell the thieves! I just got a bunch of clothes though, from my occupational therapist. Also if my speech therapist approves, I can eat with you guys. Side note, I think my handwriting is getting better. I want to write something else, so here it is. Hey, Matthew (cousin Tad) now that I can write I will be sending you a note back. Don't forget about me. I haven't forgotten about you. Me, again. I want you to know I read that letter you wrote me every day. Thank you.

My mom did a great job of getting me to the toilet today. She can help me transfer from the wheelchair to the toilet.
Kia Soul $154

Side note from Mom: Adam thinks his puddings were stolen, but nurse assured me they are safe in the staff's room where the store their food. He kept sneaking it without therapist to supervise. Well he figured out where it was. He would wheel his chair up and down the hall with me getting exercise, head into the room and grab one of his puddings and then wheel past the nurses' station which was set up in the hallway and begin flirting with the nurses. There was a bag hanging on the desk. It looked like one of those canvas shoe bags you hang in your closet, but had supplies in it. One of those pockets had plastic spoons. While flirting (they loved it and him) he would sneak a spoon out of the pocket and keep rolling. I would tell him he can't do it, but he did. He would peel the foil top off the pudding with his teeth since his fingers were not quite strong enough yet and eat it! Scared me but he never choked. I suspect the pudding thief was Adam himself!

Adam came to know all the staff and other patients. He would wheel around the halls and roll into rooms to visit, and called each one by name. He became very attached to one nurse, Jillian, and she would tease him. When he had been helpless in the sling, he would sass her, and she would tell him he was just low enough in that swing to where she could kick him in the butt. We laughed about that one. Adam knew every story about each patient too. As we wheeled along he would tell me about each person. Some could not communicate much, but lit up when Adam passed by and spoke. I felt so proud of the man he was, so compassionate and kind. I think it also drove him to heal faster.

2/24 Mom: The last note must be about the car he intends to lease. Missed you Tuesday through Saturday! Huge snow storm trapped us! The nurse just told me Adam snuck into his closet yesterday and changed his clothes ten times! They were frustrated with him, but wow he did THAT by himself! Must have taken some doing from the wheel-chair!

Adam is eating regular meals! We ate with him today! He was sitting at the desk writing in the journal when we arrived! I love that and it's legible!

We spent the whole day with Adam. I watched him pull himself to a stand twice! Dad did once, too! We each got to assist a bathroom run. After dinner he rolled to the sink and said, "I have to brush my teeth. It's my new OCD thing." (Good one to have!) Then J texted about his pudding supply which sent him straight to the pudding stock! Adam gained eleven and a half pounds in a week! Up to 110 pounds (with shoes on)!

2/25 Mom: Adam had his first meal of "regular consistency" foods today (not ground up). He took a few steps without help, too! I was too late to witness it. Hoping when we return from Sarabeth's wedding that he will walk to me to give me a hug. So proud of his progress! Adam we will miss you! Love you so much!!! Today is Monday. We will be back Saturday. Mark the date on your calendar and countdown!

Our niece Sarabeth Custin was getting married on St. Pete Beach in Florida. Joe and I flew down there to attend the wedding. We left in another snowstorm. We watched it fall from the airport windows, hoping our flight wouldn't be canceled. We boarded and arrived safely. We flew down on the twenty-sixth and flew back on the second of March.

Joe and I had a lot of time to spend with the Custin clan and enjoyed our time with them. At the same time, it was like leaving your baby at home for a week. That part was agonizing! The night of the rehearsal dinner, Adam called and wanted to talk to Uncle Steve, Aunt Debbie, and cousin Sam. All were amazed at the conversation and change in personality for the positive. Adam felt good to be able to tell them that he felt great and that he was "normal". Joe and I spoke for a long time to him, too. We missed him terribly. That night Joe dedicated a Jason Mraz song to me, called "I Won't Give Up on Us". It moved me to tears as we danced to it; tears shed for what we had lived through and still managed to hold our marriage intact at the same time. We were coming up on twenty-four years on the fourth of March. We had defied the odds! We felt proud and in love.

Joe's brother Steve participated in the ceremony. He gave a beautiful speech. He spoke of the role models Stine and Sarabeth had in the long, loving marriages on both sides of their family. Suddenly— and unexpectedly for Joe and me—he took a turn in his speech and recognized us for our commitment through what we had lived through, and really built us up as parents and as a couple. It was a very emotional moment for both of us.

While we were away, Adam wrote in the journal: *I get a six hour pass this Sunday to go out to eat with you guys. Ha! My handwriting. (It was shaky and curved up the page.)*

2/28 Liz: Adam wants his dressing changed tonight. The nurse says tomorrow. I am betting on Adam getting it changed tonight. He keeps going out in the hall and asking everyone to change it. Leena finally said they would look at it and decided he just needed more tape. Adam pulled the dressing off and showed us his sore. He got a new dressing! M.K. called tonight. Adam was really happy to talk to her. Erika came with me to visit Adam tonight. Adam is really excited to get discharged March 14th! He said it is even better than having his birthday! Liz

2/28 Adam: Jillian brought a huge chocolate cake and gave me a third of it! She is bringing me a birthday cake, too! She is very righteous!

3/3/13 Mom: Adam got a six hour pass today! First time we have seen him since we left for Florida on Monday. The Custin family all sent love, prayers and birthday wishes. Missed Adam huge! On our six hour pass we went home and visited the "girls" our dogs, Nellie and Alaska. Nellie was so excited she tried to knock him down and licked his face many times. Alaska "smiled" at him and wagged her long, bony tail! J and T came over and were so surprised to see Adam walk. So were we! And amazed at all he is doing. As promised, Adam gave me a standing hug when we went to his room! He is still wobbly and we had the chair for the outing, but he walked a little in spurts. When he tired, we used the chair. We went to the Legends to have lunch at Longhorn

Steakhouse. Adam ate and ate and ate! They brought us a birthday/ anniversary dessert called the "Chocolate Stampede". Adam ate three quarters of it and it was huge! We stopped at Walmart to get boxers, a hoodie and shampoo for Adam. We had a great time! What a day!

Adam: At Fridays you can get Jack Daniels shrimp and burger with an appetizer for $10. One of each or two of one. I got my stomach tube out yesterday and found out my discharge date is March 14th! Got my IV out too! Tube free now!!!! Getting half chocolate/half vanilla birthday cake from Jillian tomorrow!

March fourth, 2013, Adam celebrated his twenty-second birthday. My sister Kristina sent a message to many people, and he received cards and gifts from around the country. He was amazed at the caring of people, some of whom he didn't even know personally. We had a party in his room to celebrate his birthday and our twenty-fourth anniversary. Adam's friends, Cary Williams and Megan Rainey, from Tulsa came,. He was overjoyed to see them. It really boosted his spirits!

3/4/13 Wow!!!! You are back. Your body is healing! Continue the great work. Plus the new haircut looks great! Aimee P.S. You made it to 22!!!!!

Mom: Happy birthday, Adam! Twenty two years ago, God gave me the greatest gift imaginable, a wonderful anniversary gift-YOU!!! Today, He has given you back to me and your dad! My heart is full of awe and love for you! Love you so much! So proud!

3/05 Liz: A day late, but happy birthday Adam! We had a great visit. Adam talked about when he wrestled and about friends in Tulsa. He told me about his birthday and day pass. He really liked the brownies with M&M's for his birthday. So glad you made 22!

3/06 Mom: I came in and Adam is not in his room. He is doing his own laundry!

3/08 Mom: I found Adam chowing down on a regular diet. Off mechanical soft foods for good! Adam knows all the nurses codes. He said, "I can now do the LE (lower extremities) and UE (upper extremities) with my wheelchair and I'm Mod-I (moderately independent). He teaches me this stuff. That means he can go from wheelchair to walker in his room anytime.

3/09 Mom: Eight hour pass! Went to Walmart shopping and had dinner at home with Mom, Dad, Stephanie, her dog Jack, Aunt Kristina, Uncle Mark, J and T, Derek and Lauren. Lots of good conversation. Fun time!

3/10 Brief visit with Adam today. Everyone is worn out from yesterday.

3/11 Adam walked to dining hall and back! Looking good!
3/12 Liz: First thing Adam told me when I walked in was that he is going home tomorrow. Wow!
Congratulations! It has been an amazing journey!
He is walking all around tonight. He walked out to the nurses' desk to get his medicine. Adam says he does not need a knee replacement anymore. Just hard work. One of the best things about visiting every week was seeing how much he accomplished each week. The first time I visited you were unconscious, the next week you were talking, then moving your arms. Keep getting stronger. I will miss our visits. Enjoyed

watching Comedy Central tonight.

Side note: Liz continued to visit with Adam on Tuesday nights, even after he returned home. During the winter months one Tuesday, Liz didn't show up, and Adam was frantic because he could not get ahold of her. We finally got word from Becky Beers (our mutual friend from NAMI) that Liz had fallen on slippery ice at work in the parking lot. She had fallen flat on her face and broken her jaw really badly. She was unable to speak to let us know. She was in recovery herself for a very long time and is doing well today. We will always love Liz Muleski! She is a bright spot in our world—one of our angels on earth. We cannot ever repay the kindness and unfailing love she showed to our son. She is a true child of God!

Although they didn't write in the journal, my parents did come to visit Adam one time at Meadowbrook. Mom told me that Papa had driven erratically and scared the life out of her. They traveled back in the dark. I appreciated them coming. Papa brought Joe's guitar, as he had left it at their house during a visit. I could see that Papa was having difficulty getting around, and it caused us concern thinking about him driving them both home late at night.

I reflected on a couple of things that night. During the fall before the overdose, Mom was in the hospital and Aunt Jane was visiting. I was at the house alone with her and we were discussing Mom and her issues. I said, "You know, she loses interest in kids once they are walking and talking, but she is great with babies. Thank God we had you and Grandma to nurture us during those early years.

Her reply: "Yes, all babies, except you …" You could have heard a pin drop. She went on to tell me that Grandma Shultz used to yell at her to pick up her baby, and she said she didn't want "that" one. I was fifty when I heard this. It hurt me badly and I was surprised that sweet, compassionate Aunt Jane would tell me this. Maybe it was because she knew about what Papa had done, felt guilty that she hadn't done anything about it, and wanted to give me another excuse for his behavior. Who knows.

I look more like my father than I do my mother, so maybe in her pain, she couldn't face loving a child who looked like him. Today, I am in forgiveness for everything. My mom ended up being my friend during high school and beyond that. Maybe me sharing my truth with her brought out what compassion she could feel.

Chapter 43
Adam Comes Home!

More journal entries:

3/13 Adam: I get to go home today!!! Discharge a day early! As you can imagine after almost four months! OMG! So happy to be heading to the Casa!

3/13 Mom: Adam's first night home; we left Meadowbrook at 6:40 p.m. Went to CVS for prescriptions and to Panera to eat. Stephanie was working and looked up in shock to see us there! Boy was she surprised! Finally got home close to nine. Took an hour and a half to sort through all the meds, but got there! Adam slept on the couch even though he told a nurse he could climb a chair to get on his bed (very tall bed). She said, "No climbing!"

3/14 Today is our first day home. Adam has a home health care nurse, "D" He still has the bed sore inside his bottom that began the night he went comatose on 11/25/12. I always thought bed sores were small sores on top of the skin. Shocking to see up close the damage that one of them could do. He had a few small ones that didn't break the skin, yet, but this one is a whopper! I get woozy at the sight of blood, so this is scary to me. He is so thin and barely even has a butt, yet it is big enough to fit a tennis ball inside! I also had no idea they could take so long to heal and by the looks of it, I'd say we have a long way to go. Having a home nurse also gives us peace of mind as we both work. Thank God, Joe works from home so Adam has one of us around most of the time.

Adam watched a lot of Netflix today. I took him to Subway for dinner. Hopefully soon we can get back into a routine and cook meals at home again. For now we are all trying to get readjusted and rested. It has been months of go, go, go. Plus, Adam is craving every food he missed in town! At Subway a lady named Darlene was managing tonight. He told her his story. She was so impressed with his recovery she said to come in when he was ready and she would give him a job.

3/15 It is Adam's second day home. Both days we have kept in touch by phone keeping track of meds and well-being. Made it through day two. We ran errands tonight for more meds and dinner at Panda Express one of Adam's favorites. Adam has been walking everywhere, even though he was sent home with a walker. He laid it against the wall and said he won't get better using it! He is really trying hard but sometimes he overdoes it and gets fatigued and he is in quite a bit of leg, hand and bed sore pain.

3/17 The home health care nurse left her bag at our house. It had a hole in the bottom of it and unwrapped, unprotected gauze, the one she puts in Adam's wound is hanging out of it. The inside of the bag is filthy. Martin, Angie, Alex and Addie came to visit for the weekend. Angie is a Registered Nurse. She took one look at the supplies and became very angry. "After how far he has come and she could cause a very bad infection to occur. This is all unsanitary!" She had me call the lady's supervisor to report her. We sat together on speaker phone and I politely, yet firmly told her what was happening. The supervisor told me what I could and could not say to her and said I was yelling. I was not. Angie took over like a mama tigress in a loud voice, "She was not yelling. You do not tell her what she can say or can't say! Do you know this mother

251

has been through, let alone this young man? YOU may not speak to HER that way. Do you want to know what yelling sounds like?" She said "No. I will send someone new out to replace her." At this point Joe stepped in and said, "I don't think so. Your company is fired. Good-bye." I am going to the next wound care appointment to get trained to be his home nurse. In the meantime, Angie did it this weekend and I observed so I can get by until then. Queasy Mama or not, I will do this! No one will love him and care for him like his Mom and Dad. No one! We all went to Trader Joe's on Saturday and Barnes and Noble. Adam walked through both places. He drags his left leg a bit and was tired and sore by the time we got to Walmart. He drove a motorized cart in there. Made me a nervous wreck as he tried to navigate without crashing into stuff! Lol! We topped off the day with a meal at Martin City Brewery. Family is amazed at Adam's progress! We had a fun day!

Chapter 44
Adam Feels the Need to Rescue Stephanie, along with Dad

After the Martin Shultz family left on Sunday, March 17 (St. Patrick's Day), we were settling down for the evening, getting ready to eat an actual home-cooked meal. I received a frantic call from Stephanie's friend and coworker, Katie Booker. She asked if I had seen Facebook that evening. Of course I hadn't, as we'd been winding down after a big weekend and getting Adam adjusted at home again. She said that Stephanie had written an SOS on Facebook, and that she'd been injured.

Shaking, I opened the page. She had written that James had hurt her, taken her phone, and smashed it. She had crawled into the bathroom, grabbing her i-Pad on the way in and locked the door. Without her phone, Facebook was her only means of communication. Katie had already called 911, and I simply wrote back, "Oh, baby. Daddy is on his way!" We had actually been expecting her to join us for dinner, and she was thirty minutes late. I had been calling her to see what the holdup was.

Joe was instantly angry and ready to kill James. He grabbed a spatula, and I asked what he thought he was going to do with that. Well, it was one he used for the grill, very long and strong, with forked prongs hanging from the side of it. I told him to let the police handle it. The last thing we needed was for him to be in prison for murder! He left quickly in his car.

Adam, wobbling side to side and dragging his left foot, quickly went after him, shouting "I am going to kill that S.O.B.!" I told him to get into my car, and we would follow Dad, but we all needed to maintain cool heads. I was really worried about Stephanie and the extent of her injuries and about Joe for what he might do. I am forever thankful for Katie, who may very well have saved our daughter's life that night!

When we arrived at the apartment, thank God, the police had already arrested James and removed him from the premises. We sat with Steph while the other officer took down a report. He wanted to call an ambulance, but Stephie wanted her dad to take her to the hospital. She had been choked and thrown against a wall, after which she had fallen to the floor. She had been momentarily unconscious.

When she'd come to, her phone was smashed and he had ripped out the landline. While he was distracted, she'd crawled to the bathroom. Initially, she had difficulty breathing, and later she had pain in her back and stomach. She had a bump on the back of her head and on her forehead. We couldn't believe that just four days before, we had gotten her brother back home, and now this happened! I was so amazed at Stephanie's strength! What a fighter!

Thank God there were no broken bones or internal injuries. She was in a lot of pain and was given pain meds to help. She ended up going through months of physical therapy and still has back issues today, six years down the road.

So many prayers and words of encouragement came through all over Facebook, just like with Adam. We can never repay all those people for their love, friendship, and faithfulness! One of my high school friends, Kathy Morris Smith, was one of those people who never judged our life and reached out many times during our ordeal with Adam and beyond, and now with Stephanie.

The love her post brought about was overwhelming. She spoke of fighting battles alone. How frightening it must have been for Steph to keep it together all alone. Sarabeth, her cousin, had tagged onto that with: *I love you so much honey! My heart and thoughts are full of you right now. Thinking of those moments fighting this alone kills me. We will keep fighting together as a family! XOXO.*

I responded to Kathy's post: *My life's work has been with children. I have been a teacher, a scout leader, and a mother. I grew up shy, scared, and intimidated of everyone and everything because of the way I was raised. I vowed my own would never feel that way. As an adult, I put myself out there and became confident and strong as an example.*

My children were raised with love, kindness, and respect. We all loved that man who hurt her and are shocked, hurt, and betrayed. Especially Stephanie! She has had so much taken from her in life from her Type 1 Diabetes diagnosis at ten years of age. Then Adam's near death. She has had so many adjustments to make. It tears me up to see her in such emotional pain. And for what? She is so sad right now, but we will be by her side and help her through. It's what we do. Thank you so much for thinking of us, Kathy.

Unfortunately, after going to court and all, Stephanie dropped the charges and took James back into her life. Looking back, we now knew for sure that it wasn't Schizophrenia telling Adam things about James back on State Line. Those things really had been happening. We took this man into our home, loved him like one of our own, and he hurt our little girl. It was difficult to forgive him. We did our best to be supportive of Stephanie and hoped everything would turn out alright. At least James now knew he couldn't get away with anything without first being suspect. We hoped it would keep him in check.

Chapter 45
Adam Works Hard to Get His Life Back

More journal entries:

3/20 We have been home one week now. Adam went to our dentist and good friend, Dr. Jennifer McArroy. It was his first time in a year. Poor hygiene is common with the mentally ill. Even brushing one's teeth can be a struggle. He now takes daily showers and diligently brushes his teeth, plus flosses! What a reset in his brain! Dr. Mc. and staff just fell in love with Adam and he with them. He can't wait until his next visit!

Side story: when the kids were young teens, Stephanie had needed braces badly. So she had gotten them. Adam still had many of his baby teeth because his permanent teeth had never grown through his gums and were in a different lineup than the baby ones. He did not have crooked teeth, and our past dentist in Broken Arrow just wanted to keep an eye on them. When psychosis hit later, he would often try to start an argument with me about those darn teeth and how I was causing them to look bad—and therefore making him ugly—because I loved Stephanie more than him. Nothing I could say would assure him that what he felt was not true. The truth was, though, that Steph had gotten braces before Adam had become sick. His medical bills were out of this world, and at that time took precedence over braces, especially if he was choosing not to brush his teeth. Of course, I never told him that.

3/20 We also visited Dr. Galbreath, my family physician. I love this doctor! You don't come in filling out a ton of paperwork. He asks questions, records it on his I-Pad and reviews his own notes before seeing you. If your appointment is at nine, you get called back at nine! He is prompt, knows you as a patient, remembers every visit and really listens and still gets you out promptly. Adam loves him, too! Adam weighs 127 pounds! Twenty nine pound weight gain! Dr. Galbreath is happy about Adam's change in lifestyle, no drugs, alcohol or nicotine in his system! Since Dr. Galbreath's office is in St. Joseph's hospital we did a surprise visit to Dr. Southwell (the neurologist during the coma) and his ICU nurse Tess Fekas. They were thrilled and shocked to see Adam walking in to the hospital on his own!

3/22 Today we visited Dr. "B", Adam's psychiatrist. He has a dry per-sonality and was less than thrilled to see Adam. Glad I was there. He also wasn't happy about the lose dose of Zyprexa and no other psych meds. I couldn't understand why he would want to pump him full of something he obviously didn't need at this time. He reviewed records from last September and yelled, "This is not a therapeutic dose!" In-side I felt like screaming, "This is not the same man you treated last September!" I told him about the miracle and he looked at me like he would admit me! He didn't believe we had a miracle. When you expe-rience what we did you feel a responsibility to share it with others. It gives people hope and brings some to faith even!

After Dr. B we visited Adam's caseworker, Nick Pinnell. He was so hap-py and relieved as the last time he saw Adam was November of last year as we were getting ready to pull him off of life support.

Joe and I went out for two hours tonight. Adam wanted some alone time at home and we wanted to give it a try. When we got home he was cov-

ered in mud. We recently had lots of snow melt and turn to muddy slush. When we asked him how it happened he told us he walked to Quik Trip, two miles round trip! He fell, but thankfully not in the street! He was covered from head to toe! He said he needed an electronic cigarette. No! He doesn't need nicotine at all! So dangerous in his healing and could set his brain off in the wrong direction. We are trying hard to get him to understand this! He is almost four months free of nicotine.

3/23 Joe and I went to lunch today with our friends, Tony and Karen Kehres. We also visited the Nelson Art Museum. Steph hung out with Adam all afternoon. Sounds like they had a great time together. Before lunch, late morning cousin and Pastor, Gary Powell came to visit from Columbia He brought two others from his church, Nate White and Mary Foley. They interviewed Adam, Joe and I for a video Gary plans to show at his church, Revolution, in Columbia on Easter Sunday. We will be attending with much of our family that Sunday and are very excited! Gary asked Adam if there was anything he could pray about for him. Adam told him the pain in his legs gets pretty intense. He would like that to go away. He said he wants to walk like a normal person without limping or dragging his left leg and one day he wants to run again! The three of them prayed over Adam's legs. It was a very touching scene!

3/24 Still no wound supplies. Hmm.
Since I had decided to take over as Adam's home nurse, I went with him to his wound care appointments. They were in Shawnee Mission, Kansas not far from where I nannied to Tyler in Shawnee. I was trained again by Adam's doctor. Ever since we fired the home health care nurse, we had been waiting on supplies to treat the wound, plus a hospital bed

that inflated and deflated up and down, moving to help the wound heal faster. By March 25 we were anxiously awaiting the supplies and bed and still they hadn't arrived.

3/26 Supplies came in this morning! No mattress yet, though. Four months ago tomorrow Joe found Adam unconscious. Four months ago today Adam was lying in his bed all day as we were in and out of the house with early and late schedules not knowing, thinking he was finally sleeping after pacing and ranting, for night and day for weeks on end. Look at him now! Unbelievable!

3/30 We are heading to Columbia for Easter Sunday at cousin Pastor Gary's church. Adam is excited and nervous at the same time. Tonight we dined with Aunt Kristina, Uncle Mark, and Aunt Debbie at Texas Roadhouse.

3/31 Today we went to Church of the Revolution in Columbia, Missouri. Gary spoke of miracles and Jesus and how Jesus was raised from the dead. Much of the family was there, most of my siblings, Mom and Papa, Aunt Jane, cousin Donna and her daughters, Chastity and Christina. Gary spoke of miracles in our world today and then played the video of our family and the interview. We were watching it for the first time, in awe ourselves as if it didn't happen to us. It was very emotional for all of us, especially those of us who had been there when he came back to us December 1st, 2012! Gary brought us to the stage. Later, Adam stood while people streamed before him to ask him about his experience, touching him, hugging him. While he seemed to do okay with it, I felt very protective of him, not wanting him to fall or be touched too roughly. He did such a great job and we are so proud of him!

Following church we went to "The Heidelberg", an old college hang-out for all of us that attended Mizzou. It was a great weekend!

4/22 I haven't written in a few weeks so giving an update: It is six weeks this Wednesday since we brought Adam home. He is still working on walking further and gaining strength in his legs, but wow has he been building up his upper body and arms! He weighs 135 pounds up from 97 pounds! He is a dream to be around. Speaks well! I am amazed every day at his progress. You can now see his story, Adam Custin Miracle on you tube!

5/7/13 We are so busy doing life, I haven't written as often. Into Adam's six month of recovery. He is doing well, but that darn sore on his backside just won't heal completely! He had surgery yesterday to install a pump inside of it. Doctor said he could heal in a couple of weeks! No more wound changing and packing for Mom! Great birthday and Mother's Day gift for Mom! His walking has improved a lot, too. He is much steadier on his feet.

Adam was chosen for NAMI's In Our Own Voice class to be a trained speaker on having a mental illness and overcoming obstacles. With this training you go into places such as mental health hospitals where people are in-patient and tell them your story and give them hope for recovery. Tomas Hernandez was his teacher and mentor and a great friend of mine through NAMI. He is a peer specialist as a person living with mental illness himself. He is amazing, and very energetic! A wonderful mentor to Adam. I got to travel with Adam to Jefferson City as his caregiver for a weekend of training, but did my own thing while he was in class. Went to Columbia and visited family one day.

Adam already has his first presentation set up!

5/18 Went to Les Bourgeois in Rocheport Missouri with my siblings and friends. It was a beautiful on the cliff overlooking the Missouri River and MKT trail. Adam had a great time with adults feeling like he belonged. Such a long time coming in his life.

5/26 Adam still has that pump in his bottom. Hoping that will heal soon! He is getting so strong otherwise. He and Dad took pictures to-day comparing arm muscles. Adam cracks me up. Every time, every day, sometimes more than once he works his arms with weights and pull ups. Then he shows me his arms and asks, "Are they bigger than they were before I worked out?" Of course, I agree they are huge!!! Planning to go on vacation to Hot Springs Arkansas on the eighth of June and get Adam into some healing springs! Also going to Memphis to visit cousins Jeff and Susan Powell!

Sad news. Our brother in law, Mark lost his daughter, Cloe only 13 in a car accident! Adam is praying for their family as are we.

Chapter 46
Road Trip!

More journal entries:

6/8 We loaded up the car, a rental. Five of us are traveling together, Joe, me, Stephanie, Adam and our neighbor's son, Christian Poynter. Christian has been a loyal friend to Adam since we moved her. They are only days apart in age. Christian is a musician and he and Joe often jam together in our living room. He takes walks with Adam and really listens to him. Even before the coma. So happy to have him join us on this trip!

Well, we made it and have the most adorable place we are staying. It is an inn, but feels like we are in a cottage. Getting settled in. Have a lot of plans for the next two days before we head to Memphis!

6/9 We visited a spa with hot springs for all of us to enjoy. Adam loved swimming around the place, and we all did, too! Very relaxing!

When Adam was learning to walk again, I decided to get back into shape. I had put on weight sitting in hospitals, then eating bad food and drinking beer. It was difficult, and my body was in a lot of joint pain. I found out I had some allergies, and eliminated certain foods from my diet, beer included. As I walked or worked out, my mantra was, "If Adam can do it, so can I!" He even joined the gym with me after coming home. It made me nervous as he would increase the speeds on the treadmill and fall around. I envisioned him flying off the back of it and slamming into the machine behind him! He never did.

Anyway, one day we went to the tower overlooking the city of Hot Springs. Adam, wavering from side to side, dragging that left foot, began to climb the tower, and quickly! I am terrified of heights, and never in my life would I have been able to climb past the first floor of a tower, if that! Without thinking about it, because all I could think about was my man-child falling from that tower, I followed him up one flight, two flights, and eventually made it to the top! I couldn't stop him and I could not keep up. All the way, I said, "If Adam can do this, so can I, and I will not let him down!" Once I reached the top, I realized what I had done, but more so what Adam had done! That was a miracle in itself! And he hadn't stumbled once! We all took pictures together at the top and admired the beautiful view below. Later when we shared this story with family, no one believed that either Adam or I had done this! We got T-shirts commemorating the grand event!

6/10 We explored the area today. Went to this shop that had healing stones and things cut from stone. It reminded me of the stones John Green put in Adam's hands during his coma. Christian knew a lot about these, too. He went through the store explaining what each stone did for you such as relieving anxiety. Adam found this chalice made out of this light brown marbled stone. He was fascinated with it and wanted to purchase it. I noticed a crescent shaped mar in the base of it and picked out a similar one. "How about this one Adam? It isn't flawed like that one. See the flaw at the bottom?"

"Ah," he said, "Don't you understand, Mom? That is what drew me to this one, the flaw. It is flawed like me." I was moved to tears. Yes, then again we are all somewhat flawed.

6/11 We enjoyed our time in Hot Springs and hated to leave this beautiful city, but are so excited to go to Memphis and see cousins Jeff and Susan Powell. Jeff and I, were more like siblings growing up. His brothers, Doug and Gary and my siblings, Ann, Kristina, Jimmy and Martin. Sadly, we didn't meet our oldest sister, Lisa until I was eighteen. She was kept a secret. (We all caught up with one another over the years however!)

6/12 We are enjoying Memphis with the greatest tour guide ever! Jeff took us to Ardent Studios where he works. He showed us how he can cut a vinyl record. He is only one of a select few people left who has this talent! He also took us to the Stax museum which took us back in time with music. We ate delicious BBQ for lunch. During the evening we went to Etta Bena to listen to Susan sing and play the piano. She is amazing. Then Jeff took us on a foot tour of the area nearby, telling us which streets we were safe to walk on and which ones we were not. All looked the same to me!

6/13 Had a relaxing day and evening at the Powell residence. Susan and Jeff live in a huge older home. It has a ton of character, including singing dogs! Susan directs them and they begin and end at her command! Susan's kitchen has hanging pots and pans. Some too high for her to reach. She asked Adam to get one for her in her sultry, southern voice, "Adam, I need a tall, (five foot six, ha!), virile man to reach that one for me." as she fans herself. We were cracking up as he puffed out his chest and said, "I got that for you, Susan." we had the most wonderful evening filled with memories of old and new.

6/14 Today we felt sad as we said good-bye to Jeff and Susan. We are now heading to Bowling Green, Missouri on our way home to see Jeff's mother, Aunt Jane, cousin Bev Jones, and Jeff's brother and wife, Doug and Valerie. Tomorrow, Adam is going to tell his story to Aunt Jane's women's prayer retreat at her church.

6/15 Adam woke up nauseous and throwing up which we have discovered will happen from time to time with his temperature fluctuations, blood pressure issues, etc. In spite of it all, he gave a brilliant speech and was well received by all the women. They had so many questions and loved all over him! He threw up after the speech, too, but was all in on doing lunch with the family including Doug and Valorie. We had a wonderful conversation with everyone, said our goodbyes and began our journey home. We were met by terrible storms. So bad, we could barely see the road. Joe, confident as always, pushed onwards through the storm. Cars and trucks lined the sides of the highway. No place to pull over if we tried. Made it home safely! Unpacked and relaxed the rest of the day!

Chapter 47
Researching Near-Death Experiences

While Adam had lain unresponsive for so many weeks, I became that mom who snoops and searches through their kid's belongings, looking for clues and answers, and a glimpse into Adam's mind and psyche. That was when I found the contract with God. I also took the time to clean up his room and organize it for when he was coming home. (After the miracle, there was no way you could convince us that Adam could possibly die. That would have been too cruel of a twist of fate.)

I also took the time to read about NDE's (near-death experiences) to see if anything aligned with the things Adam had told us. Both the books and these persons' personal experiences and what I was about to discover among Adam's things gave me great insight and some hope, as well. I became obsessed with the afterlife. Where had my son gone? Was he still going to die? And if so, where would he go?

First, I read *Proof of Heaven* by Eben Alexander, M.D., about a neurosurgeon's journey into the beyond after slipping into a coma following a disease that only one in 10,000 survive. He awakened seven days later with memories of going to heaven and returned with stories much like Adam's, including one of meeting a deceased sister he'd never even known to exist.

Next, I read To *Heaven And Back* (the book I mentioned in the forward of this book) by Mary Neal. Then I read *Heaven Is for Real* by Todd Burpo, which was about the experience his little boy had. He was the son of a pastor who had experienced an NDE. This one was very convincing for me because it came from a small child with no preconceived ideas about this sort of thing. I also read some books with short stories about various individual's NDE's. I was so fascinated and excited at the same time. It gave me a renewed hope for the afterlife, and I knew in my heart that no matter the outcome of our son's situation, he would be okay. If he died, we knew without a doubt, he would be in heaven, at peace and without illness—happy.

All three of these books were worthy of the read, giving awesome insights into what lay beyond this life and amazing accounts. I highly recommend all three. I also read some books that compiled many people's stories about their own personal experience with an NDE.

I was especially drawn to Mary Neal, and thinking beyond the NDE, I came to realize just how connected we all really are. Beyond family. I thought of all the wonderful people who had carried us through our early years in Broken Arrow as we settled into a new territory. I thought about how one relationship or friendship led us to another, and yet another, and how we couldn't have survived life without every one of them, whether they were there only briefly or for a long time.

I thought about how it had felt as if a chain had broken when we left and moved to Kansas City; how alone and frightening it was for all of us in different ways. For Joe, in a stressful job, a new beginning. For me, away from what I knew for twenty years in my business. For my struggling kids in a foreign place. Yet, again these connections formed gradually, beginning with our jobs, then through our NAMI groups, and as time went on, through other sources, too. For each person, I can connect the dots or the chain.

During the recovery of the overdose and then the weeks of catatonia, for example, I was working as a nanny for the Wilkens. Tyler took swimming lessons at a local gym in Lenexa, Kansas. I sat in a chair during the hour, thinking or texting Joe to check on Adam. There was another lady there who brought her son. She sat alone, too. Eventually she sat near me and began a conversation. Her name is Kristen Springer. One day, she flat out asked me if I was okay. She said I looked incredibly sad all the time. "My son is unresponsive," I said.

She then wanted to know my story. I shared it with her. She then shared her story. She was a special education teacher who dearly loved her job. She is also a married mother of three. She was struggling with mania, buzzing about doing too much (she was a perfectionist), and losing sleep, only to fall into stages of depression. Finally, she got a diagnosis of bipolarity, and she decided it was best if she leave her job, as she needed to put her health first. I found it amazing that the one person I end up sitting with could totally relate to my life, but more from Adam's perspective than the family's. I was also amazed at how "put together" she seemed to me. She still juggled the schedules of three kids who were pretty spread out in age.

We quickly became friends. When swim lessons ended, we got the boys together for play dates. She became involved in NAMI, and even years later, she is a great part of what we do. She was there for me during some really rough patches. But you see how this works. She is part of the chain, a part of my life from here on out. She is not one of the ones who came and went (such as the nurses who invested themselves in Adam's recovery), even though they are just as important. Some of them have remained in touch, but there were many who were involved in all aspects of his recovery, and all of them played an important role in the chain.

Another example is my friend Lorna. We met in Tulsa during early childhood education classes. We had kids close in age. We both ran daycares from our homes. We later co-led a scout troop. She moved to Louisiana way before I moved to Kansas City, but we still travel together and visit each other when we can. She was the part of that chain that spoke to me as I rushed to the ER when the overdose occurred. She prays for me daily, and I for her, from a very long distance—a chain that will never be broken no matter where we are.

It is the same with Sarah Boyce, who jumped in and took Tyler when I had to leave to my dying son. We met at a park when Tyler was little, did the play date thing, then stayed in touch after I was with a new family. She is there when I need her, too. We meet for brunches sometimes when Sadie is at school (the child I nanny for at the writing of this book). These are just a few examples of those people we've met who we would never have predicted at the moment we met how important they would be in that chain. They are the people who help us develop and grow spiritually and otherwise.

Chapter 48
Life Begins Moving Quickly

After our return from Arkansas and Memphis, we continued with the healing process. Adam had blood work on his kidneys and other internal organs done later in June. Everything looked great! He also had follow-up MRI (magnetic resonance imaging) and EEG (electroencephalogram) tests. His brain showed damage on both sides and still had cysts in some places. Dr. Southwell, our neurologist at St. Joseph, moved to the University of Kansas Hospital and continued care with Adam.

After viewing his test results, Dr. Southwell said it was remarkable he was walking around and talking, and that he looked far better than he thought he would. He was surprised at Adam's upper body strength due to the weight training and pull ups (one-armed!) he'd been doing. Adam's left foot still had problems with dragging, and he said we needed to work on that, but overall, progress was great!

During that summer, Adam had wound care in Shawnee, so he went to work with me and played with Ty. He was really good with him and they bonded quickly. Ty's mom, Monica, had just moved into a new home, and Adam and Joe helped put all her pictures on the walls and put her furniture together. It really gave Adam confidence. By mid-July he had his last wound care appointment, and the dosages of his life-saving medicines were cut in half!

In late July, our nephew, Derek, married his fiance, Lauren, near our home, and many family members camped out at our house. Adam didn't attend the wedding. He felt overwhelmed with that, but he did great with everyone at our house. We even celebrated our great nephew,

Mason's first birthday at our house, and he also did well then.

We took the family on a tour of the fountains in Kansas City, and I noticed a man in one of the fountains who clearly had Schizophrenia. He was homeless and washing off in the fountain and loudly speaking to people no one else saw. I felt sad that he was one of the forgotten ones.

In early August, I got to go with Adam for his training in Jefferson City, Missouri, for In Our Own Voice. Since I was his nurse, this was allowed. I visited family in Columbia during the day while he was in class, an intensive two-day event. At night I helped him with his homework. He was adamant about getting it right!

In August, Adam gave his first presentation for NAMI's In Our Own Voice. He was very proud! They paid him $40. It could have been $1,000 as excited as he was! His mentor was Tomas Hernandez, a friend we'd met through NAMI. Tomas has been an amazing friend through the years I have been involved with NAMI. He is that friend who pushes you past your comfort zone and encourages you to do more and your best.

We have a joke to this day, that he and I do CrossFit training together. He does CrossFit; he tags me in all of his Facebook posts to make it look like I am with him. He challenges me for sure, but that is one thing I cannot do with joint and back issues. People actually question me about it and I just laugh. I tell him I am too old (57 at the time of this writing) to start something like that, and he says I can do anything I put my mind to. He is ten years younger than I am.

I first met Tomas in the NAMI Kansas City office. Jen Boyden warned me that he is full of energy! Boy, she wasn't wrong, but his energy inspires me! Tomas encouraged me to write this story and introduced me to Leanna Brunner, my editor, as he is in the process of writing his own book. Tomas is now a social worker in Kansas City and works with the mentally ill. He is a military vet, has served in combat, and has endured the pain of his younger sister's murder. He's had to navigate life under the burden of complicated PTSD due to multiple traumas. He is pretty amazing in my book.

Through In Our Own Voice, Adam also met Elizabeth Wilson, a lady who is about six years my junior. I had the pleasure of meeting her during a radio talk show that she, Tomas, and I had been invited to speak on. She is an amazing lady who lives with Schizophrenia and has managed it for over 25 years. She is an active advocate for those living with mental illness. I remember being in such awe of her the day we met. She spoke so eloquently. She had it put together better than I did!

She also knew my son! I felt so connected to her and wanted to give her a hug afterwards. She backed away and said, "I'm not comfortable with that." I knew better! Funny thing is, I got to know her so well from that point on, we now joke that we can't wait to see one another because we need a hug. Every correspondence she writes ends with "hugs". I will write more about Elizabeth in my second book, as she has become a major player in my life!

Also through Tomas, Adam met Michael Brown, an artist in Kansas City. At the time they met, Michael was homeless and living in an abandoned house in a dangerous part of town. He lived this way intentionally, immersing himself in the local culture. He learned a lot from his experience and drew much inspiration for much of his artwork. He has volunteered in shelters for the homeless. He has lived in an apartment now for a few years. He has mentored troubled youths, even allowing them to live with him until they get back on their feet. He is an amazing man, also ten years my junior.

Adam was very interested in Michael's way of life and asked us if he could spend a weekend in the abandoned house with Michael and see what that was like. Our first response was, "Hell no!" Adam was still in recovery from his injuries. We were not ready to be apart from him for anything, much less that!

We did, however, agree to meet Michael at a Starbucks in downtown K.C., just Joe and I. Michael laughingly told me much later that his first impression was, "Oh no, here come the Cleavers! The picture-perfect, well-to-do white folks!" He also said he was stunned to discover that we were not what we appeared to be; we were nonjudgmental, down-to-earth people who were not judging him as a black man but were truly concerned with Adam's welfare anywhere he went, even out the front door and into our own yard!

We took an immediate liking to Michael Brown. You will hear more about him in my next book, but I will tell you this: Adam did spend a weekend with Michael, and he said it changed his life for the better. Michael had to navigate around some situations that were unfamiliar to Adam: drug dealers and prostitutes heading his way. Adam, being friendly and naive in that world, just wanted to talk to everyone he met!

I had the privilege to sit in on one of Adam's presentations at Research Psychiatric Hospital. I felt anxious to walk back into the corridors where Adam had been dying during my last visit to that area of the building. He did a great job. The patients went from fidgeting around to sitting up, listening, and asking questions at the end. This was Adam's speech (it had to follow a certain format, beginning with his dark days to his journey into healing):

My name is Adam Custin. I am 23 years old. My diagnosis at twenty was Schizophrenia. I had a happy childhood and I was sur-

rounded by many friends. I can remember those times. I had a group of guys I hung out with climbing trees, playing football, video games, and camped with-normal typical life. I was in Boy Scouts and wrestling. I grew up in a loving supportive family.

My dark days began at fourteen. I knew I felt different, but didn't understand what was happening to me. So, in my head why would anyone else? At fourteen I had my first of many suicide attempts, my parents' first wake up call. They had no idea anything was wrong. During the next eight years I was in and out of hospitals and mental health facilities. My initial diagnosis was clinical depression. How could I possibly admit I heard voices? I believed they'd put me away forever. During times of darkness I self-medicated with drugs. Lots of them, including cocaine, weed, opiates, and benzos. The drugs made the voices worse. I paced the floor night and day yelling back at them, begging them to go away. They were mean and nasty and told me ugly things about myself and everyone I ever loved. I didn't trust anyone. I refused treatment because of this. Things only got worse. At the end of 2012 my dark days came to a head. I couldn't take it anymore. I took ninety-seven morphine pills. I just wanted to have peace! My dad found me the morning of November 27th in my bed, gasping for air. I was rushed by ambulance to St. Joseph Hospital. After many tests and doctor' opinions, my parents were told I was going to die. MRI's and EEG's showed no brain waves. The brain stem was the only thing functioning in my brain. As we have all been told you can't bring dead brain cells back-supposedly. I was taken off life support November 28th. Many people prayed for me. December first I woke up and spoke! No one understood why. It made no sense, but there I was. My psychosis was still out of control so after being released from St. Joseph I was taken to Research Psychiatric Hospital. For whatever reason I slipped back under. I was *moved to Research Medical Center and then to Acute Rehab there. I was out for five weeks. My body twisted up, atrophied, and I went down to 98 pounds. I had a feeding tube.*

Late January I woke up again. I could barely whisper. I could not move, eat, read, write, or go to the bathroom on my own. Things we take for granted. I went to Meadowbrook Rehabilitation Center in Gardner Kansas from there. I was there for two months relearning how to do everything.

For many years I wanted to be accepted for who I was, not labeled by my illness. During the months in the hospital I learned acceptance of myself, too. I was actually peaceful and at peace.

For years I rejected treatment. I would NEVER suggest ANYONE do what I did, but it forced me into treatment. In a coma you are helpless and depend on others. During that time I rid my body of drugs and was forced to eat healthy nutrients and take my meds. In a way I was lucky because without that time to heal I would never have followed through. I continued to heal and am the man you see here today. I continue to live drug free. I walk, talk, read, write and have memories. I keep the voices under control because I continue to see my doctors for my mind and body and I let them know if anything changes, good or bad. And I take my meds. I feel great. The voices don't torture me anymore. Treatment is so important!

Before my overdose, I used skateboarding to cope. After the coma and since I struggle with coordination, but I'm working on it. To cope now I use music, I read, and I study many things on my computer. I exercise daily, lift weights, walk, play games with my family, watch TV with my mom and we talk and laugh about things!

I have had many successes, the biggest of course being my recovery! I have trained with NAMI as a Peer to Peer speaker to share my story and give others hope. I have spoken to a group at a prayer re-treat, to United Way as an advocate for mental illness, was interviewed for a video on YouTube, and I was interviewed for the Tulsa World Newspaper (where I grew up). I was offered an application for a college scholarship and I plan on trying. I'd like to be an auto mechanic. I am still working on recovery, but I will get there!

I thank NAMI for giving me and my family support through my journey. NAMI offers many classes and support groups for both those of us who suffer with mental illness and our families who love and support us. I encourage you to become members, too. Knowledge is power!

Now, I know most of you want this to happen for you, too and if you have any questions, I will be happy to answer them!

Adam took this class in 2013 and later changed his mind about being an auto mechanic.

Adam's love and acceptance of others shined through during his recovery. Not only did he reach out to others who had mental illness, but he had no prejudice against any person, animal, or even insect. If I screamed, "Kill it!" meaning a spider in the house, he scooped it up gently in his hand and carried it outside to set it free.

A good friend of mine I have known since junior high school, Christine, came to visit. She married a man from Africa and had a step-daughter who came to live with them that year. Adam was very interested in the young lady, her country, etc. She was shy but opened up in giggles around Adam. He had a charming way of putting you at ease like that. He was curious why he hadn't met friends of mine from the past before. We all moved great distances, and Facebook was our only way of communication, it seemed.

Then he reached out on Facebook to another junior high school friend, Elise Rugolo. It was through Elise that I found out they were corresponding with each other. Elise is a mixed media abstractionist painter. Adam was obsessed with her work and wanted to purchase a particular piece of artwork, "Deluge (cool) AKA-Wet Snow" painted in 2001. I visited Elise that winter after she moved back to Columbia, and she had a copy of it in a gift bag for Adam. He was thrilled!

Adam's sister Stephanie continued to work at Panera in Kansas City. She also became a dog groomer and met a woman named Elizabeth Davis at the vet clinic she worked at. Elizabeth had three children at the time, and she and Stephanie took Adam under their wing, too, to get him out and socialize among young people again. Adam always was really good with children, and he developed an uncle-type relationship with her kids. I remember thinking: now we have a chance at a "normal" life. Adam will live a fruitful life and have a family of his own, something he dreamed of. Adam was always kind to children, animals, and insects, even in psychosis. This is something I feel is important to share, as many people believe the mentally ill to be dangerous. Statistically, they are more likely to be the victim of a crime than to commit one.

During late summer and early fall, we went to some wineries with the Custin clan, Mimi, Popi, Steve, Connie, Debbie, Joe, and Adam.

Adam was still trying to get control over his bladder and had to pee frequently. Sometimes he was foggy in his judgment, too. He was enjoying being an adult and having some beer when his bladder overtook him. We directed him to the building, but only Uncle Steve saw him head to the side of the building. He went after him. Adam just whipped it out and went on a vineyard hill. Next, he fell and rolled down the hill. He came back up to us with disheveled hair and mud on his pants. Steve explained to him why that hadn't been such a great idea, considering the fact that he could have been arrested for indecent exposure, and all! We had a few incidents that year with the toilet issue.

In mid-November, Tess Fekas, Adam's ICU nurse from St. Joseph Hospital, needed to move from an apartment in her complex into another one. She had been very ill, and Joe, Adam and I, along with a couple of her friends, got the job done. It was amazing how Adam could navigate the stairs with heavy loads! We got to know Tess pretty well following the overdose and remain friends to this day. Just another example of how our worlds intertwine for a reason.

That same month, The Tulsa World got wind of Adam's miracle, and a journalist wrote his story! Our family was also featured in The United Way Campaign, raising awareness for mental health!

In November 2013, I had the privilege of accompanying Adam for an In Our Own Voice Presentation. I was amazed at his speaking ability and his compassion for the patients in the ward, as well as the way people responded to him.

Adam went to Columbia with us for Thanksgiving, and we all had such a wonderful time. He was very entertaining to all. Someone gave him a Russian Winter Hat (a Schliapa), and he loved it. He announced the hat had "changed his life". We all cracked up. We visited what is called the "Magic Tree" while in Columbia. It is lit with multi-colored lights during the holiday season. Adam proudly took a picture in front of it, calling it the "Miracle Tree".

In the month of December, Joe, Adam and I were invited to speak to a Family to Family class about our story. Adam remarked that his dad should get the "Father of the Year" award.

Adam made fast friends with all of our neighbors, even some

Joe and I hadn't met yet. John and T, Tim and Lorrie, Joe, Adam, and I would often go to dinner together. He loved hanging with the older folks. We often said he had an old soul.

One night we went to a pub-style restaurant and sat at a long table. The waitress approached us one by one, going all around the table. She stopped short of Adam and gasped out loud. "Oh, my gosh! I can see it when I look into your bright blue eyes! Something amazing happened to you! It is almost as if you have seen the face of God!"

We were all amazed, and he said, "Well, actually I have." He shared his story and the video from YouTube, "Adam Custin Miracle". She went to the back room to view it, came out crying, and hugged him, saying, "Thank God you are alive!"

We all left thinking, "What just happened?"

Other neighbors we didn't know would encounter us on a walk on the trail behind our house or somewhere and ask where we lived. Most of the time, when we pointed to our house, the response was, "Oh, you are Adam's parents!" They all loved Adam, even when he was ill. He engaged with anyone who passed by.

At the close of December, Joe's mom, Mimi, became ill and was placed in a home. The year ended with this and became the beginning of our last months and years with our parents.

Chapter 49
2014

The year 2014 was an exciting one for Adam and the rest of us. It was also a year of ups and downs for the family in general. He was happy, carefree, and basically healed of his wounds from the overdose of late 2012. He was still living with us and had a way to go before he could be on his own, but we were realizing the true power of the miracle.

In January, Adam had his last visit with his neurologist, Dr. Southwell. Joe took him. His brain looked normal! He was doing well! Dr. Southwell was actually sad to see him go. Our whole family had a tough time with this. He had become an important part of our lives, part of our story!

I reflected on Adam's contract and how God had given him a second chance at life free from the voices. Adam had been working on his mind and body, going from a bedridden "vegetable" in a wheelchair to this strong, bright young man with a future ahead of him. He was excited and so were we. I loved to watch him do several sets of pull-ups on his exercise bar, one handed! Amazing!

He still had some childlike ways about him, though. For example, he would lift weights on any given day, ask us to look at his biceps, and say, "Do my arms look bigger than they did before I lifted weights today?" It was important to him to appear big and manly, as at five-foot-six he was a slight man. I had been calling him my man-child since the coma, and this was one of the reasons. He reminded me of his four-year-old self, wearing a Power Rangers suit, telling me how he would rid the world of bad guys. I found it endearing, but after a certain point in recovery, he sternly told me he was a man now and would appreciate it if I didn't call him a "man-child" anymore. So I never said that in his presence again. In my heart, though, he will always be my man-child!

One day while I was at work, Adam called to read me a page out of a journal he had written at the age of ten. This is what he wrote: *We just got our first dog today. Her name is Alaska. She is very sweet. In order to get rid of the voices in my head I have to die—*

"Wait!" I interrupted him. "You were only ten! You were not sick until fourteen years of age."

Very calmly, he replied to me, "No, Mom. You don't understand. I heard voices when I was a toddler. Back then I thought everyone did. I vowed to ask my best friend, Alex, every day what his voices sounded like. But he never brought it up, so neither did I."

Wow! What a revelation! On the age-old question, which came first, the chicken or the egg? The drugs or the Schizophrenia? I got my answer: the Schizophrenia was always there! He didn't cause it! He was self-medicating all along, trying to get rid of them! As a mom, this news was a huge relief!

In March 2014, Adam turned 23 years of age, and Joe and I celebrated 25 years of marriage. We three went out to celebrate together. Martin City Brewery in Martin City, Missouri, is ten minutes from our home. They had just opened up a pizza place across the street from the brewery. Adam wanted to go there first. It was very crowded, and I thought of how that would have pushed him away in the past, being too overwhelming for his mind. Now he was like anyone else, able to enjoy the atmosphere.

Later we went to a little pub in Belton, Missouri, also close to home, called Southside. It is very small and has its regulars, which we were not among. We were a social trio, though, so it didn't take long to navigate the groups of people and get to know some. Joe bought a round of drinks for the room. We were so elated to all be alive and able to celebrate together.

A woman named Nikki called us over to her table. She was sitting with another woman about to become her sister-in-law. They felt they recognized Adam from somewhere, and her friend said, "I saw you in that video." We couldn't believe someone outside our circle had seen his story!

Nikki was a joy to visit with. During our conversation, Adam felt comfortable enough to tell her he was excited about life, but due to the several-year gap during which he had been sick, he now had no friends to hang out with and was lonely. He enjoyed his mom and dad's company but needed to be with some younger folks. Nikki was around 30, but still much younger than we were. She and Adam exchanged phone numbers and became fast friends. We are so grateful to have met Nikki. She lifted him up and helped renew his hope and got him out in the world again.

People come and go in your life. Some stay briefly, others forever. They are all meant to be there for you when you need them. Nikki was one of the best—at the top of our list. She truly cared about Adam, and she brought other friends into his life, too.

Adam had friends in Oklahoma who stayed in touch with him by phone, Cary Williams, Megan Rainey, Sam Vining, Betsy Adams, Ben Ledford, Nathan Michaud, to name a few. All were lifelines to Adam, and we appreciate each and every one!

During April 2014, my father passed away, the first of our parents to do so. Two weeks later, Joe's mom passed away. Adam attended Mimi's funeral. He was standing in the entry of the church, and people began arriving earlier than expected. The family was upstairs preparing for the meal following the service. Adam took it upon himself to do the greeting of all the friends, many of which were State Farm executives. All were complimentary!

During the spring of 2014, Adam decided it was time to go to work! He approached a tree trimming company in Grandview, Missouri, where we reside, Cartwright Tree Care. They hired him as a groundsman. He basically collected the branches of trees that were trimmed and carried them off. I was worried he wasn't strong enough yet to do this, but he proved us wrong. It actually made him stronger, not only in body, but in mind and spirit. He bonded with some of those folks. I never met any of them, but someday I hope to thank them personally for their role in his growth and journey.

Adam worked for them until the early winter that year. Someone asked him why he was on disability, and he simply replied, "For Schizophrenia," which was the reason he had been put on it, but by that time, more for the brain injury, yet he never shared the story. Shortly thereafter, they told him they don't work during the winter and let him go. My brother Jimmy owned a tree trimming company for years, and he worked during the winter. I wonder if the stigma of Schizophrenia frightened them. Or maybe they simply didn't need the help.

He accepted what he was told, and that is what is important. So, whoever, I thank you for your gentle way with my son. But also I want folks to know that people with mental illness are not destined to be dangerous. Please don't fear hiring someone because of that misconception. They are people with feelings and the desire to work and be accepted like the rest of us.

Following Cartwright, Adam's caseworker with ReDiscover connected him with Job One in Kansas City. Job One helps people with disabilities get employment. Monica Roe was Adam's connection and is a friend to me to this day. She took him shopping for clothes to wear during his interview and got him prepared for his interview. She was like a coach to him. When he became employed, she was his go-to person if anything went wrong. She was so wonderful with him and always kept me in the loop of what was going on with him. We were a team—something we hadn't experienced much of with HIPAA standing between us and our son's care in the past.

Adam worked at an Army Reserve location cleaning the building. He loved it, as he could keep to himself if he had any anxiety issues, something that still plagued him following the coma. He loved his job. He enjoyed interacting with the servicemen and women and dreamed he could be in the service, too. Of course, with his history of mental problems, we knew that would never happen.

I took him to work at 6 a.m. on my way to work, and Joe picked him up at 2 p.m. We enjoyed coffee together at 5 a.m. and wonderful conversations then and on the way home. He was filled with excitement about the future. He still worked in Grandview, so it wasn't a big stretch. I remember he would carry a lunchbox with him. The first day I felt like I was leaving my baby at kindergarten for the first time. I actually had a lump in my throat.

Adam bonded with his supervisor there, a wonderful man who is now deceased from kidney failure due to diabetes. He was around our age. It was so cute when my "man-child" would innocently tell people his best friend was his boss, a black man in his fifties with a gray afro. He wanted everyone to know that! He worried so much about Richard's health. He kept up with when his dialysis appointments were, and he prayed for him. I just loved the compassion he returned with.

My sister Kristina worked for the University of Columbia in the disabilities department during Adam's ordeal. She has a close friend,

Chi Johnson, who worked with her. When the department closed down due to lack of funding, Chi moved to Colorado. She came to visit. Joe, Kristina, Chi, her husband and son, the "Mikes", and Mike's mother joined Adam and me for lunch. Chi was wearing a shirt just like Adam's, and he immediately took a liking to her. Chi is very outspoken about mental health, not just because of her previous job, but as someone who lives with bipolarity.

Another weekend, my oldest sister Elise Homeyer and her husband Herb came to visit. Herb was a judge for a teenage competition of robot making and fighting. It was on the Kansas side of the city. Joe and I took my little guy, Tyler, and his dad, Ted. It was a lot of fun. Later that evening, the Homeyers, Joe, Adam, and I went out to dinner. We ate at a Japanese restaurant. Adam had the time of his life. Unfortunately, he had a few drinks, which didn't help his ability to reason. He took a glass out of there with him and later took another one from a brewery we visited.

When we got home, he tripped and fell and broke the wine glass from dinner, but the beer glass made it home and still sits in our cabinet today. Adam's friend, Megan Rainey, later told me that he had taken her to the Panera where Stephanie worked and walked out with a bowl, presenting it to her as a gift. She was mortified, thinking they would be caught. I don't know if that compulsion had to do with the traumatic brain injury or what, but we had to nip that in the bud! She later turned the bowl into a planter as a reminder of a happy time with Adam.

In October 2014, our Executive Director of NAMI asked Joe and me if we would present to the Young Matrons Society and tell our story about mental illness and our son's miracle. The Young Matrons chose a cause every two years and raised money for that chosen cause. NAMI of KC was having financial difficulties, which we were unaware of at the time but were more than happy to pitch our cause and help NAMI. We had presented to the CIT training of police officers a couple of times, so we felt this was no biggie.

We entered the room where this was to take place. There were mostly women and a few men (husbands) there, in semi-formal attire. We dressed for the occasion, as well. People mingled around the room with glasses of wine in hand. I was thinking they were not "young", rather mostly our age or older. These were the very well-to-do of Kansas City. What would they want with us? I thought. It was very intimidating, not to mention the fact that when they sat down to hear the speakers, there were around three hundred of them! Intimidating indeed for this middle-class couple! We soon discovered that these people were some of the most compassionate people we had ever met and really wanted to help others. They were delightful.

Speaking after the Chancellor of UMKC was also intimidating, yet we somehow pulled it off. The room was silent, and tears were flowing. Following our speech, we both had lines of people wanting to talk to us. Some of them had their own stories to share with us because mental illness doesn't choose its victims based upon socio-economic backgrounds any more than by race or gender. It crosses all boundaries. Some of them told us we were brave. We have heard that so many times over the years, but we are not brave. We simply have had no choice but to walk the path that's been given us. Oh, how we had to really apply that in time!

The Young Matrons had a decision to make between us and other great causes. We were chosen!

Another Thanksgiving rolled around. This one Adam chose to stay at home while we went to Columbia. We celebrated at Mom's house and invited Joe's dad, "Popi", since both had lost their spouses

We received a call that my father's sister was in Boone Hospital in Columbia and was dying! Her sons (my cousins) Doug, Jeff, and Gary, were either there or on the way. Joe and I went promptly to her side. She was coherent and said her good-byes to my siblings and other family members. I went to hug her and she looked at me with pleading eyes and said, "You're not leaving too, are you?" We had been intending to go home, but there was no way we were going to leave her with that.

She was Papa's only sibling, and it was his would-be birthday the next day. We sat with her and "the boys" (as we'd affectionately called them since childhood). She died 24 hours later, on my father's birthday. She was like a second mom to us. Three family members gone in one year! But we still had Adam, we had Stephanie, and life was going to be great!

Christmas of 2014 was the best ever for our family. Pictures reflect such joy and happiness, along with a healed, strong young man. He was getting bigger, larger than he had ever been due to all the medications he was on. His psychiatrist kept him on a low dose of Zyprexa for Schizophrenia, as he couldn't sometimes believe he had no symptoms. He was still on anti-seizure medications from the coma, blood pressure meds, anxiety meds, meds for his stomach to ease discomfort from all the pills he was taking, and more! But, he was alive and happy. Adam began making steps to remove the "Dead Man Walking" tattoo from his arm. It was a very painful procedure that would take many months to remove entirely.

Adam continued his friendships with Nikki, Michael, and Tomas, was making other friends, and was even dating. He kept in touch with the people in Tulsa who had been a lifeline for him before and after the overdose. All in all, 2014 was a good year for Adam.

Adam also continued going out with the neighbors and family along with us. We enjoyed this one place in K.C. called Murray's, listening to bands and dancing. Joe and I had gotten to know the hostess, Mary DeVore, there. She and Adam got to know each other. Both had hilarious personalities, so it worked even though she is older than we are. She had been a huge supporter of our family and NAMI ever since. We danced and had a blast at this place.

Chapter 50
2015

2015 began beautifully! We really felt that Adam was in a great place and thriving. He had goals he was working toward. His excitement about life continued to flourish! We felt so proud of him! We enjoyed him! His brain continued to grow and learn.

In January 2015, the Young Matrons' Ball for NAMI-KC took place. It involved a silent auction, dinner, dancing, and pictures, and Joe was interviewed by a television news team. We had a wonderful time and raised a considerable amount of money.

March 4 was Adam's 24th birthday and our 26th wedding anniversary. I recently looked at a Facebook post that Joe put up on that very day: a picture of him and Adam side by side: proud dad, proud son. He publicly wished Adam a happy birthday, and several of Joe's friends tagged the post and wished Adam a happy birthday as well. Adam made a comment below theirs that he was flabbergasted that so many people he didn't even know had wished him a happy birthday and good wishes and good luck for his life ahead. He added, "I'm pretty sure this is not the last one! At least I hope not!"

It was really important to Adam to be fit and strong. He was taken off many of his medications and lost all the extra weight he had gained. He worked out constantly. We would have to stifle a giggle here and there because he would lift weights in the basement, run upstairs and flex his muscles, and still he would ask, "Are my arms bigger than they were this morning?" Of course, we would "ooh" and "aah" over them. Seriously, though, it was amazing how strong he was, considering the fact that two years before, he could barely move! He did one-arm pull ups, too! Tons of them in a row.

In March 2015, Adam turned 24. We were feeling confident that he was out of the woods of Schizophrenia. He came to many of our NAMI support group meetings to offer his support to other families and to show them that recovery was possible. He also lectured them on self-medication, not seeking help, or the taking of prescribed medications. He would sit in the middle of the room and roll around on this office chair and go directly up to the face of the person sharing. They loved it and they loved him.

In our NAMI support group, our family became close friends with a couple named Clay and Annette, who had a son, Clayton, who had been diagnosed Bipolar. During April 2015, Joe was away on a float trip with some of his male buddies, called the annual "Man Float"; it was a tradition that had begun back in Tulsa when the children were little. Now it included both friends and family. They would float and camp on the river, so they had no access to phones until the trip was through.

One Saturday, I was in our walk-in closet, cleaning and sorting things out. I usually did projects like this when Joe was gone for longer periods of time. My phone rang. It was in the connecting bathroom, and I stumbled over a pile of clothes to get to it. I answered it just in time. It was Clay. His voice was eerily calm and steady. "Heidi," he said, "Clayton took his life last night."

It took several seconds for this to register with me. We had spent some time with Clayton, and he was a likable young man, very handsome and bright. He had been an athlete and was being looked at by colleges, dreaming of going pro in baseball, until one day when psychosis kicked in. It was such a shame and such a loss to such a young, outgoing man. When he died, he was only 21. He had been ill since the age of 18, and now he was done. "Oh, God, Nooooo!" I sobbed into the phone, suddenly realizing that Clay was comforting me.

I frantically wanted to talk to Joe but wouldn't be able to reach him until the next evening. I knew that this would be a blow to him. Before, Clay and Annette would sometimes call Joe to come and talk Clayton down when it got bad, and Clayton had responded to him. In January, Clayton had run out into the night during an episode. He was self-medicating at that time, so he didn't feel the cold and got severe frostbite on his hands. We visited him in the burn unit of the hospital. It was a miracle that they saved his hands.

When Joe returned my call that Sunday night, I told him the news. Witnesses had seen Clayton driving the same route again and again—as if he was getting up his courage—then finally speeding down a big hill and crashing his car. He always wore a seatbelt but did not that night. He was thrown from the vehicle and died instantly.

Clay and Annette had been there for us during our worst nightmare. Ours ended in a miracle; theirs ended in tragedy. It reminded us of what we had almost lost. We knew we had to be there for them.

The funeral seemed surreal. Clayton was laid out in his baseball uniform. He looked unmarked by what he had been through. There were lines of people wrapped around the building outside the door. I wondered how Clay and Annette and their daughter Allie, his only sibling, could stand so calmly, greeting each person and giving each of us comfort as we struggled to comprehend what had happened to their world. Many of us NAMI folks were secretly terrified that this could happen to us. Clay was a Kansas City firefighter. It looked like all the firefighters in the city were there.

It was a beautiful ceremony. They did right by their son. Joe and I and Adam continued to reach out to them. Adam called Clay often to check on him. I was so proud of his kindness and empathy towards this family, knowing he could have put us through the same tragedy.

After Clayton passed away, we continued to hang out with Clay and Annette. One night, Clay joined Joe, Adam, and myself at Buffalo Wild Wings. I remember it was a rainy night. My friend Tracy Young called me and asked if I would talk to her friend, Frankie. Frankie's son had previously attempted suicide and was currently in psychosis. She needed help. He needed help.

We passed the phone around among us, giving Frankie references for help. Clay offered moral support, even in the midst of his grief! Adam talked to her for a long time and told her he was going to pray for her son right away. I was amazed at both Clay and Adam and their compassion through their own tragic lives.

By May, Adam was talking about enrolling in college and becoming a social worker. He decided that through his life story, he could really benefit and help other people who had the same or similar mental illnesses. We had no doubt he would be the best! He did some testing and was accepted at Longview College in Lee's Summit, minutes from home. We were so happy for him, and he seemed very excited.

At the end of May, Adam and I received letters from our beloved family doctor that he had been accepted at Mayo Clinic in Arizona. Adam had dealt with high anxiety since the coma, and his psychiatrist would not prescribe Ativan, the only medication that would ease the anxiety. Our family doctor was willing, however, as long as Adam allowed me to take possession of it and dispense it accordingly. Adam agreed, and we never had a problem with it.

Now, we were in search of not only a new doctor, but one who would be willing to prescribe this drug. We found no one. We visited his psychiatrist to ask him for help weaning him off of the Ativan, since we knew he would not be willing to prescribe it, either. He read us the riot act on how he never believed in using it in the first place, and that he shouldn't be the one having to do this. He dramatically cut Adam's dose to a fifth of what it was for a short period of time.

Adam was very stressed out about this. He had enough of the last prescription to get through July. I still get upset when I think about the way that psychiatrist treated Adam. He was put on the Ativan while he was in his coma and had continued beyond, never abusing it. This man had no reason to treat him like a drug addict or criminal. Joe and I were stressed about it too, as we knew Ativan was the only thing that helped his anxiety.

In May we also lost our beloved dog Alaska at the age of fourteen. We had lost the cats in previous years, Bear at nineteen and Fred just before our move to Grandview in 2012 at age eighteen. Jack was living with Stephanie and James, so after many years, our menagerie was gone. We now had one remaining dog, Nellie, and she was almost fourteen herself.

In June, Adam's Tulsa friends, Megan, her sister Kara, and her mom April, came to visit. They stayed in a hotel in Overland Park, and he stayed with them. He enjoyed touring Kansas City as much as they did, but come to think of it, he had been so ill since the move here he never had a chance to explore it with a peaceful mind. He loved that family so much, and so did I (and still do) because they hung on to him and loved him through all the years of struggle and beyond, never giving up on him. Megan told me a few years later, that Adam broke her heart that weekend. He said he was lonely and admitted it was depressing him. He laid in her arms and cried through the night. Looking back, I think maybe the Ativan had been keeping his depression, as well as his anxiety, at bay. Now those symptoms were showing up again.

We were also planning a trip to Glacier Park in Montana along with my sister Ann, her partner Victor, her sons Christopher and William, Victor's daughter Nikki, and a friend of Christopher's, Richard. Christopher, William, and Richard planned a remote hike through the mountains for part of our trip as this was a popular and regular activity for the three of them.

We were concerned that Adam might feel a little left out, being a young adult male, because it was so important to him that he fit in, be accepted by his peers, and be considered strong-minded and strong-bodied. But Adam didn't seem to be so concerned about this after all, and he planned the trip along with the rest of us with great excitement.

He was in constant communication with his aunt Ann, planning his shopping list and the activities that he wanted to do. He worked hard saving his money for all the supplies he would need. He purchased his own single-man tent, a brand new sleeping bag, hiking boots, and other supplies and paraphernalia. This trip was mostly what he talked about for weeks on end. He was also excited because the trip was in July, and in August, he planned to begin school. Luckily, he had enough Ativan to make it through the trip, even though he had drastically reduced the dosage.

In the meantime, there were the tests he needed to take through Longview College. Joe and I transported him there often so he could meet with counselors, take tests, etc. In May, he was accepted! He was 24 years old and excited to finally begin his life! The start date would be in August. I think that kept him going emotionally.

That July we packed up our car and met up with Ann and her truck, which was loaded with kayaks and camping gear. She had Will with her. Victor and Nikki would arrive by train after we arrived in

Glacier Park. Christopher and Richard would be traveling from Tulsa and meet us there.

Adam wanted to travel with his Aunt Ann and his cousin Will. Joe and I followed. Ann explained that we would have little or no phone reception in the mountains, so she gave us a walkie-talkie, and she kept its partner in her car. A lot of joking was going on between the two vehicles—a lot of laughter.

At some point during our travels, we stopped at a gas station to use the bathrooms and fill up the cars. Ann met me in the bathroom and said she needed to talk to me about Adam. She said he was saying some off-the-wall things along the drive. I mentioned that he did have quite the quirky sense of humor and personality.

She said that wasn't what she was talking about; that was not what she meant at all. She said he kept making weird jokes out of much of what they were saying. I said yes, it can be annoying when that part of his sense of humor comes out. She said, "I don't think you understand what I'm talking about. I think he's becoming sick again." I didn't take much of what she said very seriously at the time, but I did tell her that I would keep my ears and eyes open and be aware of his behavior, conversation, etc.

We finally made it to our destination. We set up our tents. Ann explained to us about the safety issues in Glacier Park. We had to be aware of the wildlife, especially the bears, and keep our food locked up in our cars. There were rules about keeping your camp area clean. You couldn't empty out a pan of water that had anything else in it on the grounds because the animals could smell what was in it, and they would more than likely enter your camp. There were special sinks and tubs near the bathrooms to empty these things in, which was a bit of a walk. There was a curfew at night for safety reasons.

Once we got the rest of the family in and settled, we bedded down for the first night. Adam seemed pretty excited to see his cousins and family. We all made it peacefully through that first night.

The next day, Joe had some State Farm work he needed to catch up on, so he took a hike into the nearest town and went to a little coffee shop and got to work. The rest of us explored a bit. While in Glacier, we decided to take a whitewater rafting tour. Adam had a great time, and so did the rest of us. All in all, he seemed to be having a great time.

That afternoon we walked along a concrete and stone walking bridge that looked out over the rapid water below. You could see a huge waterfall spilling onto giant boulders below. Everyone was walking in front of me. Adam was just ahead of me. All of a sudden, he climbed onto the wall of the bridge and began to fall forward. I grabbed him and pulled him back down, scolding him like a child. "You cannot walk on the wall! You almost fell off of it! I can't lose you now, Adam! Not like this!"

"Mom, calm down," he replied. "I was just playing. I had my balance. I was fine. But I am sorry I scared you like that."

That was the moment I felt that something just wasn't quite right. I didn't take my eyes off him the rest of the walk. We got in a lot of video footage of the area. There was another spot with a wooden bridge we walked over. Adam was in awe of the beauty. We all were. We crossed onto a small trail that led to a cave and walked inside it. Between the cave and bridge there was a fallen tree lying across the water. Adam was sitting on it smiling. I got a beautiful picture of him on it. I also got a couple of Joe and Adam sitting on a railing, backs to me, looking at the mountains. In all that beauty, we all felt peace. I told myself I had only imagined the almost-jumping episode earlier.

The other boys who had gone on the long wilderness hike were finishing their hike a few days later, and we took the truck and our car on this long trek to pick them up. Nikki rode with Adam, Joe, and me. Having a fairly new car (that didn't have four-wheel drive), we took it very slowly. We reached the meeting point, had lunch, and went to a lake to put the kayaks in.

Adam had been really excited about this day, but now that it had arrived, he suddenly had no interest in kayaking. He was becoming very anxious, maybe from the long drive, being closed up in the car all that time. He had developed a quick, close bond with Nikki on that trip. She was only around 12 years old, and he was 24, but he gave her kid-attention, teasing her and giving her piggy back rides everywhere. She teased him right back but also made him feel like a responsible big brother, and he ate it up. For that, we were happy that Nikki was with us.

On the return trip back to camp, Ann and her group got farther and farther ahead of us in the pickup truck. Their goal was to get to camp and get dinner going while we crawled back down the mountain. We noticed Adam getting increasingly agitated, and then he started rambling nonsense words and sentences loudly in the back seat. Nikki did her best to try to make the drive silly and fun, but it wasn't working this time. We were at the top, with no water in sight. There was just barren land with some trees—mostly burned from a previous forest fire—around us. The road was gravel.

Suddenly, Adam screamed that he needed to get out of the car. Joe stopped and let him get out, not realizing he was barefoot. Adam ran quite a distance from the car, screaming and screaming. It was then that I knew it to be true: after two-and-a-half blessed years of peace, Schizophrenia had reared its ugly head again! I know he had to be out there thinking, Why? Why? Why? I am just getting my life back on track, and somewhat normal! Why now? Oh, the agony that must have gone through him as the realization hit home. I know we were feeling the same thing along with the questions, What do we do now? Where do we go from here? Will he comply with treatment like he promised he would, should this ever return? And our fears. Can we keep him alive this time?

We were watching out the back window and noticed that he had started stomping on a large rock with his bare foot! I began to panic, and Joe ran out of the car to help him. While he attended to Adam, I apologized to Nikki, explaining that when he came back to the car, he would more than likely curse and say inappropriate things because the voices now had control over his brain again. She was so sweet and calm and replied, "It's okay. Sometimes you just got to get it out. My mom is like him." I never knew that. This little girl showed such compassion and strength for us. I will never forget that!

Joe went to Adam on that mountain. He himself was filled with fresh, instant grief. All of our NAMI training needed to be applied to our son in that moment. Adam alternated between screaming in his face and recognizing that this was his dad, who loved him more than life. In those moments, he would hug Dad close and cry loudly, mourning what he knew he had lost. Then he'd go back to screaming, then holding again. This seemed to go on for an eternity, but it likely lasted 30 to 40 minutes. Finally, Joe coaxed him back into the car. I realized then that Adam had known what was coming the day before and had intended to jump off that rock wall.

Adam was so exhausted by his psychotic break that he slept the rest of the drive back. We finally made it back, probably two hours later than expected. Dinner awaited us. Adam sat quietly by the fire. From a short distance away, I heard him say to himself that he wished he had a gun with which to kill himself. Joe heard him, too. We decided to leave in the morning and cut our trip short. We told Adam this and let him know we would seek immediate treatment. He willingly accepted this.

"We will get you help, buddy," said Joe. "Just hang in there."

We barely slept that night. I lay awake in our tent, listening. I was relieved that the boys had returned. They all slept in hammocks hanging from the trees near Adam's tent. At one point, Joe and I whispered our concerns that he had possession of his meds. I went to Adam's tent and gently asked for them. He wanted to know why. I told him what I had heard him saying at the campfire. He denied he had said it, but complied, asking if I would at least leave his morning dose with him. I compromised and gave him the morning dose.

Soon after that, I heard his tent unzip. I put my shoes on and went to investigate. "I have to pee, Mom," he said. "No big deal." So he peed and went back into his tent, and I returned to mine.

I kept listening. During the wee hours of the morning, I finally dozed off, only to be awakened by Christopher. "Adam is gone," he said. "He just left his tent and headed down the road."

Once again, I scrambled to put on my shoes and ran out into the dark, foggy night. I could barely see in front of me. I was terrified of losing Adam and of the possibility that bears were out in the night. Suddenly, I heard a strange shuffling noise—a step followed by a dragging sound. My heart pounding, I called out, "Adam!?" Seconds passed, and finally he answered as I bumped right into him. The sound was him dragging his foot, which had been injured when he had stomped the rock earlier.

"Mom, why are you out here?" he asked calmly.

"Looking for you," I answered, trying to be calm. "You can't be out here, honey. It's past curfew and there is the danger of bears."

"I am not afraid of bears, Mom. But I will come back because of curfew. I have to finish my cigarette first."

"Okay, let's walk back while you do that." Then I jumped because I bumped into Joe, who was out looking for both of us! We all calmly went back to camp. Adam went to sleep at that point, and Joe and I decided that while he rested, we would break camp and start packing so we could head out ASAP. We were not going to sleep anyway!

Shortly after that, we packed up Adam's things, said our goodbyes, and hit the road. Ann and her crew finished the trip and traveled to Yellowstone on their return. It felt like deja vu; years before, on another family road trip, she had told us that our daughter was ill and had continued on the trip without us. Now, she had warned us about Adam, then continued without us.

We drove through Sturgis, South Dakota, on the way home, a place neither Adam nor I had been before, but Dad talked about it from a past motorcycle trip. Bikers were just getting set up for the big annual ride, so we saw quite a few motorcycles, but it was not as crowded as it would be in a day or two.

We went into the shops that were already set up and picked up a few t-shirts. Adam actually enjoyed himself that day and took a lot of pictures with his phone. We relaxed a little and felt confident he would receive help once we were home.

That night we stayed in Sheridan, Wyoming. First we stopped at a restaurant called The Rib and Chop House. Adam had been going on and on about how he had never had a New York Strip Steak before. Joe said, "You can have anything you want!" Joe and I had plank salmon. We let Adam order a beer to calm his nerves a bit. He was getting agitated waiting for the food. He asked me why the family at the table next to us was staring at him and talking about him. I told him they were not; they were not even looking our way. He said he was going outside to smoke a cigarette while we waited for our food. He came back in with bloodied knuckles. The food was good and we all enjoyed it, but I think Joe and I just wanted to get finished and get the heck out of there before another episode started.

We checked into a two-story motel in the area and got Adam his own room. The building he was in was at an angle to ours, and we could see his room out our window. Both rooms were on the second floor. I told Adam he needed to stay in his room for his own protection, so no one would call the police if he had an episode. I went on to say that maybe they didn't have CIT officers to help if that happened, and we didn't want him getting arrested. He agreed, calmly, thank God. I gave him my phone charger so he could talk to a friend all night long if he needed to. We had no incidents during the night.

What happened to Adam on that mountain? Did the high altitudes create a shift in his brain? Was Schizophrenia always there, lying dormant, ready to rear its ugly head? Why the peaceful two-and-a-half years? What was it all about; what was it for? To help us learn from this experience?

If so, we did. We became less judgmental, more compassionate and understanding of others. The little problems in life seemed not to be such a big deal anymore. And Adam brought so many back to God. Had it been the Ativan that had been keeping the voices away? Was it the magic cure? We believe it had been, as the voices in Adam's head hadn't returned until he was coming down off of this medicine. He had very much reduced his dose the month before.

Later on, Megan told me that when they had visited, Adam had admitted that he felt depression coming on, as well as a lot of anxiety and whispers in his mind. Not voices he could understand but whispers. He thought it was his anxiety and racing thoughts that came with it.

Joe later told me that he had noticed this in June as well, since he had been working from home and could hear Adam complaining about it. It just hadn't been full-fledged voices until he was up on the mountain.

The next morning following breakfast, we drove nonstop all the way home. Adam was much calmer and relaxed once we got there. We arrived late, went to bed, and called the doctor in the morning. Adam was immediately set up with a home caseworker again. This time it was Tyler Sharpe, a young man who would become a big part of our lives from that point on.

Adam was started on a new medication regimen and regular doctor and psychiatrist visits. Sadly, Adam didn't get to start school in August—another blow to his world.

Early in September, SASS (Suicide Awareness Survivor Support, an organization started by Micky and Bonnie Swade ten years before in honor of their son who had taken his life) had their annual walk to raise awareness and give peace to the families who also lost loved ones to suicide. Along with the walk, there were speakers, as well as prayer and beautiful music. The names of lost loved ones were spoken, never to be forgotten, and doves were released. It was so beautiful. Joe, Adam, my neighbor T, and I, along with some other NAMI friends, came with the Hugills to support them and honor Clayton.

I was amazed that Adam came, as he was suffering again himself. He was so loving to the Hugills and Clayton's previous girlfriend, Savannah. He talked with her for a long time and befriended her on Facebook.

Shortly after the walk, after we had returned home, something strange was happening next door to us, as well. We had been so wrapped up in the problems with Adam that we didn't get out much with the neighbors, although occasionally we joined Tim and Lorrie for a meal. John and T were always "busy". It began to dawn on me that something wasn't quite right because every time I saw T, she ran back into her house, ignoring me.

This went on until early November, when Joe ran into John and asked if everything was okay. He said it wasn't. They went for coffee and he told Joe about an incident that had happened at their house in September. This is what we were told:

Adam came over to see T, a common occurrence. They were joking around as they always did. Adam was slight in build and T was tiny herself. He just adored her, and she always gave him loving attention and kindness. This particular day, he asked her if she had ever played "Good Game".

Now on the Shultz side of the family, this had started out as a joke during a Mizzou football game several of us had attended. Someone got slapped on the bottom by surprise, and the person who did it yelled out, "Good Game!" Our family is goofy, and we have a lot of fun. To us, this was all innocent fun. To Adam, T was family, and to him this would be funny. This is how the mind of someone who suffers, not only from Schizophrenia, but also from a traumatic brain injury, who doesn't always think through consequences or think he is doing anything wrong, like crossing boundaries), works. T said that no, she hadn't played Good Game before, and he promptly smacked her hard on the bottom. Her response was to slap him in the face and yell at him and send him home.

For several weeks, we never knew what had happened, yet it was us she was mad at, and she refused to speak with or acknowledge us ever again. This person we considered a very good friend had just written us off like that. Now that we knew the story, we wanted to make things right with John and T.

As it happened, John was about to have surgery on his foot that week. It had been crushed in an accident at his place of work. It was outpatient surgery, so when he came home, we brought food over. T seemed very receptive to this and welcomed us into their home, thanking us profusely. Joe was visiting in their room with John, sharing some laughter as is common around John. He always has us in stitches, and on heavy pain medication, his humor seemed to double.

T and I were right outside the bedroom door. I took the opportunity to apologize to her for Adam's actions. She was embarrassed, not knowing yet that Joe and John had spoken. I nodded my head, equally embarrassed by my son's actions and showing sympathy towards her. She knew him well, knew he had no filter for inappropriate things, and sometimes, like a child, had to be told about boundaries. I did not lecture her on this because I knew that she felt violated. I still couldn't figure out why she was upset with me for something Adam had done and of which I hadn't had any knowledge of. Anyway, I did my best to make it right. I asked her that day if we were okay. She said that we were.

We checked in on John the next few days, and every time she raved about the food we had brought and how it had lasted three days! We were glad because we know how it is when you have a hospitalization and are sent home. You just want to take care of your loved one, not shop and cook. The fourth day, T sent me a text message thanking me again. I replied to her that after all they had done for us since we had met them, we could never repay their kindness. She replied with, "Oh, you've done more than enough."

Then, once again, I didn't hear from her in weeks. That's when I realized that her text had not been intended to be kind. I was perplexed, but it was winter, and I figured I was imagining things. Maybe we didn't see them due to the weather, and we were so busy trying to figure out how to deal with Adam's illness returning that we had little time to socialize with others anyway.

In November, shortly before Thanksgiving, Adam begged to be put in Research Hospital. He was feeling suicidal and asked for help. Pre-coma, he would never have reached out like that. He had been doing everything right: taking his medications, seeing his psychiatrist, not using illegal drugs, working the program with his clinical case worker, Tyler, and setting goals for the future. He was also seeking counseling with Aimee, the one he had bonded so closely with at Research. She now had her own practice in Harrisonville, just thirty minutes away. Joe drove him there weekly, because she was worth it and deeply cared for Adam.

Intake was interesting. Joe and I were in the room with Adam. The lady was typing away his responses to her questions. When she asked Adam what his chief complaint was, he told her that Stalin was in his body. "Who?" she asked. We explained that Joseph Stalin had been a Russian dictator. She looked at all of us like we were crazy. You would think she'd have heard it all before, working in a mental health hospital. So he went on to tell her that all the Stalins were inside him. "All?" she asked. He said that the Stalin from every age he had ever lived now lived in him, from childhood on. He couldn't help the way he was because it was his job. Oh, boy! I was sitting beside him and he said, "You can hear them, can't you, Mom? The ones in my stomach are so loud!"

Adam spent the week at Research (no surprise) as they tweaked his meds and tried new ones. He also made an appointment for early December to see a new family physician, hoping he could get put on Ativan again. We prayed a doctor would approve it. The pacing and shouting had returned with the voices. Our hearts were breaking. We felt, though, that after his near-death experience, and with his asking for help, that suicide attempts were hopefully a thing of the past. We also wondered if thinking about Thanksgiving and dealing with family were stressors, and if he might feel safer in the hospital. It gave us a little respite and relief for a few days.

At home, Adam would tell me about the voices and how ugly they were, and he said that if I supported him, I would yell at them and tell them to leave him alone. I had no problem with that. It was how and what I said. Not being one to yell, I would sternly tell them to get out of Adam's body and leave him alone! He would tell me that wasn't good enough; I had to yell loudly, "Get the f*** out of Adam's head, you motherf*****s." Wow. I did exactly as I was told, no matter how uncomfortable it made me, because he had to know I supported him, believed him, and wanted to help him.

We spent Thanksgiving day with family and brought food back home for Adam. He was such a different person to visit with than in previous years. He was genuinely concerned about the patients and their families at Research Hospital who visited them. He even hooked a couple of families up with our support group. I really felt hope for him to get this under control this time.

We also had our annual C.I.T. Award Ceremony in November. I recall a conversation with Adam during that time about the financial state NAMI Kansas City was in. Joe became president of the board that year and was gravely concerned about it. We had raised thousands of dollars at the Matrons Society Banquet earlier in the year that had disappeared into a black hole for past debt. Had he known this beforehand, he never would have taken on the position.

The last thing we wanted to see was NAMI KC folding and losing the precious people who we loved who worked there. There had already been several layoffs prior to this, and now we understood why. Funders were backing out, and now we stood to lose government support. We brainstormed ways we could raise money. Adam commented to me that I had said a while back that NAMI KC had never had a walk, and that I should take it on. Somehow, it had gotten around the NAMI circle that I was going to do this. I got some positive responses and some negative ones, such as Why did I think I could do this when no one else ever could? It was kind of a self-esteem blow. I didn't think I really would take it on. Then Adam said, "Let's do this, Mom! I have a great idea! Let's call it 'Runs Like Crazy'!"

I wasn't so sure about the name. It might sound offensive or stigmatizing in some people's minds. But he added, "Hey, I have Schizophrenia and it doesn't offend me, so let's do it." He let me win the debate on the name of the event, but said no one could prevent him from having the team name he wanted. He said, "I am of Native American descent from Dad and your mom. I am also of German descent from your dad. So our team will be called Runs Like Crazy, as that is now my Native American name, but it will be written in German on our shirts so as not to offend most people (only the German speaking ones, LOL), Laufen Verrückt." I agreed that is what we would do. For NAMI, but mainly for Adam, I would attempt to form a team and do some research and begin planning this walk. The idea terrified me!

In mid-December, Joe confronted John again about the strange distance of T. Every time I walked outside and she saw me, she did the hundred-yard dash into her house. I couldn't figure it out. I thought we had made amends. John told Joe that T said it was because of me and how I had treated her when we had brought the food over after his surgery. So, I wrote her a long letter, which took a lot of energy considering the stress and worry at home, but I thought she was worth the time and friendship. I told her how much I loved her. I told her how sick Adam was. I told her again and again how I treasured the friendship and wanted to save it.

She came over that evening. We were getting ready to go out to dinner with Tim and Lorrie (a dinner they declined because we were going). This was awkward timing, for sure. Adam was in his room close to the living room where she sat glaring at me with intense anger in her eyes.

"What did I do wrong?" I asked. "You have been angry with me for weeks on end, first over something I knew nothing about. I apologized profusely, once again for something I didn't do, and you are still angry, and I don't know why."

She replied that it was because of when I had been at their house with the food, which was a "cover-up". What? A cover-up for what? It is the kind of thing we do. Apparently, she realized that after enjoying the food for three days. Then, when we had talked about the incident with Adam that day following John's surgery, I had reacted inappropriately. I asked her how I had done that. She seriously said I tilted my head forward with a sympathetic look when I should have had an open-mouthed shocked look. Huh? Now she was reading my intentions into my expressions. It was at that moment I realized the problem was not with me, but with her. I had done everything I possibly could to right this situation.

Then a car horn honked, and Joe said, "Tim and Lorrie are here and ready to go." With that, T got even angrier. "You are going out with them?" I mentioned that they had been invited to several outings recently, only to decline every time. On her way out, she yelled, "There is nothing wrong with your son!" like I was making excuses for his behavior. I chose not to say anything more. What more could I say?

We went to dinner. Tim and Lorrie had no idea what was going on with John and T. We chose to keep silent for the time being and didn't want to jeopardize their friendship with them.

Also in mid-December, we had Clay and Annette Hugill over for dinner and games. Adam was having the best time, laughing and joking. He had quit smoking, so we were surprised when he suddenly got up and said he needed to take a break. We all got up and stretched.

To our surprise, Adam went out on the front porch and lit up a cigarette. He was pacing and yelling at the voices. I heard him say that there would be consequences for smoking again, that it was not allowed. We didn't stop him from smoking or argue with him. He obviously was going into psychosis again, and we didn't want to fuel the fire. He jumped off the porch and walked away from the house for a few minutes. When he came back inside, he plopped down beside me on the couch. His face was contorted and scary looking. I turned to look at him, and I know my reaction must have been a look of horror. His blue jeans were blood-red on his thighs. Trying to maintain calm, I asked, "Adam, are you bleeding?"

"No!" he yelled angrily. "Didn't you see me fall off the porch? This is mud!" But I knew better. What in the world had he done? Did he need a doctor or stitches? I was stunned and didn't know what to do. So I did nothing.

We resumed the game. It was weird. All the training we'd had, and we didn't know how to respond. Adam calmly told me later that night that the second coming of Jesus was to be in Grandview. "Blood is going to flow freely down the streets of Grandview, Missouri," he said. I didn't know what he meant by that, but it scared the hell out of me!

We all went to bed that night and not a word was spoken about the bloody pants again. He seemed to be okay during the next week; no sign of infection or anything. If anything, his mood lifted. He seemed content. I felt relief. Maybe the meds were finally kicking in and working!

Chapter 51
Christmas 2015

Christmas was quickly approaching. Adam was working the program and seemed to be leveling out a bit. On December 23, Joe and I were preparing for an overnight stay at my mom's house on Christmas Eve, which had been a longtime tradition. The kids still did not want to go, so we decided to go for one night and come home on Christmas Day to celebrate with Stephanie and Adam.

James would not be with Steph that year. She opened up to us that Adam had been correct all along; James had been abusive and had never stopped hurting her, even after the incident in 2013. They had been living like roommates for months, and she had been seeing someone else—someone we prayed would be kind to her.

On the 23rd, Adam said he needed to do his Christmas shopping, so he and I went to Academy Sports. He said, "Mom, you wear your tennis shoes into the ground. I am getting you new shoes for Christmas." I got some and was also browsing the gloves and ear bands. Adam said, "Mom, you get so cold in winter. Let me get those, too." I told him he was spending too much on me, and then he worried that Dad would think he loved me more because I got more things than he did. He actually spent more on Joe, but it was a gift certificate. He wanted me to tell Joe that I had bought the other stuff so his feelings wouldn't be hurt.

Adam was also insistent on buying a new pair of jeans for himself, along with a gray hoodie with no words or brand names printed on it. He searched and searched for the perfect ones. He wanted to look good on Christmas Day.

On the morning of the 24th, Joe and I got ready to leave for Columbia. Adam suddenly became agitated with us and wanted to know if we were planning on getting him a new phone charger for Christmas because his was not working very well. I said I would bring one back for him. He wanted mine, but I had not charged my phone and needed it in case of emergency. He was not happy and pitched a fit. We left annoyed with each other. We did exchange hugs, and all of us said, "I love you," but everyone was on edge.

We got to Mom's house, but neither Joe nor I felt right about it. We watched the interactions of the siblings and some of their children, so happy and carefree. Later in the evening, Joe wrestled his little nephew Jude. That was the highlight of the night. A small boy. No worries. Carefree. Just like our boy once was. It was bittersweet.

At around 8 p.m., Adam called. He said his battery was getting low, so this would be the last contact we'd have with him until we saw him in the morning. He said he needed to hear a real voice for a while and told me how calming my voice was. He said, "I love you, Mom." I told him I could come home right away if he just said the word. He told me to enjoy the family, and we would see each other in the morning. I said, "I love you, Adam." We ended the call.

We continued with the family, played with the children, and took family pictures surrounding my mom (which would be the last ones taken in which she still lived at home, although we didn't know it at the time).

I have five brothers and sisters, they have children, and some of the children have children. So, you can imagine how crowded a sleepover in that three-bedroom house was! Many of us camped out in Mom's basement on couches or air mattresses, or in sleeping bags.

I fell asleep feeling a bit uneasy. I missed my kids. Everyone else had someone with them—an extension of themselves—at Mom's house for Christmas. I always have Joe, and he has me, but we miss the laughter and joy the others are blessed to experience through their children and/or grandchildren. I longed for that, for a new baby grandchild of my own to hold and love—for my own children's happiness. Why? Why did we have to endure this cruel twist of fate? Things had been going so much better, we had thought. Adam was going to have a full life. Then Schizophrenia returned, and our daughter had been traumatized by abuse.

I finally drifted off to sleep, only to be startled at 3 a.m. I sat bolt upright in bed and gasped out loud, feeling panic.

Ann was awake and aware. She has always had this tuned-in connection to me, and she has this knowing way I can't explain, except by saying we are sisters (born fourteen months apart) who shared everything growing up, from friends, to classes, and later to a dorm room in college. She lives in St. Louis, and I live in Kansas City, at opposite ends of the state. We don't call each other a lot, but she knows when I need her to. It is an amazing bond we share. She called out to ask if I was okay.

"No, Ann," I replied. "Something bad just happened. I felt it."

"Is it Adam?" She also shared a unique bond with Adam. They did speak by phone quite frequently as well as travel together through the years.

"Yes, it is Adam." I was scared. I was exhausted, too. I had only been asleep for a couple of hours. I fell back to sleep.

In the morning, I told Joe about the night. He had slept through it right beside me on an air mattress. We gathered our things, said our goodbyes, and stopped at Waffle House to grab breakfast before hitting the road. Adam's phone had died, as we knew, so I couldn't call him.

We drove in silence, both lost in our own thoughts. We stopped to pick up Stephanie as scheduled, as if a normal, methodical process would change what we thought we might find. The unspoken fear. We didn't say anything about it to Stephanie. I kept convincing myself it was only a fear—a night terror based on my apprehensions. We kept the conversation lighthearted on the way home.

It was almost one o'clock by the time we got there. The lights were on upstairs in every room. That was odd. I walked in, calling out to Adam, racing through every room. He wasn't there. Dread filled my entire soul and body, and I turned to Joe and said, "Do not follow me." He had found Adam prior to the coma and had been so traumatized by it.

I knew what I would find. I just didn't know how he had done it. I knew at that moment that it had been his spirit I had felt leave his body at 3 a.m. I headed to the basement stairs. I slowly took each step down. Halfway down, I froze and then collapsed. A sound escaped my lips that came from the depths of my soul. I didn't recognize it myself.

There was my baby, my boy, my man-child, my only son born alive, hanging from a noose like you'd see in Western movies. His back was turned to me.

The scream brought Joe and Stephanie running down the stairs and to my side. Steph ran screaming back up the stairs and fled the house, tearing through the neighborhood.

Joe ran to his boy, his love, and wrapped his arms around him, sobbing, "Adam, Adam, oh Adam." He tried to lift him up and down off that noose.

Adam's eyes were closed, his face relaxed, and his knees bent, as if he had powered through it, his hands held out and down in front of his body. His body was cold and rigid. He was dressed in the clothes

314

he had purchased at Academy! I had helped him shop for the clothes he planned to die in!

I watch a lot of crime dramas—forensic type shows. Suddenly I thought, what if they look at this like a crime scene? "We can't take him down, Joe," I said. "We have to let the police do their job here." He agreed. He called 911.

The hours that followed were surreal. Just writing it today takes me back, and I feel the shock, pain, agony, and despair of it all over again. The police came quickly. We brought them here for this on their Christmas, too. It wasn't fair that this should be a memory for them, as well as us! They ushered us into Joe's office, a room where we wouldn't see them bring his lifeless body up the stairs and out the door.

I called Ann, who was waiting to hear from me after the night before. "Ann! He is gone!" I said. "Adam is dead! He hung himself!"

"Oh, Heidi!" she replied. "Oh, God, no!" She agreed to notify the others on our side of the family.

Next, I called Joe's sister, Debbie. Calmly, but through tears, she said she would come ASAP and would let all the Custins know. I was so thankful that I didn't have to repeat those words to the others.

The police officers were very respectful, patient, and kind with us. They asked if we needed a chaplain. We did. They brought in Pastor Kevin Hardy. I can't tell you what he said that day, but I remember the feelings we had. He gave us comfort. He was gentle with our souls.

An officer said, "Was that your daughter I saw running, screaming and crying through the neighborhood in a pink hoodie?" I told him it was. He went to go find her and brought her home to us. She sat silently crying, curled up on the couch. She was in shock. Why, oh why, did we pick her up and bring her home first? Now she has to live with the image, too!

While the police were still here, a friend from our NAMI support group, Holly Behrens, just opened our front door and walked right into my arms. I wasn't sure how she knew, but she was the first to arrive, and I needed that.

Moments later, my brother Martin came in. He looked so distraught and devastated, as I knew he would be. He too had spent a lot of time on the phone with Adam. They had been close. Martin and I were close, too. I had been his second mom growing up (he is almost eleven years my junior). I felt the need to comfort him, but as he took me into his strong arms, I knew I needed him more.

As the hours progressed, it felt like the day of the overdose. Joe's brother Steve and his wife Connie arrived from Atlanta. Thank God for them. They guided us through the funeral planning process. Joe's sister, Debbie, and my sister, Ann, took care of the obituary and finding pictures of Adam. Debbie put together a beautiful film presentation, and Ann put together boards to display the pictures on. I recall sitting with them, looking through bins of pictures, laughing and crying at the memories. It was too much for me. They just took over, and I was grateful.

I was searching for clues, like a suicide note. Ann said she sensed there was one somewhere. She searched his room and basement. She said, "One day you will find something."

Eventually, I did, months later in his notebook on his desk. I don't know why I had overlooked it before. In the notebook, on a torn piece of cardboard, were the words of Frank Sinatra's song, "My Way". I had listened to that song many times before. It was a song of my mother's era—one of her favorites.

A couple of days after Adam's suicide, Ann, Debbie and I were sitting at the kitchen table. They worked on plans, while Steve, Joe and Connie were at the funeral home hashing out details. I remember them saying the funeral home was arguing over doing a service on New Year's Day. I guess Connie stepped up to the plate on that one. It was said that she catapulted across the table and gave them hell. I guess they were suggesting we have visitation after New Year's and then the funeral days later. People were already in town from all over the United States. She wanted to know why they would want this family to have to drag out this anguish any longer than was necessary and possibly not have the family there to support them. Another hero of ours. Go, Connie!

I was looking through Adam's phone messages and pictures. I saw his legs and what he had done to them a couple of weeks before when Clay and Annette had been at our house. One leg had slices cut all over his thigh. The other had a deep, wide, trench dug into it. I wailed and became very dizzy, and they took the phone away and took me to bed. I never found those pictures again. I am certain that Ann or Debbie took care of that for me! How in the world had he made it through those weeks without infection or complaining about pain?

Many people arrived that week. Some stayed with us, while others were put up in hotels nearby. Popi (Joe's dad), Steve and Connie, their daughters, Alesha, Abby, and Sarabeth, along with spouses and kids, stayed in a hotel.

My mother became ill and stayed at home. Debbie, Ann, nephews Chris and Will, and niece Jessica stayed with us. Martin and Kristina went back and forth and stayed in Columbia. Kristina's daughter Brittney and her kids were in town from California and had to fly back before the funeral. Friends from Tulsa came: Cary Williams, a friend to Adam from their junior high years until he died, our dear friend, Aric Kohl, and Ben Tedder, who had taught Joe how to play the drums and become close with all of us. Ben used to stay with our kids when they were teens, and we had traveled. He was twenty years younger than Joe, so he had been close enough in age to relate to them. He later became a nurse in the mental health field, but we already knew he was good at that!

One of the arrangements that needed to be made was finding a location to have the services. We had lived in Kansas City for six years and had tried so many churches, yet none of them felt like home; not like the one we had attended in Broken Arrow. But we felt the service had to be in a church.

Our friends, Brad and Tracy Young, came in and saved the day on that issue. They live in Pleasant Hill, thirty minutes away from where we live, and attend the Methodist church there. Their pastor spoke with our cousin, Pastor Gary Powell from Columbia, and let us have their church for the services and the following reception. The Youngs also housed Kristina and her daughter, Jessica.

Another thing I had to accomplish was to get appropriate clothing for Adam's visitation and celebration of life. Ann took me to Kohl's. I found the perfect outfit for both gatherings, along with boots to wear with the dress for the celebration of life. The lady working in the dressing room was about our age. She said, "Wow! I wish I had a figure like yours. I would wear that, too!" Without emotion and in a monotone voice, I replied, "I have to look just right. My son is dead. He took his life, and now we have to do this."

She mumbled "I am sorry," and shuffled off.

"Why did I do that, Ann?" I asked.

"You are in shock," she said. "It's okay." She gave me a pass on anything I said or did.

A couple of days prior to Adam's celebration of life, Kristina,

Joe, Brittney and her boys, Jessica and I went out to eat before Kristina took Brittney to the airport. Even that lunch felt surreal to me. Byron, Brittney's husband, who was back in California on military duty with the Air Force, called and prayed with us over speaker phone. There we sat in 54th Street Diner, normal, everyday conversation going on at our table and around us. I joined in, but it felt like I was someone else, and was hovering over all of them thinking, "This is not normal, guys! How can we just sit here and eat and act like this is just like any other day or time?" It was surreal.

Our visitation was scheduled for New Year's Day. We had a houseful on New Year's Eve and celebrated Adam with our wonderful extended family and friends.

Many people wanted to go to the basement. I went, too, but was frightened. Not of Adam, but by images and fears for him and how he had felt that night. Being down there begged all the questions:

- Was he frightened?
- Did he cry?
- Did he pray?
- Did he think of me or Dad or Stephanie in his last moments?
- Did he regret it at the last moment?
- Did he suffer? (The most agonizing question of all.)
- Did he feel relief immediately upon entering heaven?
- Was he even in heaven?
- Where was he?
- Was he a lost spirit, wandering up and down our basement stairs over and over, leaving the imprint of his soul and last moment for-ever?
- Did he love us?
- How could he have left us like this?

I stayed down there for quite a while. Christopher, Will, and Ben sat with me. We talked about serious things, such as Joe's and my mental health following this. I don't remember all that was said, just their concern. I remember telling them that our friend, Tony Kehres, had taken Joe's guns at Joe's request.

Three months prior to this, Joe had stopped drinking, and everyone was concerned about that. Joe has stayed sober to this day but has said himself, if he had not have stopped when he did, he wouldn't have cared, and probably would have killed himself drinking. Thank God he quit when he did.

I know I did things others found strange, like immediately going through Adam's things and giving his stuff away, telling a story about him or the object as I went along. Cousins and aunts and uncles and friends were grateful to have these things. Someone asked me if I was sure I wanted to do this. I had to keep busy, and this was one way to do it. Martin said to put all of the t-shirts aside and that his mother-in-law would make something out of them for us.

I don't remember if anyone stayed up until midnight. I don't remember anyone acknowledging the coming of the new year. We had a big day the next day.

Chapter 52
The Celebration of Life
for Adam Patrick Custin

January 1, 2016, was the day of visitation. We had chosen to cremate Adam's body. The funeral home allowed us to have a gathering of family before they removed his body. I don't think they realized how large our family was, but they didn't argue. They also allowed us to have a Catholic priest, Father Anthony, who had stood beside us since the coma in 2012. Adam was very fond of him and would have wanted this. And for Popi since we were having a Non-Denominational Celebration of life the following day.

Father Anthony delivered a wonderful message and made certain we understood that God would not judge someone who did not have total control over their own mind—that Jesus took care of the sick. He said it clear and so true. Adam already lived in Hell here on earth. He gave us so much peace. Popi needed to hear that, too.

Family viewed the body and went outside the room, so we could have our last moments with our son and brother. I stared at every line on his face and touched his hair and his hands. I looked at the marks on his neck, the bruising on his ear, the faded remnants of "Dead Man Walking", the tattoo that he never finished removing. I laid my head on his chest, wanting to hold him somehow and feel his body one more time. Of course, it was cold and rigid. I didn't care. This was my baby's body. Just once more!

"Uh, Ma'am," I heard a man say. "The table is not stable. Better not do that." Oh, God no. I would have been mortified if he had slipped to the floor and the table had collapsed! I asked if before they took him away, could I see his feet? He had beautiful feet. I was memorizing everything I could about him and remembered Joe lovingly washing his feet during those weeks of unresponsiveness. I had to see them one more time. They complied with my wish. We then watched them tote our only son's body away. We know he wasn't in there anymore, but it was the body that carried him almost twenty-five years. This would be the last time we would ever lay our eyes on it again.

From that moment, we went directly into visitation. The line moved through for four hours. I was amazed at the number of people who came to shower us with love and support. State Farm was well represented, our family from near and far, NAMI folks, friends of Adam in Kansas City, people who worked with Adam, and my family whose children I take care of, Craig, Lisa, Nick, and Sadie Peterson, some of my other heroes in this life. I have no idea what I would have done without their support, and it continues through today. Many said they came that day and would not be able to make the celebration the next day. So, I figured the next day would be a small group.

I play "Words With Friends" with a guy who the game picked at random. He lives in Grandview, too, by chance. We corresponded about our struggling kids and created a friendship. I had never met him in person. At the very end of the line stood a man whose face I had never seen—either not even a picture. He said, "Do you know who I am?"

"I do, I think! Are you Dave Allen?" He was! How incredible is that? I was touched by so many, but that really meant a lot. Joe and I have run into him a couple of times since. Joe will say, "Hey, isn't that your friend, Dave?" Sure enough. We also met his daughter once, who is doing so much better, I am happy to say.

Visitation was so exhausting. We wondered how in the world

we were going to go through this again. We smiled and greeted and comforted others all day. How did we do that? Where did the strength come from? I remembered Clayton's Celebration of Life and how his parents did the same. I didn't understand it then or now. Maybe it is God's comfort and our angels carrying us through. Who knows? The breakdowns come soon enough, however.

Joe and I slept little that night—really the whole week and weeks to come. We lay in each other's arms sobbing all night long. He is my rock—always was and is. We vowed to never let this or any other storm tear us apart. Nothing has. We are blessed that way. I thought of the song Joe had played for us at SaraBeth's wedding in 2013 and later practiced and sang for me in our bed and on the front porch of our home. "I Won't Give Up On Us", by Jason Mraz.

I prayed those words would ring true. We all hear the horror stories of families ripped apart by the loss of a child, and in the case of suicide, it can be even more stressful as people tend to want to blame someone.

The morning of the Celebration of Life was chaotic. We had several people to get through two bathrooms to get ready, and the drive to the church was thirty minutes away. Joe and I were in our bedroom getting ready when James, the man Stephanie whom broke up with, arrived at our door. He asked to speak with us in private, so he came into our room. We were not happy but still in shock and not wanting to fight anyone on that particular day, so we listened to what he had to say. He was in there a long time.

Each of our siblings took turns knocking on the door to see if we needed them to escort him out the door. We declined but were not sure why we did that. We just wanted no controversy on our day of honoring Adam. He told us he was sorry for the loss, how he loved

Stephanie, but he was going to move on with his life, blah blah blah. He told us she was on drugs. Why, on this day, would you say that? I needed to focus on the loss of Adam, not stalk my daughter and look for signs.

What kind of person does this? When my mind cleared much later, I saw the sociopath that he was and that he was manipulating us, working on our emotions as our weakest, most vulnerable moment. Horrible! He finally left. Our family was not happy about this at all!

It was shortsighted of me to think it would be a small group at the funeral. I was shocked at the crowd. Many of our friends showed up from Tulsa, Oklahoma, including Ben Tedder, Cary Williams, Megan Rainey, Ben Ledford, Mike and Kathleen Michaud, Carol and Rene Ogden, and Adam's first friend since the age of three, Alex Foster. With it being the holidays, many people sent regrets due to travel elsewhere. Susie Green, whom we had known since Tulsa and then had lived in the Kansas City area, but now resided in Colorado, was there! My previous family I nannied for when I first moved to Kansas City in 2009 came. Monica Wilkens was the mom. She knew all too well young loss, losing both of her brothers, one at seven by a hit-and-run driver and the second at 29 years, due to a rare disorder that caused his heart to stop suddenly.

I could see her own pain through mine, and as I know now, we relive it through others' similar losses. It brings back the pain. Monica's former husband, Ted, his brother, Chris, and daughter, Josie, who spent a lot of time with Adam the summer of his recovery as she stayed with Tyler Wilkens and me while I was a nanny to him.

We learned that Susie Green also lost her step-son to suicide on Christmas Day 2012, and we never knew! She had spent all that time taking care of us and Adam. We should have been there for them! She calmly explained that she was strong enough to handle both her husband, Glen's, grief and ours, because they were not her biological sons. She was like a second mom to Adam as a child, however. She didn't tell us then because she didn't want us to lose hope! Not only is that true strength, but love, support, and friendship beyond expectation!

More NAMI people arrived and more extended family from all over and more State Farm folks. Friends whom Adam made in Kansas City, Nikki and brother Zak York, and their gang came. My close friend, Lorna Hesskamp from Tulsa, who now lived in Louisiana, could not make the trip, but her daughter, Jacy, came from Tulsa to represent the family. She actually transported a group of Adam's friends whom she only met that day. I felt overwhelmed with gratitude from all of the support.

First, "He's My Son", by Mark Schultz was played, the song I prayed through prior to the coma and played as we removed life support in 2012. Cousin Pastor Gary, who performed the ceremony, opened in prayer. "For Baby" by John Denver was played next. Gary spoke of the life of Adam. Steve and Ann spoke on Adam's life. Our executive director spoke on behalf of mental illness and those like Adam, whose lives are robbed because of this.

I love how she let everyone understand that Adam was not responsible for his death, that Schizophrenia was the culprit, and she really pushed for advocating for mental health. She had some health issues and had difficulty climbing the stairs to the pulpit. This was my first observation of Stephanie's new love interest as Marlon graciously arose and escorted her up the stairs. I was very touched by this.

Our niece, Jessica Ziulkowski, read Scripture: Romans: 6 4-11: [4]We were therefore buried with him through baptism into death in order that, just as Christ was raised from the dead through the glory of the

Father, we too may have new life. [5]For if we have been united with him in a death like his, we will certainly also be united with him in a resurrection like his. [6]For we know that our old self was crucified with him so that the body ruled by sin might be done away with, that we should no longer be slaves to sin [7]because anyone who has died has been set free from sin. [8]Now if we died with Christ, we believe that we will also live with him. [9]For we know that since Christ was raised from the dead, he cannot die again; death no longer has mastery over him. [10]The death he died, he died to sin once and for all; but the life he lives, he lives to God. [11]In the same way, count yourselves dead to sin but alive to God in Christ Jesus.

A lady named Jean Pinkston from Pleasant Hill United Methodist Church followed with "O'Holy Night" for us, accompanied by Michelle Camacho. It felt it fitting, though, unusual for a celebration of life song, since Adam passed away on Christmas during the wee hours before dawn. I didn't know her then, but I do now. She was part of Tracy Young's women's Bible study group, and they had all actively prayed for Adam and our family since the coma of 2012. I was so touched by this. These ladies, with the exception of Tracy, didn't even know us, yet they prayed for our son's miracle to happen. Now here was one of them singing for us! We could definitely feel God working in our lives through tragedy.

Cousin Pastor Gary followed with the eulogy. "In the Arms of the Angels" by Sara McLachlan, played next, followed by the closing prayer with Gary. Throughout the service, Debbie ran the presentation with pictures of Adam's life and the people in it.

We adjourned following, "Starry, Starry Night" a song, by Don McLean about Vincent van Gogh, an impressionist artist during the 1800s, who died by suicide and struggled with mental illness himself.

Adam was drawn to his artwork as it reflected many of his thoughts and moods. The song was eerily like Adam, too. Such powerful lyrics were written during the early 1970s by Don McLean at a time mental health awareness was not a movement as it is today. Don McLean had much insight into the mind of one who suffered so greatly. Sometimes I think we are still not listening, but it is getting better. More people need to speak out on mental health and work to change this. One person at a time, I say.

It was during this song, that a second sound that no one—not even me—recognized, escaped my inner being. Someone told me the wail sounded like a wild, wounded animal, and it scared a few people in their silence. I felt like a wild wounded animal! I knew I would never be the same person again. I didn't feel human at all. The pain was so deep, so intense; it felt as if I had fallen into a tiny hole with no oxygen, and it was closing in on me by the second. Surely, I would not survive this! How any mother had survived a child loss was incomprehensible to me. Or a father! Would WE survive this or our life together after this? How? Could we ever crawl out of bed again? Face the world?

Sometime during the service, Popi (Cliff, Joe's dad) stood up in the front row to speak. I was in such shock I cannot remember word for word what he said, but it started out with something about Adam being raised Catholic and the beliefs of suicide as a means of death. Those of us in the Custin clan held our breath a moment as it seemed he was going to say something about the non-denominational service in a Protestant church that maybe offended him. Or that Adam went to Hell. Popi always spoke very slowly as if tasting each word as it came forth. He put much thought into everything he uttered always. He was a great storyteller and sometimes took so long to tell it, you wondered where he was going and if there was a point. He was a brilliant man who always came full circle with everything he delivered well into his old age. At this time he was eighty six. At the end of his speech, he repeated the words Father Anthony spoke the day before as if to reiterate to the other Christian churches that his grandson was indeed in Heaven! He said it beautifully, tastefully, without judgment, and with much love and protection of Joe's and my hearts.

Following the service, we were led out first so we could greet people as they were going into the reception room. I had to pee so badly, so I darted into a bathroom in the hallway. Joe was already in place at the end of the hall. I came out just as the crowd filled the hallway and there I stayed, greeting people. A few joked and down the way, Joe seconded the greeting. I was overwhelmed by the numbers of people once again, but the love that flowed gave me strength to go through with this. We always say at times like this, it is like a family reunion and question why it takes death to bring us all together.

Food was provided, but I had no appetite. Ann kept trying to encourage me to eat. I was also visiting with so many people and wanted everyone to know how thankful we were to have their support. Along with providing food, Ann and Debbie had put an awesome display of pictures on a table for us to look at. So many memories were on those picture boards, happy memories! How could life that began so well end like this?

As everyone departed, Alex Foster stayed behind. As Adam's first friend, his best friend in life, I knew how difficult this was for Alex. When Adam became ill at fourteen, he was making choices Alex couldn't comprehend, the self-medicating, the reckless behavior. Alex had chosen during these years to leave the large public school and attend a private Christian school. It seemed his values differed from Adam. He didn't understand any more than we did the reason why. He only knew he couldn't behave like that, so he went down one path and Adam went another. He lamented if only he knew, he could have offered support and maybe helped him and changed the outcome of all of this. We assured him we didn't hold anyone responsible and were proud of him for his choices. No one can be blamed for what they didn't know or understand. That is why with NAMI, we push so hard to educate so this kind of thing doesn't happen to another family. With knowledge comes power. With power comes change. Unfortunately, we still have a long, long way to go. Alex returned for a visit a while later. We all went to dinner and spoke of old times and what was new with Alex.

After we parted with Alex at the church following Adam's service, we returned home. Some family members had already left. A couple of them stayed for a few days to help us get settled in our new normal, whatever that was. Nothing about this was normal. We were stunned. We walked around our house crying constantly and holding onto one another. Everywhere we looked, we were reminded of Adam. We could smell him, including the lingering scent of cigarettes after he came inside on a cold day after smoking. At night, we thought we could hear him walking up and down the stairs. Our dreams and nightmares were all about Adam. It was clear to us that Adam was still with us, even though we couldn't see him. During the few years following Adam's death, we would continue to bear witness to miracles and incredible events set in motion by the life of Adam Custin.

Epilogue

When I was young, I allowed events and things that happened to me to define me. As a child, I lived under the hand of abuse. As a child walking the halls of school, I allowed that to create in me a child who was frightened of everyone and everything around me. I allowed that abuse to steal from me who I was inside. As I grew older, it became more and more difficult to function in the outside world. I look back on that experience and try to compare it to the feelings that must have come over Adam at the age of 14 with the abuse that went on in his own mind.

When I went to college, I made a decision to change, as most people did not know me or who I had been before. I decided to redefine who I was. I changed a bit, but inside I was still that frightened child. It affected my relationships with men and with friends and family.

After I met the man who was to become my husband and life-long partner, I was still frightened inside. With his help and understanding, and after many years of working on myself, I was finally able to redefine who I was, and who I was really intended to become all along. Stephanie and Adam helped me to redefine who I was. This was Adam's story, and I intended to write it back in 2013 after he had experienced his miracle. For some reason, I couldn't complete that task at the time, partly because I did not want to embarrass him, and partly because the past was very painful, especially the parts about him. I did not want to relive that at that time.

Now that he is gone, it is not only his story. It has become my story as well because he was a part of me, and now this has happened to me. It has also become my husband's story and my daughter's story, and the story belongs to anyone who was a part of Adam's life and anyone who loved him.

When my children were born, I made a conscious effort to become that redefined person because I owed that to them as a parent, I owed it to Joe as his wife, and I owed it to myself. I became involved with things I never thought I could do because they took social effort, like leading the Girl Scouts, owning my own business, becoming a mental health advocate, becoming a support group facilitator for NAMI, and becoming a public speaker. That is something I would never have foreseen.

As a parent, I felt that by getting involved in my children's lives, by volunteering or becoming involved in a church, by providing them with a quality education and background, by simply being supportive and kind and loving, my children would grow up to be well-rounded, determined, and strong, and would be motivated to carry out their own sense of self and self-worth. They were given a life as children that was completely opposite of my own. What I learned through the experience as a mother and parent is that it really makes no difference how you were raised, what opportunities you were presented with, or the amount of love that was given to you or taken from you. When illness hits, it changes the dynamics of things. It changed the dynamics of all of our lives. In many ways, it made me a stronger person. It made me bolder because I had to fight for my children. It made me more outgoing because someone had to send a message to the world. Without having known Adam or Stephanie, I would never have had the courage, strength, or determination to write this story.

I have learned that there is no particular definition of me. I am constantly redefining who I am. Ultimately, I am evolving through my experiences in life, whether they be good or bad. My life is shaped by these experiences. When I come to terms with each event that happens in my life, I realize that I am evolving, not only in body but in spirit. And I realize that none of these events is coincidence. I see now that we are all tied together from the beginning to the end. As for the idea of "normal", I realize that there really is no such thing, as it is a constantly changing notion, as well. We will always be looking for the new normal. If I find it, I will let you know.

As for Adam's Contract with God, was it fulfilled in his mind? I think as he was recovering from the trauma of the morphine overdose, he felt a lot of hope in recovery. If not, would he have worked so hard to become strong and well again? And during that recovery, as he changed, grew, and became more of the man he intended to be, I think he did believe God was honoring his contract.

But then, everything went very wrong. We will never understand why. But what do I believe now? I believe that Adam is in heaven and that it is everything he ever wanted to be in this world. All of his dreams are fulfilled. He is free of voices and free of any pain—mental and physical. So, yes, God kept his promises, even though as a mother, I would have preferred that they had come to fruition here with me.

As I say this, I do not condone Adam's actions. I believe in life and the natural process of life. Nor do I suggest consuming one hundred morphine pills as a way to fix the voices in one's head. We had a miracle; medical science will tell you that he shouldn't have had the three last years that he did.

I believe that Adam's miracle was meant to teach us here on earth about many things. The day Adam returned, he brought many people to faith in God. He gave us hope for a cure in the future. And most of all, he taught us to love with all our hearts. Faith, Hope and

Love. And the greatest of these is love!

On that note, I wish to make it clear that I also have a lot of forgiveness in my heart. My wish was not to hurt anyone through the writing of this story. I simply want others to see how mental illness impacts an individual and how trauma can affect someone this way. For instance, my father had a good side to him, too. Trauma created some mental issues within him that he unfortunately took out on his children and wife.

My mother's trauma caused her to drink, and the drinking became an issue for her and those around her. I don't know what caused Mimi to act and react the way she did, but I know that deep down, she had a good heart. She did many things to help out the poor and people who were down on their luck. She had a wonderful laugh when things were going smoothly, though I know she was hurting on the inside. Diane had trauma in her life as a child, which in turn triggered her depression.

As for T, I don't know what caused her to do the things that she did, but I do know that hurt people hurt people, so something must have happened somewhere. I forgive them all. I love them, too, and have faith and hope that if I ever hurt anyone, they will forgive me, too.

When I decided to write *Adam's Contract with God*, my editor Leanna Brunner said I really had more than one story to tell. I could write about miracles, advocate for those living with mental illness and their families, tell Adam's life story, talk about Schizophrenia, or delve into navigating through the loss of a loved one by suicide. I felt the need to write on all of these themes, and I hope I did Adam justice by incorporating these into two books.

This first one is more about the time before Adam's suicide, and the next one is about life beyond it. I wrote the second one because my life did not end with Adam's life nor did miracles. I invite you to read on in *Living the Legacy of Adam* (a title inspired by my pastor and friend, Chris Pinion), to discover how we learned to live again,. For my beloved son, Adam Patrick Custin, 3/4/1991-12/25/2015. Rest in peace, my love, until we meet again.

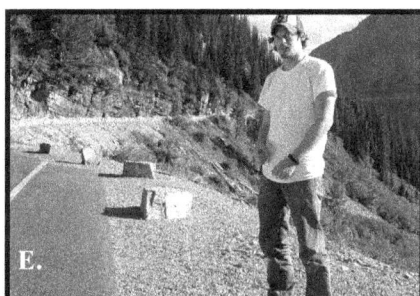

A. Challis from Hot Springs Arkansas, with a flaw in it that Adam chose because he was "flawed". B. Cover artist, Michael Brown. C. My parents, brothers, and sisters the night we removed Adam from life support, November 28, 2012. D. Teenage Adam before official diagnosis. E. Adam on the mountain in Montana the week psychosis came back. F. Our last Christmas together as a family in 2014. G. Sister Stephanie.

A. *Adam during recovery years. B. Adam and Dad showing off their muscles in the fall of 2013 after months of relearning everything following the overdose of 2012. C. Adam after coming out of the coma in December 2012. D. Adam at the top of the tower in Hot Springs Arkansas with Mom, Dad, Stephanie, and friend, Christian. E. Adam and Dad celebrating Adam's birthday and our anniversary March 4, 2014.*

www.ingramcontent.com/pod-product-compliance
Lightning Source LLC
Chambersburg PA
CBHW072050020426
42334CB00017B/1453